BATTLE BENEATH
THE WAVES

also by Robert C. Stern

The Lexington Class Carriers
Type VII U-boats

BATTLE BENEATH THE WAVES

U-boats at war

ROBERT C. STERN

CASTLE BOOKS

This edition published in 2003 by Castle Books ®
A division of Book Sales Inc.
114 Northfield Avenue
Edison, NJ 08837

This book is reprinted by arrangement with
The Orion Publishing Group Ltd.
Orion House, 5 Upper St Martin's Lane, London WC2H 9EA

First published by Arms and Armour 1999
Cassell Military Paperbacks edition 2002

British Library Cataloguing-in-Publication Data
A catalogue record for this book is available from the British
Library

Designed and edited by DAG Publications Ltd

ISBN: 0-7858-1682-8

Printed in the United States of America

Contents

Acknowledgements

This work could not have been completed without the immeasurable assistance of a number of people. I have to thank Rod Dymott and all the others at Arms & Armour Press for their infinite patience as the completion date slipped time and again. Much of the material in the book came from files stored in the depths of the US National Archives, Washington DC and Suitland, MD, and I owe the respective staffs a tremendous debt for their help. Ken MacPherson of Port Hope, Ontario, offered his kind assistance when I was just starting my research and arranged for me to meet a number of U-boat survivors whose recollections enliven this work, as well as my previous books. Included on that list are Ernst Schmidt, Willi Brinkmann, Johan Albrecht and Werner Hirschfeld. I want to thank, once again, Dave Herrling who read over the manuscript and offered valuable suggestions. My wife, Beth, also read it through. Whenever she asked, 'What does this mean?', I knew she'd found another subject that required better explanation. I know there are others who contributed materials or information along the way. If I have failed to mention any of these, allow me to apologise.

As always, the many who helped have made this a far better book, but any errors of fact or inference are mine alone.

Again this book is dedicated to my wife, Beth. If she can put up with me when I'm writing a book, she can survive anything.

Introduction

This is a collection of stories relating to submarine warfare, as experienced by the men who served in the U-boats of the German navies of the First and Second World Wars. These examples have been selected as a fair cross-section of those types of incident actually encountered by U-boatmen. The reader must understand, however, that the episodes recounted here can in no way be considered typical – and for two primary reasons.

First, these incidents reflect moments of action or great stress. Yet the old saw about combat being 'days of boredom punctuated by moments of stark terror' was never more true than in the case of U-boat warfare: except that instead of 'days of boredom', it should probably read 'weeks of boredom'. No attempt is made in this book to describe those tedious weeks. The reader is left to imagine what it must have been like to spend weeks on end living in a narrow steel tube, standing watch, eating bad food and sleeping in a bunk just vacated by another man who smelt as bad as himself. Because they tell of combat action, therefore, these incidents are very much the exception, not the rule, in terms of the time a sailor spent on board his submarine. And the reason why many of these tales, particularly in the second half of the book, describe the sinking of the U-boat in question, is because after May 1943, most encounters between U-boats and the enemy placed the submarine in mortal danger.

Many of the U-boat survivors with whom I talked couldn't remember much about the various attacks they had made on convoys. Performed correctly, such an attack is a rather unexciting affair. Sneak in, shoot some torpedoes, sneak out. Just another day on the job for a U-boatman, but, of course, potentially much more eventful for those at the other end of the transaction. What stood out in their minds were the times when, for one reason or another, things went wrong: and when this happened, the end result often was the loss of the boat itself.

The second reason why these stories are untypical is that they were all told by survivors. In the First World War, almost 30 per cent of the officers and men who served in U-boats died in that service. This horrendous loss rate was trifling, however, compared to the casualties of the Second World War, when approximately 70 per cent of men serving in U-boats lost their lives. (Just to put that number in perspective, during the same war, the

Submarine Service of the US Navy suffered the highest casualty rate of any branch of the US military: its losses amounted to approximately 15 per cent.)

The men who survived to tell these stories, particularly those of the Second World War, considered themselves, quite rightly, to prove the exception to the rule. I had the good fortune to sit in Ken MacPherson's comfortable living room in Toronto and talk with a small group of U-boat survivors. When I asked them to remember and describe a particular event, their minds must have turned to the many friends and shipmates who never returned. They all agreed that by the very act of surviving, their experiences could no longer be considered typical.

This book, by definition, is about combat, about the attempt by U-boats to sink enemy ships and the enemy's attempt to protect his shipping and sink the submarines. But running through a number of these stories is an interesting sub-plot that touches upon the issues involved in the treatment of survivors. In an ideal world, no survivor should be left to drown at sea. Once an enemy ship is sunk, the men in the water cease to be combatants; so they should be treated humanely and, as far as possible, their safety should be assured. But often that is more easily said than done. In earlier periods of naval warfare, humane treatment of survivors at sea had traditionally demanded that they should be taken on board the ship that sank them and dropped off at the next port of call. If that proved impossible, then it was understood that the survivors would, at the very least, be provided with adequate lifeboats, directions to the nearest land, and food and water sufficient for the voyage.

Such 'traditional' interpretations, however, dated from an age before the invention of the submarine and the airplane. The stark reality of modern warfare was that submarines had neither the space to take on board any significant number of survivors, nor the spare lifeboats or provisions to supply these to survivors in the water. Even stopping to offer limited assistance was potentially dangerous, particularly in the later stages of the war when Allied airpower over the Atlantic made surface operations extremely hazardous. Much propaganda was generated to depict the U-boat as a cruel weapon and U-boatmen as cold-blooded killers; yet in the clear light of hindsight, it is impossible to fault U-boats (or the submarines of any other nation) for slipping away from the scene of a sinking as rapidly as possible and leaving the victims to fend for themselves. After all, no-one faults aviators for not stopping to aid the survivors of ships they sank. Is a U-boat that different? In any event, moreover, orders from headquarters reinforced the obvious wisdom of abandoning survivors to their fate.

Fortunately, most U-boatmen never had to confront directly the question of whether or not to save men in the water. Nevertheless, in several of these tales, U-boat commanders of U-boats did have to face the reality of survivors in the water in an unexpected way and were forced to make a hard decision.

Although this book is in no sense intended to be a history of U-boat warfare, I have chosen, nevertheless, to use that history as a thread to tie together the individual accounts. The stories, therefore, are related in more or less chronological order. Each chapter outlines enough of the ongoing historical background to place that particular incident in context. Additionally, some of the chapters include relevant 'detours' – discussions of important forms of technology which materially affected the operations of U-boats, both in attack and defence.

The heart of the book, however, consists of the actual stories of U-boat warfare, chosen because they are illustrative, unusual or just plain interesting. I have attempted, to the best of my ability, and without going over the top or indulging in melodrama, to describe the feel and smell of life aboard a U-boat in combat. Above all, nothing has been invented. These accounts tell the stories, as far as possible, exactly as they happened.

— 1 —
U9

Already Obsolescent

SMS U9 was already obsolescent at the outbreak of war in August 1914. When U9 set out on the first offensive patrol of the war, it was accompanied by nine other U-boats, all just about as old. (U-boat is an anglicised version of *Uboot* in German, short for *Unterseeboot* or 'underwater boat'.) Frankly, none of the ten boats that made up this first patrol, a sweep northward into the North Sea in an attempt to locate the Royal Navy's blockade lines, was truly modern. Germany began the First World War with only 20 submarines; only four of them were fully up to contemporary standards and none of these four were in this first patrol sweep.

The ten boats that comprised this first organised submarine sortie were still rather fragile, somewhat experimental attempts at producing an underwater warship. Like all the other submarines dealt with in this book, they were in reality submersibles – surface warships that made occasional, brief and often dangerous excursions below the surface in order to carry out a stealthy attack on an enemy vessel or to escape pursuit. Any other type of vessel with similar characteristics of speed, protection and armament, but without the ability to dive beneath the surface, would certainly have stood little chance of success. Once underwater, a clock began to tick, counting off the brief hours before the boat had to rise to the surface to replenish air and recharge batteries. If prevented from resurfacing within the normal span of a few dozen hours of underwater endurance, whether by reason of mechanical failure or enemy action, the boat and the crew would perish.

The results of this first patrol were typical of what might be expected from these early vessels. One boat, most likely U15, sighted a British battle squadron and launched at least one and possibly three torpedo attacks on enemy battleships, with no success. U15, probably suffering from engine problems, was discovered stopped on the surface by HMS *Birmingham*. The cruiser rammed the U-boat at high speed, slicing it in half, sinking it with all hands. U13, also in that first sweep line, disappeared without a trace, probably after straying into a minefield. U9 never even got into danger, turning around after two days when its engines broke down.[1] No enemy vessels were sunk or even damaged by any of the ten boats. The results of this first war patrol were clearly educational. Peacetime training had not prepared these fragile boats or their crews for the rigours of war. Boats had to be better prepared and crews honed to a finer edge. And some luck wouldn't hurt. U9's next patrol would surely be better.

A Brief Backward Look

Practical submersible warships were but fourteen years old when U9 left port at Heligoland on the morning of 6 August 1914. The first vessel to fit that description is generally considered to have been USS *Holland*, built as a private venture by the American designer John Holland, purchased by the US Navy and commissioned in October 1900. *Holland* was the culmination of several centuries of experimentation and technical advance that had seen any number of abortive attempts to use vessels in naval warfare that could partially or wholly submerge. Typical of earlier attempts was CSS *Hunley*, also named for its inventor, built for the Confederate States Navy in the US Civil War. *Hunley* was a 40-foot-long steel craft. It was designed to submerge entirely, but in order to carry out an attack, it was supposed to creep up on its target with its hull awash, with only a few small hatches above water for the commander's head and to provide air for the crew of eight men labouring mightily below. Labour they did, because *Hunley* was propelled by a single screw driven by a crankshaft, which was turned by the sheer physical effort of the crew. *Hunley* could attack only by dragging an explosive charge up against the hull of its target and hoping that it could be detonated close enough to cause fatal damage.

All of the technologies required for a modern submarine were present in *Hunley*: a means of propulsion that would work under water as well as on the surface, the ability to submerge and resurface, and a method of delivering an explosive charge to an enemy's hull. However, these technical developments were in such primitive form that *Hunley* represented a far greater threat to its own crew than to the enemy. It sank at least twice during training, each time killing some or all of the crew. Still, crude as this craft was, CSS *Hunley* would go down in history as the first submersible to succeed in sinking an enemy vessel. Raised again after each foray, more volunteers were recruited for its next action. Finally, on the night of 17 February 1864, *Hunley* crept alongside one of the Union Navy's blockade ships outside Charleston, SC, and detonated its charge against her hull. The victim was USS *Housatonic*, a 1200 ton, 11-gun screw sloop. The damage to *Housatonic* wasn't devastating, but it was sufficient to cause her to sink slowly. *Hunley* never returned. The backwash from the explosion flooded the boat and sent it to the bottom in deep water, never to be raised again.

Between 1864 and 1900, each of the nascent technologies present in *Hunley* would advance through a myriad of large and small innovations to the point that John Holland was able to combine them into a practical and reasonably safe vessel. USS *Holland* wasn't revolutionary in any sense. Rather, it represented simply a combination of technologies now mature enough to produce a reliable result. Similar experiments had been underway in other countries, most notably France and Germany. The French, in particular, saw the submersible as a relatively cheap and easy way of neutralising the long-standing naval superiority of its traditional rival, the British. In 1886, the French Navy began pouring significant resources into submarine development. They saw the vessel as a coastal defence weapon, capable of defeating the Royal Navy's primary tactic for dealing with a continental enemy with a weaker surface fleet: a close blockade that would bottle up the enemy's navy and cut off vital imports. The submarines which the French began producing in numbers were for the most part small, short-ranged craft with heavy armament.

Germany, logically, should have shown the same interest as France in a weapon designed to counter the Royal Navy, but the Germans had greater ambition than the French. Under Navy Minister Von Tirpitz and the young Kaiser, they contemplated challenging the British on the surface and showed no early interest in submersibles, despite active experimentation by private firms, particularly the Howaldtwerft in Kiel. The British reacted to submarine development with alarm and more than a bit of self-deception. Like the French, they understood that submersibles would give a weaker power the ability to challenge the Royal Navy, but they chose to ignore the threat, on the presumption that any danger they did not acknowledge wasn't real.

Holland's submarines were designed for the US Navy, a force with no fear of close blockade, but still concerned about the possible arrival of an enemy fleet unannounced somewhere off its long coastline. (The theories of a professor at the US Naval Academy at Annapolis, MD, Alfred Thayer Mahan, author of *The Influence of Sea Power upon History*, had become very popular among officers in the US Navy at this time. Mahan argued, in brief, that commercial conflict led' inevitably to military conflict. The logical conclusion, therefore, was that although the Americans had much in common with the British, the latter's status as the world's leading trading nation – a position to which the Americans aspired – meant that the Royal Navy was the most likely enemy to be faced by the still small, but growing, US Navy.)

Having recovered from the Civil War, America in the late 19th century was a cocky young nation getting late into colonial expansion and determined to catch up with its European rivals. Submersibles could provide for a relatively inexpensive coastal defence capability while allowing the admirals to concentrate on building up their battle line. In 1888, the US Navy announced its first competition for a submarine design, a competition won by John Holland seven years later. The submarine that eventually became USS *Holland* wasn't the same boat for which the US Navy contracted in 1895. Meddling and constantly shifting requirements meant that this boat was never completed. USS *Holland* started out as a private venture, Holland's sixth such, designed to show the Navy the boat they should have been building.

For armament, Holland used a single torpedo tube. The Whitehead-type torpedo, invented by the Italian Giovanni Luppis, was first manufactured by the English engineer Robert Whitehead, working as manager of the Fiume Iron Works on the Dalmatian coast of the then Austro-Hungarian Empire. Whitehead attached an 18-pound explosive charge to the head of a small self-contained underwater apparatus 14 feet long and 14 inches in diameter. Propulsion for the weapon was provided by compressed air that drove a turbine which in turn drove a single screw. The first version, tested in 1866, had a speed of six knots and a range of 700 yards, enough to give the launching vessel safety from the explosion that would damage and even possibly sink its target. Improvements followed rapidly. Gyroscopic control added stability. Vickers Ltd came up with a much improved propulsion system that used an alcohol and water mixture burned in compressed air to generate high pressure steam that significantly increased range and speed.

For underwater propulsion, Holland used a battery-driven electric motor. Since the 1870s, when the first practical storage batteries had been manufactured, this form of underwater propulsion had become the standard for the various experimental designs being produced in America and Europe. It was relatively light and compact and, most importantly, consumed no oxygen. Its primary drawback was the low power and minimal endurance provided by the batteries then available. For surface propulsion, Holland, from his first experimental boat onward, had favoured internal combustion engines. For USS *Holland* he adopted the gasoline-powered Otto engine, designed by the German inventor Nikolaus Otto. This engine gave tremendous advantages over previous surface propulsion systems. Rival French boats were mainly powered on the surface by steam engines, which had numerous disadvantages, being extremely bulky and giving off tremendous residual heat after the boat submerged, so as to make interior conditions in a submerged boat all but unbearable.

The disadvantages of a gasoline engine all centred on the fuel. Gasoline is volatile and its fumes explosive, and in more than one instance, Holland's boats suffered serious internal explosions that killed crewmen. The obvious solution was the use of a heavy oil engine, such as the compression-ignition engine developed by Rudolph Diesel in 1895. The first diesel-powered boat was the 1902 Laubeuf boat *Aigrette* built for the French Navy. Early diesel engines were far from a total success, being very unreliable, and it was a number of years before the diesel gradually was adopted as the standard means of surface propulsion for submarines. Nevertheless, despite the disadvantages of gasoline propulsion, the Holland design was clearly superior to those that had preceded it. Holland sold his boats, or the right to manufacture boats to his designs, not only to the US Navy, but also to the Royal Navy, whose A class was an enlarged Holland design, as well as Russia, Japan and the Austro-Hungarian Empire.

Submarine Development in Germany

Von Tirpitz and the Imperial German Navy still displayed no interest in the type. A Spanish engineer who had worked for a time with Maxime Laubeuf in France, approached the famous armaments manufacturer Krupps, which had recently gone into the shipbuilding business after acquiring the Germaniawerft yard in Kiel, with a plan to build a submarine modelled closely on the design of *Aigrette*. Given the repeatedly stated lack of interest on the part of the German Navy, Krupps was unwilling to build a full-size copy of *Aigrette* (172 tons; 118 feet), but was agreeable to backing the development of a diminutive version of the design as a speculative venture. The resulting boat, named *Forelle* (Trout), was so small (15.5 tons: 39 feet) that the two torpedo tubes had to be mounted outside the hull; and because there simply wasn't room for separate surface and submerged propulsion systems, it was powered solely by a 65hp electric motor. This gave it a speed of four knots and a range of 25nm on the surface. It was faster submerged than surfaced, because it possessed a simple spindle shape with very little in the way of superstructure. It did have a tiny conning tower pierced by a Zeiss periscope, which gave it an ability to attack while submerged not shared by many of its contemporaries. German naval authorities looked over *Forelle* after its completion in late 1903, but showed no inclination to buy it or the larger copies that Krupps was attempting to sell. In 1904, however, the Russians found themselves at war with the Japanese and sent a mission to Germany with the aim of strengthening their inadequate naval forces. This commission inspected *Forelle* and bought it, at the same time placing orders for three of the larger, more capable version.

These three boats were full-sized, fully functioning submersibles, on a par with their contemporaries. Not trusting the state of maturity of diesel engines,[2] but unwilling to accept the known risks of the gasoline fuel used by Holland's boats, Krupps elected to use the equally untried Körting engine. This was a more conventional internal combustion engine, differing from the gasoline engines used by Holland in the use of kerosene or lamp paraffin for fuel, both far less volatile than gasoline. The Körting engine, however, had at least four serious disadvantages. The lower volatility of the fuel meant that it had to be pre-heated in order to burn properly in the combustion chambers.

This proved difficult to do, particularly when the engine and fuel were still cold; a number of different engineering solutions were tried before one was found (blowing pre-heated air into the cold cylinders) that succeeded. Even with pre-heating, the heavier fuel burned less completely than gasoline and caused a dense white exhaust plume. The two biggest problems, however, were related to the design genesis of the engine. This was conceived and was being produced by the firm of Körting Brothers as a power plant for trucks and motor launches. It was designed to run at a constant speed, with the desired revolutions of the drive shaft being achieved by means of an automotive-type geared transmission. Since no such transmission existed for the size of engine required for the Russian boats, the only way to attain variable speed in the water from a constant-speed engine was to use a variable pitch screw. The power loss due to the inefficiency of the screws was estimated to be as high as 40 per cent. Finally, Körting had never attempted to build engines as big as the 200bhp units ordered for the Russian boats. In fact, the largest they had built prior to these was an 8bhp truck engine. Engine production slowed the completion of the three Russian boats, and engine reliability remained a problem.

In the autumn of 1904, with construction of the Russian boats well advanced, Von Tirpitz finally relented and consented to a contract for the first submersible for the German Navy.[3] U1 (*Unterseeboot* 1) was largely a copy of the Russian boats. The differences were minor, primarily entailing a slight increase in the diameter of the pressure hull and alterations in the external hull to improve streamlining and to prevent oil leakage from the external fuel tanks. Once again, the Körting engines were delivered late. When U1 began its trials in August 1906, a year after the scheduled delivery, it did so on electric power only because the main engines still hadn't been delivered. Not an auspicious birth for the dreaded German *Ubootwaffe*.

The Desiderata Boats

U2 was ordered before trials began on U1. Having decided to build submarines, the German Navy realised they had let most other navies get far ahead in both numbers and quality of boats. After all, this was the era of naval competition among the 'Great Powers' and even if a nation felt less than fully enthusiastic about a weapon type, as was clearly the case with the German Navy and submersibles, it still couldn't afford to let its potential enemies get an advantage. In 1908, when U2 entered service, the US Navy had 12 submarines; the French, with their early start, had some 60, though most were already obsolescent; the Royal Navy, which, like the Germans had started late, had applied its massive shipbuilding capability to produce submarines and was approaching the French totals, all but one of them being Holland-type boats.

The Germans continued cautiously. U2 was almost half again larger than U1 and had two 300bhp Daimler paraffin engines in the place of the latter's 200bhp units. The problem caused by the need of the Körting engine for constant speed was solved by adding two extra electric motors on each shaft and using the paraffin engine primarily to generate electricity for the motors. Only when moving ahead at normal speed were the engines connected directly to the drive shafts. Still, like U1, U2 was considered too short-legged and generally too fragile to be an ocean-going submarine. (In contrast, the Holland boats were proving themselves to be fully ocean-going boats. The five American C class boats sailed from their US port to Guantanamo Bay, Cuba, and then on to the Panama Canal, the second leg crossing 700nm of open ocean, a feat considered daring at the time.) U3 and U4, ordered a year later, were 200 tons heavier and had greater endurance, but still were considered too small for the task of combating the Royal Navy in the open ocean. It was clear, even to the German Admiralty (*Marineamt*), that not only were they building fewer boats than their rivals in the naval arms race, but that, in most cases, the boats they were building were inferior in quality. In order to ensure that future construction would at least be of the required quality, if not quantity, the *Marineamt* drafted a set of *desiderata*, a list of requirements that the next boats ordered (including U9) should meet in order at least to equal, and in some aspects surpass, foreign rivals. The list came to four requirements. [4]

The list of *desiderata* covered the four main aspects of a submarine's performance: speed, range, underwater endurance and armament. In each of these areas, the Navy wanted significant improvement over current capability, as embodied by U3. For example, the desired speed was 15kt maximum on the surface and 10.5kt submerged. U3 was able to achieve 11.8kt and 9.4kt respectively. U9, one of the *desiderata* boats, was faster on the surface, able to reach 14.2kt, because its main engines were almost twice as large as U3's. However, it was slower underwater, 8.1kt, because its displacement was 25% larger than U3's in order to accommodate the larger engines and the larger crew needed to service them, but its electric motors were only marginally more powerful than older boat's. In the other three areas, U9 represented little or no improvement over its predecessor.

All in all, U9 and its contemporaries in German service fell short of the desired characteristics in almost every category. Of the series of *desiderata* boats, only one, U16, met most of the standards. Like all the boats, it failed the crew size and endurance requirement; this one, perhaps, was unattainable. Compared to their contemporaries, these boats were rather bigger but slower than the French, which were more specifically designed for coastal defence, but were roughly similar in characteristics to British and American designs of the same period. All the major combatants – those who would face one another in the First World War – were evolving boats of at least 500 tons which possessed adequate range for open ocean warfare in the Atlantic and adequate armament to inflict some damage once an enemy was found.

U9 Makes Its Mark

After its abbreviated and fruitless first patrol, U9 was repaired and readied as rapidly as possible for its second sortie. Nevertheless, it was late September 1914 before U9 reached its assigned patrol area off the Dutch coast in the North Sea. The honour of achieving the first success against an enemy target had been denied U9, but something far more spectacular awaited. (The credit for the first sinking of an enemy warship by a U-boat went to Otto Hersing. On 5 September 1914, Hersing's U21 found the small cruiser HMS *Pathfinder* off St Abb's Head on the Scottish coast and sent her to the bottom with a single torpedo under the forward funnel. It took only ten days for the British to even the score; E-9 sank SMS *Hela*, also a cruiser, six miles south of Heligoland.) Even though they had missed out on this particular honour, U9 and her crew had already accumulated an enviable record of 'firsts'. When U9 participated in its first fleet exercise, the 1912 spring manoeuvres, it was credited with 'sinking' three battleships; for the first time, the notoriously conservative admirals of the German fleet knew they had to take this new weapon into account. Still, it was not until the Kiel Week festivities in June 1914, when the Kaiser personally inspected the tiny U-boat flotillas, boarding several boats, including U9, that the crews truly felt part of the fleet.[5]

U9's crew were proud of their boat and of their skill, a seasoned veteran unit. Despite their youth, many were 'plank-owners', meaning that they had been with the boat since its commissioning. They were drilled to a fine edge of readiness, eager, like their commander, to take on the enemy. The Commanding Officer from the beginning had been Otto Weddigen. Even as a young Leutnant, Weddigen rapidly obtained a reputation as a cool thinker and a grimly determined warrior. He was by nature an innovator, always looking to improve his boat and his service. And, like the best warriors, as Napoleon pointed out, he was lucky. It was luck, more than skill, that put U9 on the surface some 20 miles north-west of the Hook of Holland soon after dawn on 22 September 1914. It was luck, not skill, that revealed a wisp of a masthead on the southern horizon. But it was skill that then took over and enabled Weddigen and his boat to pull off quite the most extraordinary feat in the still brief history of submarine warfare.[6]

U9 had spent the night resting on the bottom in 100 feet of water, riding out the tail end of a North Sea storm. Dawn on the 22nd brought calmer weather and Weddigen ordered the boat to the surface. The IWO (*Erste Wach*

Offizier – First Watch Officer, the boat's second-in-command), Johannes Spiess, had the watch and it was he who sighted the masthead and then three faint trails of smoke on the horizon. He recognised the masthead to be that of a warship and, given the location, not far from the Dutch coast, knew that it had to be an enemy warship. Excitedly, he called Weddigen up from his breakfast. The CO's first order was to shut down the main engines. U9 was so small and low in the water that he was certain that he hadn't been sighted, but those damned Körting engines emitted a plume of white smoke that would be a dead give-away if he approached on the surface. After a brief study of the three smoke trails and the mast, he ordered the crew below and the boat submerged to periscope depth. As long as he was running on electric motors anyway, he might as well reduce even further his chances of being sighted. He set a course of south-east, towards the masthead. Judging from the smoke plumes and the masts coming into view, he concluded that he'd happened upon a flotilla of three cruisers. U9 was about two miles due north of the left-most of the line. The time was 0630. If he maintained his present course, to the south-east, and the cruisers maintained their course as well, he would be in position to attack the middle target in less than an hour.

What Weddigen indeed had seen as U9 crept closer was a patrol line of three cruisers, steaming slowly in line abreast towards the north, with about two miles between ships. Because of the angle at which he was seeing the ships and the mere glimpses he had of the targets during the brief periods he allowed the periscope to be raised, he mistook the three cruisers for much newer vessels than they actually were. Maybe a bit of wishful thinking entered into it as well since it was well known among the flotillas that HMS *Birmingham* had rammed and sunk U15. He initially identified the three ships as town class cruisers; perhaps one of them was *Birmingham* herself. Word spread quickly through the boat that U9 was about to avenge U15. Amazingly, the three cruisers held their course and their slow patrol speed, never swerving for the full 50 minutes it took U9 to draw within torpedo range of the middle target. It took very little of that time for the torpedo men to check their 'eels' and check them again.[7] Mostly, it was standing by their stations, talking in hushed voices, trying to conceal the nail-biting tension with small-talk and wisecracks.

Finally, at 0720, Weddigen took one more glance through the periscope. The target was dead ahead, 500 yards away. One shot would do it.

'Stand-by Tube I! Fire I! Down periscope! Right full rudder! Depth 15 metres!'

The orders came one after the other in rapid-fire succession. Each had a purpose. The first one made sure everything was ready to fire the first bow tube. The second actually launched the torpedo towards its target. The remaining orders brought in the periscope that might leave a tell-tale wake, turned the boat away from its target and angled the boat down to counteract the tendency to breach the surface after launching a torpedo. (Launching a torpedo lightened the bow of the boat by more than 1000kg. Later U-boats had torpedo trim tanks that would automatically flood to compensate for the lost weight and allow boats to maintain trim. Early boats, like U9, had actively to point the bow downward right after a shot in order to prevent broaching.)

All that done, the crew could only wait. It only took 31 seconds before the sound of a dull explosion and then a louder blast was heard throughout the boat. A quick check through the periscope revealed a cruiser heeling to port as water poured in through the hole torn in her hull by the torpedo. Weddigen was surprised to find, now that he had a good look at his victim, that she wasn't one of the new, fast town class cruisers; what he had hit was, in fact, a much bigger but far less valuable ship. His victim was HMS *Aboukir*, a 12,000 ton, 13-year-old, relatively slow armoured cruiser. She was a ship designed to counter a threat, French commerce raiding cruisers, that no longer existed, so she and two of her sisters were relegated to patrolling the Dutch coast, protecting the shipping lanes further south that were steadily plied by merchantmen carrying the vital supplies needed by the BEF in France.

So novel was the submarine as a weapon that the crew of *Aboukir* and of her two sisters concluded without hesitation that they'd happened upon a German minefield. The thought that they had been the victim of a U-boat attack apparently didn't occur to any of the British sailors watching *Aboukir* in distress. As *Aboukir* settled aft, her two sisters altered course to close the sinking ship, intent on picking up survivors. It was a brave act, but incredibly foolish. Even had their initial assumption been correct and they had indeed wandered into an uncharted minefield, nothing could have been more dangerous than for *Aboukir's* two sisters to manoeuvre through that same minefield in a well-intended but clearly ill-conceived attempt to rescue survivors. Instead, as U9 looped to the right and then settled on a north-easterly heading, Weddigen watched with amazement as the ship from the right of the formation swung left towards him, moving slowly, watching for non-existent mines. They passed close by each other on opposite headings and then U9 swung across the cruiser's wake and turned up along its port side.

U9's well-practised crew meanwhile had reloaded Tube I with one of the two spare torpedoes, so the boat again had all four tubes ready to fire. Continuing his steady turn to the right, Weddigen brought his boat bow on to the second cruiser, let the range drop to 350m and, at 0755, fired both bow tubes. Again, U9 turned away to the right and set its bow planes to angle the boat downwards. This time, the boat was so close to its target that there wasn't room to complete the turn. Weddigen quickly ordered both motors reversed and tried to back the boat away from its victim. Lighter at the bow by the weight of two torpedoes and pulling backwards with bow planes down, U9's bow broke surface. Her victim, HMS *Hogue*, had been hit by both shots and was settling fast on an even keel, but still had enough fight left in her to begin a heavy fire on U9's exposed bow. Weddigen took hasty corrective action, reversing the bow planes and dragging the bow back underwater. Luckily for U9, *Hogue's* shooting was poor and the U-boat resubmerged without damage. Within five minutes *Hogue* rolled over and sank, and, by now, *Aboukir* too was gone.

That left the third sister, HMS *Cressy*, name ship of this ill-fated class. Incredibly, *Cressy* came on, apparently oblivious to the fact that a submarine was lying in wait. U9, having backed away to a safe distance from *Hogue*, resumed its turn to the right and, completing the loop, settled on a south-westerly course. *Cressy* was approaching *Aboukir's* survivors from the south-west, so the two were approaching on opposite headings. U9's batteries, not fully recharged in the brief time it had spent on the surface before sighting the cruisers, were now approaching exhaustion. (It was necessary to retain at least 800 amp-hours worth of charge in the batteries, because the Körting engines were started by an electric starter motor that required that much charge. Later, diesel-driven U-boats used compressed air, another limited resource, to start their main engines.)[8] Weddigen had no intention of letting the third cruiser slip away; he would take his chances. The single remaining spare torpedo was loaded in Tube II in the bow; both aft tubes still had torpedoes.

As *Cressy* slowed to start picking up survivors, U9 approached from the east. At 1000m, Weddigen swung the boat around to bring the aft tubes to bear and at 0820 launched both aft torpedoes. Lookouts on *Cressy* spotted the oncoming torpedoes (the alcohol-burning torpedo of the day left a highly visible bubble track that could alert a victim), but it was too late to do much. Still having some way on, *Cressy* tried to turn left to avoid the danger, but only managed a partial turn before the torpedoes arrived. One torpedo passed ahead but the other hit forward on the starboard side. Not sure that the single hit was fatal, Weddigen swung U9 around to the right and at 0835 fired his remaining bow torpedo at the stationary *Cressy* at 500m. *Cressy* quickly rolled to starboard and slipped under. U9 crept away to the north, finally surfacing at 0850, clear of the scene.

U9 had left behind a scene of devastation. Three large, old cruisers were gone. More importantly, 1460 officers and men were to drown at the scene.[9] The British naturally condemned the event as a typical case of German 'dread-fulness' (*Schrecklichkeit* – a term first used by British propagandists to describe the occasionally brutal treatment of the Belgian civilian population by the invading German army during the opening weeks of the war). Propaganda aside, it did shake a basic belief on the part of all combatants. It was clearly now no longer safe to stop to rescue the survivors of a sinking. Within days, the order came down: survivors were to be abandoned, the area cleared, until it was certain there was no more threat from the attacking submarine.[10]

U9 went on to one more significant success, sinking another old cruiser, HMS *Hawke*, off Peterhead on 15 October. *Hawke* and another cruiser of the 10th Cruiser Squadron, employed in the Northern Blockade that had already so effectively shut off Germany's commerce, apparently stopped to exchange mail. Weddigen, never one to pass up such an opportunity, put a torpedo into *Hawke* at a range of 500m, sinking her in eight minutes. The other cruiser, HMS *Endymion*, followed orders and steamed off at high speed, leaving the survivors to their fate in the icy North Sea. In the end, only 73 out of a crew of 544 were rescued. First Sea Lord, Jacky Fisher, commented that U9 had caused the Royal Navy more casualties than were lost in all of Nelson's battles combined.[11]

An event more significant than any of U9's exploits occurred with little fanfare two days before Weddigen sank *Hawke*. U17 caught up with a small merchant steamer, SS *Glitra*, off the Norwegian coast. *Glitra* was stopped and searched strictly according to the provisions of international law. Having determined her cargo to be contraband war materials, KL Feldkirchner instructed her crew to take to their boats and then scuttled the abandoned steamer. The instructions given to U-boat commanders had been to ignore merchantmen, but Feldkirchner thought the opportunity too good to pass up and his superiors back home concurred. Clearly, the event was a watershed, far more portentous than either of Weddigen's more famous exploits. Much debate in Germany and outside would be expended over the next few years in determining what rules should apply to the use of submarines against technically non-military targets. For the moment, Germany was committed to the strict observance of Prize Law.

The magnificent crew trained by Weddigen didn't stay together too long after the sinking of *Hawke*. A crew this good was needed to season the crews of other boats, particularly the new construction that would soon add many more capable boats to the U-boat flotillas. Soon Weddigen himself was detached from U9, taking over the newer U29, bigger, faster and better in almost every way. Weddigen took U29 out for the first time in March 1915. He sank four steamers off the Scilly Isles, each time scrupulously following the letter and spirit of the law. So strict was his observance of international law that he received praise from the Commander of Submarines in the Royal Navy and even got dubbed the 'polite pirate' by *The Times*.[12] On 18 March, U29 was headed home around the northern tip of Scotland when it stumbled on the Grand Fleet. Engrossed in trying to line up a shot on one squadron of dreadnoughts, U29 was surprised and rammed by HMS *Dreadnought* herself and was lost with all hands. In his short career, Weddigen had become the first great U-boat ace and the first U-boatman to win the *Pour la Mérite*, the so-called 'Blue Max', Germany's highest honour. Some notion of the esteem in which Weddigen was held by his compatriots can be surmised from the fact that when Germany began to build U-boats again in the 1930s, the first flotilla of the new *Ubootwaffe* was named after him.

Johannes Spiess took over U9 and commanded it until November 1915. It was relegated to a training role in 1916 and survived the war, finally ending up ignominiously beached off Dover when it broke its tow en route to the salvage yard. Spiess proved luckier than Weddigen or U9. He commanded UC27 briefly in July and August 1916. Then, he took over U19 through June 1917. He had some success in command of U19, sinking the armed merchant cruiser *Calgarian* in March 1917. He commanded U52 between September and October 1917 in the Mediterranean, and ended the war in command of the brand new, large *Mittel-U* U135. (The term *Mittel-U* referred to 'mainstream' U-boats. During the First World War, U-boat designs evolved into several distinct lines of development. The *Mittel-Uboote* continued the development of standard ocean-going U-boats that started with U1. During the course of the war, *Mittel-Uboote* became ever larger and more complex and, at the same time, slower and more expensive to build. There were also the *U-Kreuzers*, a separate line of even bigger boats intended for long-range raiding. Finally, there were the UBs and UCs, which were smaller boats.)

Together with a torpedo boat and a detachment of marines, Spiess was instrumental in putting down an attempted mutiny in the fleet at Schillig Roads in late October 1918. The crews of several of Germany's powerful battleships refused to sail when the Admirals of the High Seas Fleet ordered one last desperate sortie rather than submit tamely to surrender to the British. Spiess's efforts were ultimately in vain; only a week later, a better organised attempt set up a Workers and Soldiers Council in the fleet and effectively took control of the once proud High Seas Fleet.

— 2 —
UC74

Unrestricted Warfare

By the spring of 1917, Britain's vital lifeline, its seaborne commerce, was under vigorous and successful attack. The Germans had come somewhat reluctantly to the conclusion that unrestricted U-boat warfare was the only chance they had to counter the slow strangulation caused by the Royal Navy's blockade of their commerce. Although a continental power, the Germans had built up their economy before the war to depend on extensive imports of oil and many strategic materials, particularly nitrates from South America used in the production of fertilisers and munitions. Effectively cut off from all imports from the first day of the war, in August 1914, the German economy was slowly failing; the ability of German industries to build the machines of war and of its agriculture to supply its fighters and particularly the civilians back home with food and other necessary materials was steadily diminishing.

Some inside Germany had argued even before the war that an unrestricted campaign against Britain's own commerce was inevitable and proper. But others, more cautious or more old-fashioned, had argued both against the necessary barbarity of such a course and, more practically, had realised that unrestricted U-boat warfare would eventually lead to incidents involving American shipping and would lead sooner or later to America's entry into the war on the opposing side. Three different times the Germans had declared unrestricted U-boat warfare and three times they had backed off, mainly due to American protests. (These periods had been February–September 1915, March–April 1916 and October 1916–January 1917. The American position here was ambiguous; while maintaining strictly neutral status, and carrying on a vigorous trade with Britain, the Americans protested only briefly and feebly against the blockade of Germany while issuing repeated strong protests against German sinking of American ships, particularly when they were sunk without warning.)[1] Finally, in February 1917, bowing to the unavoidable conclusion that Germany could not win the war on land and would eventually starve unless Britain could be convinced to quit the fight, the German High Command issued its fourth and final declaration of unrestricted warfare against Britain's commerce.

The critical point was the unrestricted element of these campaigns. International law always allowed warfare against an enemy nation's commerce, but required that steps be taken to protect the lives of crew and passengers.

Further, that law permitted contraband war materials in neutral hulls to be seized or the ships sunk, but only after the ship was stopped, its manifests examined and, of course, provision made for the safety of crew and passengers. The British, in their blockade of Germany, had no trouble following these rules, since their warships controlled all the main water approaches to Germany. U-boats, on the other hand, were increasingly endangered by these rules, especially after the British armed their merchantmen and ordered them to fight back. (The British never admitted that the general arming of their merchant ships and the issuance of instructions to fight back when a U-boat ordered them to stop amounted legally and morally to removing them from the class of non-combatants, which were subject to the protection of prize law, and made them auxiliary warships, which could be sunk without warning under existing maritime law. The critical point was that U-boats could only find out whether a potential target was an auxiliary warship by putting themselves in mortal danger. It would be difficult and probably pointless to argue which side 'broke the law' first, as both sides bent the rules as they saw fit and took legalistic positions which justified their actions. Ultimately, geography and a powerful fleet put Britain in the position to safely follow more of the niceties of prize law in its blockade of Germany, while leaving the Germans little choice but to break those same rules in their attempted counter-blockade.)

Before the start of the first campaign of unrestricted warfare, U-boats had been sinking only a small number of British merchant ships.[2] Given the small number of U-boats available and the demands of prize law, successes were few and far between. The beginning of the first period of unrestricted warfare brought an immediate fourfold increase in sinkings that, with minor fluctuations, gradually grew to the point that by the end of this period, September 1915, British shipping losses for the first time exceeded the rate at which new shipping was being built. Political pressure from America brought this campaign to an end; economic pressure started the second one the following spring. (The decision to restart unrestricted warfare was also influenced by an American pronouncement in November 1915 that it had no objection to such warfare as long as neutrals weren't attacked without warning. The Americans conceded the point, argued by Germany, that armed merchant ships should be treated as warships. U-boats, in theory, could identify neutral shipping, even from a submerged attack position, because neutrals were supposed to carry large, highly visible neutrality markings that included the ship's name, country and large depictions of the country's flag painted across the ship's side. However, in poor visibility or at night it was not always possible to see these markings, and the British, as this chapter shows, had no qualms about disguising its warships with neutrality markings. The Germans, to be fair, used the same ploy in both wars.)[3]

This campaign was brief, lasting only two months in early 1916, before the Kaiser lost his nerve in the face of renewed American protests. Nevertheless, during those two months, sinkings shot up and then they dropped back down again when the campaign was halted. The cycle was repeated during the winter of 1916–17, until finally, in early 1917, the U-boats were released from all restrictions. The rate of sinkings had been holding steady through late 1916 at about 300,000GRT per month; with the final resumption of unrestricted warfare in February 1917, the rate shot up first to 500,000GRT and, in April, to an incredible 800,000GRT.[4]

Q-Ships

The Royal Navy, still invincible on paper, was losing the war. The German High Seas Fleet, the Kaiser's pride, had challenged the British only once, at Jutland in May 1916, and had held their own, but by the end of the day, the Germans were headed back to port and, with only the briefest interludes, would remain there until the end of the war. The Grand Fleet was invincible, but in the open ocean around the British Isles, the Royal Navy seemed powerless to stop the U-boat assault.

The British attacked the problem with typical energy. Various anti-subma-rine weapons and tactics were tried, but unfortunately proved almost entirely unsuccessful. Static measures were attempted: minefields of ever increasing depth and complexity, including drags, sweeps and nets of every variety. Despite the immense effort, virtually nothing was gained. The Germans continued to use every strait and narrows the Royal Navy tried to block. Active measures concentrated on patrols by destroyers, sloops, motor launches and drifters. While the numbers of craft available for such duties increased dramat-ically as the war progressed, the tactics with which they were employed were simply ineffective. The standard procedure was to maintain standing patrols in high-traffic areas, for which, of course, the U-boats were on alert and which they generally avoided with ease. When a U-boat was sighted, anti-submarine craft were dispatched to the location. As a rule, by the time the patrol arrived, the U-boat had cleared the area.

One tactic that seemed to be producing satisfactory, though sporadic, results was the use of decoy ships. The ploy, as old as warfare, was to lure the enemy into attacking a seemingly helpless target, only to find that the intended victim was a well-armed and well-protected warship. In the First World War, the British converted over 180 merchant vessels into 'special service vessels' popularly known as Q-ships.[5] These ships were designed to look perfectly innocent; their guns, generally at least four in number, were hidden behind easily removed camouflage screens designed to resemble ordi-nary deck-hamper. In place of a standard cargo, their holds were generally filled with empty steel drums or bales of cork or some similar material that would aid floatation in case the ruse failed and the ship was torpedoed.[6] Despite this protection, 27 out of the approximately 180 Q-ships were sunk by U-boats. In turn, the Q-ships accounted for 11 U-boats. Most of those victories came in 1915 and 1916; as the war progressed, U-boats learned to be cautious of small, single targets and became more likely to attack without warning. Still, even at the beginning of 1917, an inviting target could draw a U-boat to the surface, looking for an easy kill without wasting a valuable 'eel'. Even during the periods of unrestricted warfare, a strong temptation remained for U-boats to attack smaller targets on the surface, using their deck gun. For most of the war, only the biggest U-boats had more than four torpedo tubes and more than eight to ten total torpedoes; many had less. Consequently, commanders learned to reserve their torpedoes for larger, more valuable targets, accepting the known risks of surfacing to engage smaller targets by gunfire.

HMS *Wonganella*

One such encounter occurred on 11 March 1917. The Q-ship was HMS *Wonganella*, operating mainly in the Mediterranean, regularly patrolling between the Atlantic and Malta. Originally the merchantman SS *Thornhill*, *Wonganella* was converted into a warship by the installation of a pair of 4in and a pair of 12pdr guns, one of each on either broadside. This arrangement of guns was far from successful. *Wonganella's* captain, Basil T. D. Guy, reported, in a post-war account of the action:

> I had 2 guns in action ... but they were not well calibrated to shoot together at that range – they were any old guns we could get hold of and spotting was very difficult with two guns of different calibre that did not shoot together at any given range.[7]
>
> *Wongonella* was capable of 9½kts with a clean bottom. However, her bottom was far from clean in the late winter of 1917. On Monday, 5 March 1917, she left Malta for Gibraltar; this time she was to continue on to England for docking and a good scraping. In the meanwhile, she was still a Q-ship in His Majesty's Navy and so, as usual, she decked herself up in 'war paint' before leaving Malta:
>
> On this cruise I was disguised as a Spanish ship, flying the Spanish ensign and carrying a large painted flag on each broadside, together with the name of the ship and port of registry painted in large letters on each side.

The thinking behind the disguising of Q-ships as neutrals, was that a U-boat would not pass up a juicy neutral target, but would have to surface to inspect its papers because neutrals could be sunk, under prize law, only if they were carrying war materials (or other contraband) for the other side, and that could be verified only by examining bills of lading. Since carrying contraband was extremely profitable for neutral shipowners, a high percentage of neutral shipping in the Mediterranean and around the British Isles was indeed liable to be sunk under prize law, so that a Q-ship painted with neutrality markings would be a tempting lure for an unwary U-boat. In this case, though, the disguise proved to be useless and, in fact, dangerous:

We met very bad weather and I had to shelter off Cape Bougaroni; a French customs officer pulled out to me and talked Spanish, which I could not do, so he became very excited and suspecting me probably of being a German raider in disguise, he dashed ashore to get assistance – so, fearing arrest, I had to put to sea in the gale.

We had secret signals with French *naval* patrols, but not with shore officials.

I was of course soon arrested at sea that night by a trawler, but he let me go on receiving my secret signal; however I was again arrested next morning (Saturday) and taken nearly into Algiers by two trawlers who ignored my secret signals, until just before reaching Algiers they let me go again.

Meantime I had been frightened by the possibility of unpleasantness with the Spanish consul and had painted out my disguise and become an 'allied' merchant-ship with no name or colours showing.

On being released off the entrance to Algiers I proceeded on my cruise but could not resume the disguise again because the paint had not yet dried.[8]

So, temporarily undisguised, HMS *Wonganella* proceeded westward near the North African coast in the direction of Gibraltar.

UC74

Early German U-boat development seemed to follow a simple line of evolution: each succeeding class was bigger than the previous. This was fine as long as the primary tactic remained the strict observation of prize law, as adopted at the beginning of the war. Bigger boats meant longer range and the ability to carry more torpedoes and larger deck guns. As long as U-boats were thought of only as traditional commerce raiders with the added ability to submerge (and as long as anti-submarine measures remained largely ineffective), this line of evolution made sense. As the war progressed, two additional factors led to the development of smaller, less complex and more quickly built series of boats. One was the gradual improvement of British anti-submarine measures, which increased the chances of losing a boat in action, which, in turn, militated in favour of more, smaller and cheaper boats as opposed to fewer, bigger and more expensive ones. The other was the decision to use U-boats for the laying of mines. This latter factor led to the building of UC74.

There was nothing very unusual about UC74. That, in and of itself, distinguished it from the bigger U-series boats. Those boats were built in small classes; the whole process from design to construction to deployment was slow and the number of boats was never enough. It was only when the war was actually under way and after the Belgian coastline had fallen into German hands, that plans began to be made to build numerous, smaller boats to supplement the small number of bigger ocean-going boats. The first small, short-range, coastal minelaying U-boats were ordered in October 1914.[9] This initial UCI series was truly tiny, just 168 tons surface displacement, with six open vertical mine-tubes, each capable of carrying two UC120 mines, and no torpedo tubes. They were designed to make short trips from Zeebrugge or other Belgian ports, to lay their mines off some English port and to head straight back to base. Unlike the massive minefields laid by both sides to protect their ports – minefields whose basic size and location was well known by both sides – these U-boat-laid minefields, of up to a dozen mines, took a slow but steady toll of shipping and tied up huge numbers of small craft in constantly sweeping the approaches to ports.

Only 15 UCI boats were built before it was decided that a somewhat bigger boat might carry considerably greater offensive punch over a longer range and still be much faster and cheaper to build than the big mainstream boats. These enlarged small minelayers were dubbed the UCII class. They were more than twice as big as the UCIs, at 417 tons.[10] Surface range jumped from 750nm to over 9000nm. A raised deck-casing forward allowed for longer mine-tubes, which permitted the UCIIs to carry 18 larger UC200 mines in their six free-flooding tubes. They also carried three torpedo tubes, a total of seven torpedoes and even mounted an 8.8cm deck gun. This new boat was an extremely successful design and was produced in significant quantities; 73 were ordered, and 63 were completed before the end of the war.

UC74 was a UCII. It was ordered from Vulkan Hamburg in 1916 and put into service in November of that year. Its commanding officer was ObltzS Wilhelm Marschall. Marschall took the boat through its working up in the Baltic and then departed Kiel for the Mediterranean on 17 February 1917 on UC74's first war patrol. They found and sank the Dutch tanker SS *Ares* (3783GRT) off Portugal and passed through the Straits of Gibraltar on 10 March.

An Unlikely Duel

At 0145 on 11 March 1917, UC74 was well inside the Mediterranean, about 25nm off the Habibas Light (which would put the U-boat close to the southern shore between Oran to the south and Cartagena to the north). At 0215, a steamer was sighted off the starboard quarter heading south-west, but wasn't pursued, since it was too close to the shore and had too big a lead; anyway, it was heading away from Pola, UC74's destination. (Pola was the primary naval base for the Austro-Hungarian Navy. Located on the eastern shore of the Adriatic, at the tip of the Istria peninsula that partly forms the Gulf of Venice, it is now called Pula and is part of independent Croatia. During the First World War, Pola was the principal base for German U-boats operating in the Mediterranean.)

At 1015, another steamer was sighted, this time two points off the port bow heading north-west. This one was headed away from Pola as well, but the intercept solution was easy and could be achieved without any backtracking, so Marschall ordered the bow swung to port, keeping the target eight points on the starboard bow. The weather was cloudy and the wind and seas calm. Visibility was good, but the merchantman seemed unaware of the U-boat closing on the surface. UC74's log reports the initial encounter in just a few words:

Opened fire at 8000m; steamer turns away and attempts to escape the beating by course-alterations; ceased firing; continued pursuit.[11]

Wonganella was in fact genuinely surprised when UC74 opened fire, but recovered quickly. The irony of the moment – a Q-ship caught unawares by its intended quarry – passed unnoticed as *Wonganella* immediately fell into its alternative guise of the frightened merchantman fleeing an attacking U-boat. (By having painted out its neutrality markings, *Wonganella* lost the use of its primary tactic, that of waiting for the U-boat to heave to and send over a boat with an inspection party before opening fire. As a British merchant ship, it had to feign panic to lure the attacker close enough for a quick kill.)

Guy continues:

About 9.30 a.m. Sunday 11 March 1917, a gun was fired on my port beam and we made out a submarine very indistinctly about 6000 or 7000 yards distant. I hurried away to run and he continued to fire 7 or 8 rounds which mostly fell over (beyond) me, after which he ceased firing and chased me.

I gave him a run of 15 or 20 minutes, going slow myself, and even stopping my engine occasionally and saw him settle down to a fast chase.[12]

The deception worked. UC74 saw only a panicked victim and set off in pursuit, never suspecting for a second that its quarry wanted to be caught. When the range had dropped sufficiently:

> Opened fire again at 4000m; steamer stopped and turned, leaving UC74 on his starboard side; we turn to starboard. No flag and no neutrality markings. Firing for effect; 7 hits observed. 2 boats are let down into the water.[13]

Marschall was playing right into Guy's hands:

> I was hoping that he might run right up to me, but in any case I had to wait until he fired again before I could "abandon ship", there being no obvious excuse if one is not being "shelled".
>
> When he had closed to about 3000 yards he turned to starboard and resumed firing: this was my opportunity, so I ordered "abandon ship".
>
> This order takes everyone to the boats except myself, the gun crews, the chief engineer and one stoker.
>
> I then hurried to starboard, broadside to the submarine, went astern with my engine, blew my steam siren and did everything possible to let him know I surrendered (except make a signal by flags) . . .
>
> Thus he could see two boats being got out on his side and I assumed he would cease firing until the boats were away. Never was an assumption more in error, he delighted in firing on the personnel of what he then thought was an unarmed ship and sprayed my after well-deck as fast as he could – in other words 'frightfulness'.[14]

The U-boat's continued shelling ruined *Wonganella's* carefully practised ruse, damaged the boats she was attempting to launch and began to threaten the ship. (The British log complains at length about the U-boat's continued shelling after *Wonganella* started to launch her boats, but completely overlooks the moral issues associated with feigning surrender in order to lure the U-boat to its destruction.)

> The abandon-ship idea seemed no longer feasible, I had not a sound boat to put the wounded into, nor enough of anything to take the crew detailed to abandon ship. At least one shot had hit me on the waterline and water was pouring into my holds. The holds were empty except for about 3–4 feet deep of sand, as ballast.
>
> At this stage I decided that my only hope of getting the submarine was to open fire now. It was most disappointing, the range between

3000–4000 yards was by no means a certainty, it was not even probable that we should hit him under such snap shooting conditions, but there seemed no chance of getting him closer and his shooting was quite good enough to sink us at any minute.[15]

The confusion on board *Wonganella* was increasing by the minute. Far sooner than he wanted, Guy ordered his two starboard guns to open fire:

> The din was indescribable, shells bursting, cries of wounded men, the steam from the burst winch pipe and above all our own boiler steam blowing off – you could not give an order and be heard at 2 feet away. Fortunately the casemates where the guns were situated were quieter and they received my order 'open fire'.
>
> The next thing was to get all hands on-board again. The noise was so frightful that nobody except the gun crews knew that we ourselves had opened fire and so all continued to man the boats.[16]

Wonganella shooting back changed the complexion of the encounter. UC74 had been engaged in a leisurely shelling of an apparently helpless victim. U-boats had been doing this with great success for over two years. Suddenly, and quite unexpectedly, the helpless victim was fighting back. Fortunately for Marschall and his crew, his aggressive attack on the freighter had forced her to open fire at a greater range than she would have liked and the resulting fire was sufficiently inaccurate to enable UC74 to get her gun crew below and dive without being hit:

> Steamer opened rapid fire at 3000m after 6th hit, from hidden gun mounts, the muzzle-flashes indicate 2 guns amidships (1 in front of and 1 abaft the funnel). (Calibre about 5 cm).; then a larger calibre gun also began a rapid-fire from amidships...[17]

The initiative had briefly swung over to the Q-ship, but once UC74 was below the surface, the U-boat was once again in control of the situation. Guy had no choice but to get the crewmen out of the boats and back on board as quickly as possible. Retrieving the boats themselves was out of the question:

> The submarine had submerged as soon as we commenced firing (at that time I judged from the number of rounds we fired that he was under water in 45 seconds) so we must expect a torpedo at any moment.
>
> I shouted to and beckoned the starboard boat to come alongside. The men began climbing inboard up only one rope ladder. I managed by

working the engine very slowly to turn the ship's head 8 points to starboard, thus heading for the spot where the submarine had dipped: this undoubtedly gave us another 7 or 8 minutes grace, as he had to steam 3000 yards underwater to my new beam before he could attack with a torpedo.[18]

As soon as the last man was inboard I went 'full speed ahead' and turned to port to swing my propeller clear of the boats which I left behind...[19]

Marschall wanted nothing more than to finish off the pesky Q-ship with a torpedo, but Guy's tactics ruined his shot:

Alarm, fast-dive. Underwater, we continued the attack on the steamer, which is now flying the English battle-ensign from her gaff. Shot from 2nd tube (distance 500m) missed forward, becausethe steamer made a hard starboard turn and gathered way on a NW course, leaving her empty boats behind. Steamer had anyway, at 5-10m in the calm sea, seen the torpedo's exhaust bubbles.[20]

The torpedo missed because *Wonganella* had indeed seen the telltale bubbles caused by the torpedo's launch and had been able to turn away from the torpedo.

As suddenly as it had started, the encounter was over. Two hunters had met and neither had prevailed. HMS *Wonganella* continued off to the north-west at her best speed of eight knots, on the lookout for the U-boat, expecting to see it re-emerge at any moment, but no more was seen of UC74. As long as UC74 remained submerged, that speed was enough to assure *Wonganella's* escape. Swinging gradually around to the south-west, *Wonganella* met up with HM Yacht *Jolanda* at dusk and was escorted the rest of the way into Gibraltar.

UC74 continued submerged, trying to get into position for a second shot, but the target was soon forgotten as the U-boat found itself entangled in what it believed was a net or other underwater obstruction left behind by the fleeing Q-ship. Only by diving deeper was the boat able to free itself of the net.[21] By the time UC74 resurfaced, at 1340, the steamer had long since disappeared.

Aftermath

This was just another of the many encounters between a solitary steamer and a U-boat. It differed from most only in that the intended victim had teeth and was designed to trap the hunter. Both lived to tell their story. UC74 continued on to a successful career in the Mediterranean for the rest of the war, sinking a total of 37 ships of almost 100,000 GRT.[22] It eventually was interned at Barcelona on 21 November 1918 when it began to run out of fuel while trying to return to Germany at the end of its last patrol. Marschall had turned over UC74 to OLzS von der Luehe long before, on 17 December 1917. He was promoted to Kapitänleutnant and given the command of UB105, also operating out of Pola in the Mediterranean. This boat also was successful, sinking 25 ships of almost 70,000 GRT.

After the war, Guy and Marschall went in very different directions. Guy settled on a farm in Surrey and raised chickens. Marschall stayed in the much reduced *Reichsmarine* after the war and prospered, rising through the ranks until, in the reborn *Kriegsmarine*, he became probably the most successful German surface ship commander of the Second World War. Reaching the rank of General-Admiral, he was in command of the surface fleet in 1939–40, but he argued continually with Grand-Admiral Raeder over the degree of tactical independence a fleet commander should be allowed when at sea. Finally, tired of Raeder's 'micro-management', he went on sick leave for almost two years before coming back as Commander, Group West in 1942, after the surface fleet was effectively bottled up by the Royal Navy and Hitler's fear of another *Bismarck* disaster.

UB81

The Silent Enemy

UB81 was a brand new boat, but its crew was experienced and its captain was extremely popular. It was one of the growing number of UBIII boats entering service in late 1917. The UB series were developed in order to augment the woefully small number of mainstream U-boats (*Mittel-Uboote*) being built in Germany's yards. Just as the UC series was developed to provide smaller, cheaper and, above all, easier-to-build minelayers to supplement the few big minelayers coming into service, the UB series was intended to add many more submarines to the fleet in a short period of time. As with the UCs, the first UBs had been tiny, but, having gone through two redesigns, the UBIII boats had grown to become fully capable ocean-going U-boats. At more than 500t, with five full-sized torpedo tubes, an 8.8cm deck gun and a range of 8500nm, they were indeed a potent weapon to be appearing in numbers in the waters around the British Isles.

UB81 was built at the AG Weser yard in Bremen, having been launched, in nearly complete condition, in mid-August 1917. As was normal for a new boat, the crew began to assemble even before the launching. The LI (*Leitender Ingenieur* – Engineering Officer) came to the yard as the boat was being built. Then the engine-room chiefs and the remaining officers and gradually the rest of the crew assembled so that the boat was fully manned at commissioning and ready to begin trials. The officers and petty officers were, for the most part, well experienced. Almost all had joined the Navy prior to the war and had served on other U-boats before coming together to form the crew of UB81.

The captain of UB81 was a particularly successful and well-decorated U-boat veteran. OLzS Reinhold Saltzwedel had commanded four other boats (UB10, UC11, UC21 and UC71), all operating out of the Flanders bases, prior to being assigned to commission UB81. He had claimed sinkings totalling 230,000t, sufficient to cause him to be awarded the coveted *Pour le Mérite*, known popularly as the 'Blue Max'.[1] His best-known engagement, the one that led directly his receiving the award, was his attack on the Q-ship *Dunraven* on 8 August 1917, while on his sole patrol in command of UC71.[2]

Saltzwedel was popular in part because of his success and bravery, but mainly because he was a good commander. He had a reputation for treating his crew well and bringing them back alive, two very important traits, from the point of view of those who served under him. Like the average U-boatman, by the end of 1917, Reinhold Saltzwedel had already been to sea on too many missions with too little time to recover between patrols. In less than two years, he had been in command on no less than 11 patrols. The longest stretch of time off duty during those years had been a break of slightly less than a month between his first and second commands, and that had been back in June 1916. As a rule, U-boatmen were well treated. The naval command understood both how important the U-boat offensive was to Germany's chances of success in the war and how dangerous the job was for individual U-boatmen. So, while the German civilian population got by on slimmer and slimmer rations, U-boatmen still fared well. For purely logistical reasons, those in Flanders did better than those based in Germany proper:

> The Submarine Officers in Flanders appear to have a much pleasanter time than those in Germany. They are all billeted in private homes in Bruges and take their meals in the *Offizierkasino* (Officers' Club). The food is excellent, and there is no lack of wine and spirits; in fact, during the short interval between two consecutive cruises, the officers appear to enjoy themselves freely. There are no restrictions as in peace time; they can go where they please in uniform or plain clothes, and they are not interfered with if they are seen in music halls or other localities in uniform.[3]

The free availability of alcohol was particularly important to submariners. Almost to a man, they found solace in inebriation. Saltzwedel was no exception:

> On one occasion, however, after OLzS Saltzwedel had been in harbour for 5 days and had not been sober the whole time, he came around and turned him out of bed and told him to get away to sea again.[4]

Perhaps it was the fact that he shared the same fears and sought the same relief as his crewmen that accounted, at least in part, for him being such a popular commander.

UB81's crew was all in place and presumably sober for the boat's commissioning at the Weser yard on 18 September 1917. It took the rest of the month to complete work on the boat and then from early October through early November it went through acceptance trials. Those trials found the boat to be in good shape and only minor corrections were required from the yard before it left Kiel on 9 November for Flanders and combat. The boat passed westward through the Kiel Canal, down the Elbe estuary and, under close escort, along the East Frisian Islands as far as Nordeney, where the escort departed and headed back to Cuxhaven. UB81 then proceeded alone along the Dutch and Belgian coasts using the swept channel codenamed 'Black', arriving at Zeebrugge on 11 November. There they trained for two-and-a-half additional weeks, including a two-day practice patrol into the North Sea. Finally ready for offensive combat, the boat provisioned and fuelled and departed Zeebrugge, heading south-west along the Belgian coast towards the Straits of Dover. They passed through the Straits on 29 November without difficulty. South of the Dover Barrage, Saltzwedel brought the boat back to the surface, and he was operating on the surface when, near midnight on 30 November, UB81 found and attacked a convoy, sinking the 3200GRT steamer *Molesey*. Satisfied with this success, he took the boat south to the shallows close under the French coast and put it on the bottom, in 24 fathoms of water, until late afternoon on 1 December. At that point, the boat was surfaced and proceeded through the long winter night due west across the Channel, anchoring again in shallow water off the English south coast until just before dawn on the 2nd.

Despite the one sinking already achieved, Saltzwedel was far from satisfied with the performance of his new boat. He had encountered no fewer than four different convoys in the Channel within as many days. Each time he had been on the surface when the convoy was sighted. Each time he had attempted to dive the boat once he'd gained a favourable attack position. However, on three of those four occasions, the boat had plunged out of control when the dive was made and, by the time it was brought back under control, the targets had slipped away.[5] Bad as that was, things were about to get worse. Preparatory to surfacing at 0610 on 2 December, an attempt was made to raise the anchor, which had been dropped to prevent the boat's slipping while resting on the bottom. Instead of raising properly, the anchor cable parted, and the anchor and about 50m of cable were lost.

Once the anchor was lost, nothing else seemed to work right. Saltzwedel brought the boat to the surface and the LI adjusted the trim as best he could, but the boat never really handled correctly after that. Despite these problems, Saltzwedel spent the daylight hours of 2 December patrolling, mainly on the surface, along the eastern shore of the Isle of Wight and into Spithead as far as the Owers Light. But he failed to sight a target and had taken the boat south again to a point about 10nm south-east of Dunnose when, submerged to a depth of 25m, a dull explosion was heard aft. Moments later, two crewmen came running into the control room and announced that water was pouring into the after torpedo room, the aftmost of the boat's compartments.

A Weapon of Infinite Patience

Of all a U-boat's enemies, a mine was the least feared yet, in some ways, the most deadly. It is natural not to think much about mines as a threat; after all, mines don't chase you. There is no animus, no personifiable human malevolence on the other end of a mine. Instead, mines wait with infinite patience for you to make a mistake, which is part of what makes mines such a dangerous weapon. You can travel through a minefield 100 times and on the 101st passage you might get caught. You can pass 2m away from a mine and be blithely unaware of its existence, but slip over those few metres and your brief time on this earth will probably end: which is another part of the curious nature of mines as a threat. Every other weapon in the enemy's arsenal might hit you, but it is far more likely to miss by some distance and then perhaps inflict a measure of damage depending on how far away it explodes. Mines, almost always, are far more binary in their effect: which is what makes the story of UB81 so unusual. This time, there was an encounter with a mine and there were survivors to tell the tale.

Most First World War U-boatmen sailed from harbours, whether in Flanders or Germany, into seas liberally strewn with mines. There were mines everywhere. Both sides laid extensive minefields and, more often than not, each side knew where the other side's fields were. The location of your own minefields was, in theory, a carefully guarded secret. Germany had an elaborate set of fields along its North Sea coast, with regularly swept entrance and exit routes, coded with colour names. When each U-boat left harbour, it carried not only its standard navigational charts, but also an 'Eyes Only' chart of the latest information on minefield location that only the commander could see. That way, if the crew was captured, it would have no detailed knowledge of the minefields to divulge, either accidentally or on purpose.

Even so, it wasn't such a bad strategy to let the other side know where your fields were, because that would restrict their movements into narrow, swept channels, where they would be easier to find. And, of course, periodically, it was good strategy to lay some mines in the enemy's swept channels, just to keep them on their toes. Maybe you could sink a ship or two before they caught on and reswept their channels. Germany's UC-type minelayers were particularly good at laying a few mines at a time in places the British thought were safe, off harbours and in swept channels.

Laying a minefield took careful thought, particularly if your intent was to sink (or prevent the passage of) submarines. If your target was surface shipping, the problem was much easier. In that case, you sowed some mines at or very near the surface and waited for the enemy to stumble on them. Catching a U-boat is much harder because it's a small target and it can dive. A sparsely sown minefield would have little if any deterrent effect. If the odds of hitting a mine were low and the alternative routes were longer and not much less dangerous, as was the case with the Straits, U-boat commanders would choose the shorter route and accept the risks. And if all the mines were at the surface, the boat could always dive underneath them. To block the passage of U-boats, you had to sow a field that was both dense and arrayed its mines vertically as well as horizontally. This took a lot of mines, intimate knowledge of the topography of the ocean floor, careful selection of location and considerable skill in minelaying. It was not easy to do. For example, the British tried from early 1915 onward to block the Straits of Dover against U-boat transit, using nets and mines. Despite all this effort, the Royal Navy estimated that throughout 1917, as many as 30 U-boats a month were passing through the Straits without harm. Therefore, in late 1917, the Navy decided to abandon the existing net and mine defences and replace them with a deep new minefield across the narrows between Folkestone and Cap Gris Nez.

It would seem that if any stretch of open water could ever be mined, the Straits would be among the easiest. After all, the Straits are, at the narrowest point, slightly more than 20nm across and are deeper than 50m for only a short part of that distance. Nor was it necessary to mine the entire distance, since a navigable channel had to be left open in the shallow waters under both shores to allow normal traffic to pass beneath the watchful eyes of shore-based observers and their guns. Except for these open passages, the rest of the Straits were sown in late 1917 with more than 9500 mines in 20 parallel rows covering a breadth of six miles.[6] This improved barrier was more successful than the previous systems. It did account for 12 U-boats before the end of the war. Nevertheless, more than 25 boats per month continued to pass through the barrage up until the end of the war.[7] UB81 passed south through the Straits without incident.

Thus, UB81 sailed into an ocean literally strewn with mines, both enemy and friendly, where minefields were a known and accepted hazard. To the maximum extent possible, the danger was mitigated by knowledge of the location of minefields, which allowed them to be transited quickly or avoided completely. Nevertheless, UB81 was mined on 2 December 1917. At least, it must be assumed that the explosion was a mine detonating, but there are a number of factors that cloud the issue. First, there were no known minefields in that location off the Isle of Wight.[8] It could have been part of a recently laid German minefield about which Saltzwedel had no knowledge, but that was unlikely. It is far more likely, as happened regularly, that the mine was a drifter, one that had broken free from the Dover Barrage or another field and had drifted on the tide. Second, the explosion was of such low order that the mine may have been defective or perhaps it exploded some distance from the hull. Either is possible. The U-boat's survivors theorised that the boat was still trailing a long length of its broken anchor cable (which would also account for the boat's poor handling) and that this might have snagged the mine's mooring cable and caused it to explode well away from the hull. Regardless of the cause, UB81 now had water coming in aft, the result of detonation some-where outside the hull.

Desperate Choices

There was no panic. The officers and petty officers of UB81 were all experi-enced and it quickly became obvious that the situation was serious but not critical. A quick investigation of the damage showed that the leaks right aft were unstoppable; no simple shutting of valves would stanch the water coming into the boat, so Saltzwedel ordered the compartment abandoned and the watertight hatch between it and the engine room shut. If the leaks had been restricted to the aftmost compartment, UB81 might have been able to limp home, but the next report was of multiple leaks in the engine room as well. They were neither as numerous nor as serious as those in the torpedo compartment, but they too were unpluggable and it became obvious to Saltzwedel that UB81 was sinking. (With both the engine room and the after compartment flooded, the boat would be without power, and, anyway, it would be far too heavy to float.)

The crucial questions were how long it would take for the boat to sink and whether it would be possible to save the crew. The most logical next step would be to bring the boat to the surface, and Saltzwedel ordered just that, but it was already too late. The stern of the boat had been steadily dropping due to the water coming in there, and when the LI attempted to surface the boat, it was discovered that the lines from the compressed air flasks to the aft dive tanks had been damaged in the explosion and the aft tanks couldn't be blown. This only caused the boat to take on a still greater upward angle, since the bow tanks had successfully blown. As a result, within a few minutes, the boat came to rest with its stern on the fortuitously shallow bottom at a depth of 28m sloping at an upward angle of 53deg. The bow of the boat was at or near the surface. That was obvious from the way the bow rose and fell with the motion of the waves. Unfortunately, there was no easy way of telling whether it actually projected above the surface of the water.

The situation was difficult, though not yet desperate. But every moment that passed made their chances a little more bleak. Water was still entering the boat aft, and the air pressure in the boat was increasing in direct propor-tion to the amount of water taken in. The higher the atmospheric pressure, the greater the physiological stress on the bodies of the men in the boat. (One seaman, noticing that his heart was racing as his lungs laboured to cope with the increased pressure, counted his pulse rate and found it to be 127 beats per minute.) Some of the battery acid had already escaped into the bilge due to the angle taken on by the boat, and, as the water level slowly rose aft, sea water would hit cell after cell in the battery space just aft of the control room, each time releasing another dose of highly poisonous chlorine gas into the boat. (The chemistry involved is simple. The batteries carried on U-boats were wet-cell, lead-acid units. The acid was hydrochloric [HCl]. When the acid contacted seawater, the hydrogen atom bonded strongly with the trace metals in the seawater and chlorine gas was released.) Fortunately, chlorine gas is heavy and tends to sink; so it sought out the lowest parts of the boat. Nevertheless, enough gas mixed with the rest of the air in the boat to make breathing more difficult as time went on. Finally, the water that continued to leak in made the boat heavier, and with each passing moment, the tilt decreased slightly. Even if the bow was now above the waterline, eventually it would sink below it, and escape would become much harder, if not impossible. All in all, every moment that passed made the chances of escape less likely. If an attempt was to be made, the sooner the better.

Saltzwedel understood the situation very well and the limited options available. He developed a plan and put it into action in a matter of minutes. Any escape would have to be through the forward torpedo tubes. On the assumption that the bow was free of the water, it should be possible to push men out through the tubes and thus effect an escape. The most immediate obstacle was that all four forward tubes were occupied by torpedoes – objects that are heavy and awkward to handle under the best of circumstances. With the boat lying at a greater than 50deg downward angle, and the deteriorating conditions inside the boat sapping men of strength and hope, removing a torpedo from its tube would be cruel and dangerous work, but it had to be done. To make matters worse, Saltzwedel ordered that the tube to be emptied would have to be one of the upper tubes, because that would increase the odds that the outer end of the tube would be above the waterline. It was a horribly difficult task, but there was no choice. Anyone not needed to handle the torpedo was asked to leave the forward compartment; then, with all the torpedomen standing by to catch the 'eel' when it started to slide out, the inner door to the upper starboard tube was eased open. Predictably, the torpedo started to slide. After all, it was extremely heavy (c.1000kg/c.2200lb) and it was covered with a coating of grease, applied deliberately to ease the task of sliding torpedoes in and out of the tube when the boat was horizontal. The torpedo would have been a G/6 model. A torpedo of that type had a diameter of 50cm (19.5in) and a length of 6m (c.18ft). More than a dozen sweating desperate men fought to grab onto the torpedo as it slid. Fortunately, it started to move slowly enough for its progress to be stopped and eventually it was lowered gently to the deck and its detonator disconnected.

The plan that Saltzwedel had worked out was simplicity itself. Three men, all volunteers, were selected to attempt to squeeze their way through the torpedo tube and out to the surface. It required extraordinary courage to allow oneself to be pushed upward into the narrow, cold, greasy and dark tube. (The tube was slightly over 20in in diameter, fractionally more than the 19½in diameter of the G/6 torpedo.) All the more a courageous act because there simply was no way of knowing what would greet the volunteers when the outer torpedo tube door was opened. If the bow was below water and if the outer door couldn't be closed again, there would be no way of pulling the men back in and equally no way for them to extricate themselves on their own out the top. (The outer tube doors were designed to be closed with the tube flooded. They were not designed, however, to be closed against an inrushing flow of water. It is likely, but far from certain, that they would have closed properly had it been necessary.) The volunteers would be condemned to drown without even the minimal comfort of movement.

In the event, one man allowed himself to be pushed into the tube and then a second behind him, so that the first was standing on the second's shoulders, and then a third. Finally a wooden box was pushed in under the third man. And then the entire crew held its breath while the torpedo mate opened the outer door. After what seemed an eternity, a faint cheer was heard from up the tube and then the crew noticed a rush of air through the tube as the pent-up over-pressure found release. The crew quickly pushed with every available tool against the bottom of the wooden box. When the first man emerged from the tube, he climbed the steeply angled bow of the boat and made fast to the hawse the line he had tied around his waist. Once the line was secure, he was able to pull the other two men in the tube up and out. With the tube clear, they were able to yell down that it was a windy and cold night and that the tube opening was perhaps a foot above water.

A collective sigh of relief passed through the crew as rescue now seemed a reality. However, it was clear that big problems remained. There were no lights in sight, although they were near a busy shipping lane, but soon they noticed numerous ships passing well out to sea. Clearly, they had to attract the attention of one of those passing ships. Flashlights and a Very pistol were hauled up the tube and activated. Meanwhile, seven more crewmen, led by the LI and the IIWO (second watch officer), were pulled up the tube, so that a total of ten men were perched on the bow. (Dropping into the water wasn't an option. In December in the English Channel, the survival time of a swimmer was measured in minutes.[9]) As the minutes dragged on, the initial enthusiasm among the men hanging onto the bow began to wane. It was now perhaps 2200 and the cold wind and the certain knowledge that it would get much colder before dawn drove three of the ten to decide that they would rather die in the relative warmth of the boat's interior than freeze to death or drown when they inevitably fell victim to hypothermia and dropped into the water.

The LI, the more senior of the officers outside the boat, realised that going back inside meant giving up what slim chance existed of rescue; so he decided to follow the three back inside in an attempt to talk them or any others into returning with him. He found that conditions had deteriorated dramatically inside the boat. Water had continued to rise and, as a result, the concentrations of chlorine gas were reaching toxic levels. (The open torpedo tube provided ventilation only to a small area around the tube door itself. Without functional ventilation fans, the quality of the air in most of the boat continued to deteriorate.) The rising concentrations of chlorine gas and carbon dioxide were affecting the crew's mental state as well. Most seemed to have resigned themselves to death. The LI's attempt to persuade others to follow him failed. No one was interested. Even Saltzwedel had become lethargic. The LI begged the captain to order his men out of the boat, but Saltzwedel refused, saying that each man had to make that decision on his own and that, anyway, some of the crew simply were too big to fit into a 20in torpedo tube. The LI then urged the captain himself to come outside, arguing that the men would follow him if he led, but again Saltzwedel declined. He said he wouldn't leave the boat while any of his crew remained on board. The LI was frustrated by the captain's adamancy, but he knew better than to try to argue with his commanding officer. Not only had he failed to persuade anyone to follow him outside, but he found it hard to dissuade them from taking their own lives.[10]

When the LI had himself pulled up the rope and outside again, nobody else came with him. Thus, there were only seven men clinging to UB81's bow when, just a few minutes later, the Royal Navy patrol boat P32 gingerly approached out of the dark. Once the captain of the patrol boat had satisfied himself that UB81 represented no threat, he brought his boat in close to rescue the desperate men hanging on the U-boat's bow. Given the darkness of the scene and the force of wind and waves, and the laudable desire of P32's captain to take the survivors directly off the bow, rather than forcing them to jump into the icy water, it was perhaps inevitable that the patrol boat should bump against the U-boat's bow. Add to that the fact that the U-boat had continued to take on water slowly for the hour that had elapsed since the first men had emerged from the torpedo tube, so that the foot of clearance between the open tube's lip and the waves was now just a few inches. The effect of the bump was to drive the opening of the torpedo tube beneath the surface. The rope leading from the bow back into the boat prevented the closure of either tube door, so there was no way for the men inside UB81 to check the inrush of water down the now submerged torpedo tube. The end, then, must have come quickly for the 28 men still inside the boat. Those who didn't drown in the first rush of water, who found an air pocket in the overhead, surely were quickly asphyxiated by chlorine gas as the sea water found the forward bank of batteries.

The sailors of P32 rescued all seven of the men clinging to UB81's bow. However, one of them, a machinist's mate, died of wounds before getting to port. The remaining six, the two officers, the navigator, another machinist's mate and two seamen, survived to undergo interrogation and internment in a British POW camp. Saltzwedel went down with his boat, but his reputation lived on. Just as Otto Weddigen (see Chapter 1) was remembered by the naming of the first flotilla of new U-boats after him in 1935, Reinhold Saltzwedel's name was given to the second flotilla the following year.

— 4 —
U152

The Behemoth

Mainstream U-boat development and production continued into 1918 at the same slow pace as before. It was augmented by the relatively more rapid, large-scale production of the UB and UC series of smaller boats, intended to make up for the disastrous shortfall in offensive power to be found in the small number of larger boats. Incredibly, the Germans continued not only to pursue the costly development of the mainstream boats, ranging in size from just over 700 tons surface displacement to 900 tons, but also built significantly bigger boats. These boats were not built in large numbers, but they nevertheless took up inordinate planning resources and yard time to design and construct. Several series of these bigger boats were planned simply as enlargements of the mainstream *Mittel-U* series.[1] Two series of still larger boats, which came to be called the *U-kreuzers* (U-cruisers), also were built.

The evolution of the U-cruiser series was unusual, to say the least. By 1915, not even a year into the war, the Royal Navy's economic blockade of Germany was already devastating Germany's war economy, just as the British had intended. What made it worse was that Germany possessed no effective means of ending or breaking the blockade. The High Seas Fleet, easily the second most powerful naval force ever assembled, was still so inferior in numbers to the Grand Fleet that a direct confrontation would probably prove catastrophic. (That confrontation indeed did take place in May 1916 off the Danish coast at the battle of Jutland. While not a disaster for the Germans (they actually succeeded in sinking more British ships than they lost), nevertheless it was clear after Jutland that the Germans lacked the power to move freely in the North Sea and, without that power, they were unable to break the blockade.)

Desperate situations breed desperate solutions and, in this instance, the same solution was conceived almost simultaneously in at least three different places. Probably the first to conclude that a large, cargo-carrying submarine should be able to break the blockade with impunity was the State Secretary for the Treasury. When, in mid-1915, he approached a Bremen wholesale merchant named Alfred Lohmann with his idea, he found that Lohmann had already thought of it and, indeed, had already initiated discussions with potential business partners.[2] As patriotic as he was imaginative, Lohmann approached the German government later in the year with an offer it couldn't afford to ignore.

Lohmann's proposition was simple. If the imperial government would guarantee the principal and promise to pay interest on it at the rate of 5 per cent per year, Lohmann and his partners, Norddeutsch Lloyd and Deutsche Bank, would undertake to raise 2,000,000 marks in order to build and operate an ocean-going cargo submarine. All commercial profits on the sale of the cargo – and they were expected to be considerable – would go to the government. Lohmann, true to his patriotic intent, offered to handle the purchase of the export cargoes, on the German end, free of charge. The German government was being offered a good deal and took little time to accept the proposition. It did so formally on 8 November 1915. The Deutsche Ozean-Reederei GmbH was formed by Lohmann to raise the capital and begin negotiations for the design and construction of the boat. Lohmann had earlier approached AG Weser with the idea for a large ocean-going cargo U-boat and some informal designs had already been prepared when the project was officially launched.

Krupps, the large munitions firm, had already been toying with the same idea that Lohmann proposed because it had large stocks of metal, particularly nickel, stored since the beginning of the war in warehouses in the US for lack of a means of getting it back to Germany. Krupps planned to design and build their boat at their Germaniawerft yards and present it as a gift to the nation, with the sole proviso that its first use be to carry their nickel back home.

Vulcan Stettin, the other yard in Germany already building large U-boats, got wind of these schemes in October 1915 and submitted a plan of their own to the Navy for the conversion of two large UE minelayers already under contract at their yard.[3] When this plan was rejected, Vulcan tried again quickly with a project to build two new boats to the same modified-UE pattern.

Although not initially involved in the negotiations for the construction of Lohmann's boat, the German Navy soon realised that the selection of a yard to build the cargo U-boat would have an impact on its own production schedules; so it rightly included itself in the decision-making process. It examined each of the rival proposals and quickly opted for the Germaniawerft offer, in part because that yard promised the shortest building time for a boat twice the size of the Vulcan plan, but mainly because Krupps stood by their proposal to build one boat free of charge to the nation and, along with the boat paid for by Lohmann's company, was thus offering to build two boats for the price of one. For a price of 2.75 million marks, the estimated cost of one boat with a 600t cargo capacity, Germaniawerft agreed to design and build two boats. One would be owned by the Deutsche Ozean-Reederei GmbH, the other by Krupps, but both would be operated by Lohmann's consortium.

The boats proposed by Germaniawerft were to be twice as large as any previously built in Germany – 65m long, with a beam of 8.9m and a displacement of over 1500t. They weren't sleek by any definition. Unlike more warlike U-boats, these two were designed to maximise internal capacity and, therefore, they were much beamier than the biggest contemporary boats. Not being designed for military use, they were given unusually weak surface propulsion, both to save room in the engineering spaces, which would leave more room for cargo, and because there simply seemed to be no need for high speed. Their diesels produced a total of 800hp, a third of the surface horsepower put into contemporary military U-boats. As a result, they had a maximum surface speed of barely 12kt, 3–5kt slower than their military counterparts. (That speed disparity only became critical later, after these boats were militarised, when the ability to chase down a fleeing target could make the difference between a sinking and another frustration.)

The pressure hulls for the two boats were of unprecedented size and, given the fact that Krupps's Germaniawerft yard was already booked past capacity, were in fact built at the Flensburger Schiffbau yard, but the assembly of components and completion was done at Kiel. Given the urgency of the project, existing components, particularly in the power-plant, were used to the greatest possible extent. The diesel motors, for example, were 400hp units originally intended as auxiliary power generators on battleships also under construction at Germaniawerft. The first of the two cargo U-boats, named *Deutschland*, was launched on 28 March 1916 and was ready for trials barely six weeks later. The second, named *Bremen*, was launched shortly after its sister. As soon as it was ready, *Deutschland* set out for Baltimore, Maryland, on 14 June 1916, where Lohmann's agents had assembled some 1800 tons of rubber as well as smaller quantities of other commodities in desperately short supply back home, and where Krupps had its nickel stored. *Deutschland* arrived off the Virginia Capes on 9 July, well-laden with a cargo of gem stones and, more impressively, 163 tons of dyes and chemicals, which sold on the US market for $1.4M.

For almost a month, the German crew was the star of what would today be called a 'media circus'. The men were wined, dined and repeatedly photographed and interviewed. The boldness of the idea of using submarines to break the British blockade seemed to strike a sympathetic chord with the Americans, who were not yet in the war and who have traditionally sided with the underdog. (It has to be remembered that at this time, American public opinion was far from being strongly pro-British. Many Americans, particularly those of German extraction, were sympathetic to the German side. This was particularly true of Baltimore, where *Deutschland* was docked, which had a large population of German immigrants. The American decision to enter the war on the side of the Allies just a year later was far from universally popular, although public opinion had for the most part swung against the Germans, due mainly to well-publicised incidents of U-boat sinkings causing the loss of American lives.) On 2 August, *Deutschland* departed Baltimore, carrying a cargo of rubber, nickel and tin conservatively valued at several times the cost of building both mercantile boats. This phenomenal success was offset by the unexplained loss of *Bremen* on its maiden outbound voyage.[4]

Prior to the loss of *Bremen*, in fact, before *Deutschland* returned from America, enthusiasm for the idea of merchant submarines had risen to the point that the German Navy ordered six more *Deutschland*-type boats from Krupps. Again, as with the first two, Germaniawerft was so busy that it couldn't make space in its building slips for the new boats; so it distributed the contracts for the hulls of the six boats to other, smaller yards which had little or no experience of U-boat construction, but which had unused building slips. Three hulls were ordered from Reiherstieg, and one each from Flensburger Schiffbau (which had built the pressure hulls for *Deutschland* and *Bremen*), Atlaswerke and Stülcken Sohn. This time, Germaniawerft was responsible only for the diesel motors and for final fitting out; completed hulls were to be delivered to Kiel by each yard. Work proceeded quickly and the first of the boats to be launched, the single hull from Flensburger Schiffbau, was christened *Oldenburg*. However, the brief day of the merchant submarine was already over. The boat was quickly renamed U151 and its fitting out was halted while plans were made to add a pair of torpedo tubes to its bow and four large guns (2x15cm and 2x8.8cm) were added on deck. On 16 December 1916, the decision was made to convert *Oldenburg* and the three hulls completing at Reiherstieg (which were designated U152-4). Less than two months later, *Deutschland* was taken over by the Navy as U155 and the boats being built at Atlaswerke and Stülcken Sohn were similarly militarised (as U156 and U157 respectively).

(The decision to abandon the experiment in blockade running by submarine was made, in part, as a result of *Deutschland*'s second voyage. At the same time as *Bremen*'s doomed voyage in September 1916, the German Navy had dispatched one of its military U-boats, U53 under KpLt Hans Rose, on a mission to harass British shipping off the American coast. In retrospect, it is hard to imagine what the Navy's High Command intended to accomplish with Rose's mission. A great deal of good will had been generated by *Deutschland*'s initial visit. It was predictable that the news that a German predator was lurking just outside American territorial waters dispatching 'innocent' merchant ships as they emerged from harbour would erode that good will. At issue was not the reality of the war being fought in the Atlantic, rather a matter of perception. The Germans consistently misunderstood the stakes in the battle for the hearts and minds of the American public. More importantly, they had no idea how to influence public opinion in their favour. Had they understood the stakes, they would never have dispatched Rose to American waters. As it was when on her second voyage *Deutschland* arrived at New London, Connecticut, on 1 November, its reception was cool. Even worse, when it was leaving port a few days later, *Deutschland* accidentally rammed and sank its escorting tugboat with the loss of five of the tug's crewmen. After repairs, *Deutschland* set out for home on 21 November. It was to be its last commercial voyage.)

The militarisation of *Deutschland* and its six unfinished sisters resulted in the German Navy gaining possession of seven of the largest U-boats yet built. However, the very same qualities that had made them well-suited for their intended purpose as cargo carriers conspired to make them less than fully satisfactory combat submarines. So much of their displacement had been reserved for cargo space and, conversely, so little for machinery and the storage of fuel and provisions, that they were slow and short-legged both on the surface and submerged. Even worse, their unusually broad hull-form, which made them excellent sea boats and stable gun platforms, gave them very poor manoeuvrability, particularly underwater. In general they reacted sluggishly to the helm and, most critically, would dive very slowly.

The comments of KL Adolf Franz, who commanded U152 on its last war patrol, are instructive. U152 was one of the three hulls built by Reiherstieg and was officially launched on 20 May 1917 at Germaniawerft, Kiel. Franz took over the boat on 29 August 1918, its third commander in as many war patrols. The first two patrols had been moderately successful, consisting of long operations in the Bay of Biscay and in the vicinity of the Azores and the Canary Islands. As was common later in the war, Franz came to U-boats from the surface fleet where he had been a gunnery officer at Jutland, but he'd already commanded U47 for one patrol in the Mediterranean and he joined U152 after a stint as commander of U30, a training boat. (Franz was replaced as commander of U47 by a KL Canaris, who went on, between the wars, to achieve the rank of Admiral and commanded the German military intelligence agency, the *Abwehr*.). As a gunnery officer, he was ideally suited to command one of the former mercantile boats, which were primarily submersible gun platforms.

After watching a juicy convoy slip past just out of range on 18 September, Franz bemoaned his boat's sluggishness and handling problems:

> Our low surface and submerged speed had forced us, when we came within sight of that first convoy to cross our bow, to abstain from attacking. Had we been in any of the newest German U-cruisers, we would surely have been nipping at the heels of that convoy, in the

confident expectation that we could gain a good position ahead of the target and achieve a quick success. As it was, we had to be content with radioing the sighting of the convoy back home and hoping that some of the many U-boats on standing patrol west of England would be notified...[5]

In a choppy sea when there was much wind or in a heavy swell, the boat had shown us its shortcomings in regards to its dive characteristics, which urged much caution in combat. We quickly found out, from both practice dives and during attacks, that, if we were even the least bit sideways to the seas, the boat dived extremely slowly, that it seemed reluctant to dive, as if it wanted to stay on the surface for what seemed like minutes, instead of putting its nose down and vanishing under the waves. Also once the boat was submerged, there were plenty of shortcomings in its underwater handling; it was often so ill-mannered that the officers and the helmsmen and planesmen in the Control Room worked up plenty of sweat.

Their biggest problem, as a class, however, was poor range. *Deutschland's* specifications had called for a boat with excellent range, in excess of 25,000nm, but, in reality, the boats fell far short of that goal. So short that less than three weeks into his mission, Franz was seriously worried about his boat's ability to complete its planned patrol:

In the 17 days, so far, of this patrol, we'd covered some 2200nm, which makes an average, in 24 hours, of 130nm and gave us an average speed of 5.4 knots. Given our operational orders, it was going to be another 7000nm before we made it back to our home port in the Baltic. Having gone one-fifth of the entire way of 9200nm, we should have consumed up to now approximately one-fifth of our oil supply. Our operational orders were: 'Conduct attacks against merchant targets en route to the American east coast. Once there, begin operations in a patrol area between Savannah and New York, stretching as far north as Halifax, which operations are to include the cutting of underwater cables and mining of likely locations. On the return journey, continue operations against merchant shipping. Any enemy warships encountered are to be sunk.' We still have approximately 2400nm to cover to get to Savannah. The distances along the American coast amount to approximately 900nm. From Halifax back to the Faroes is about another 2600nm and from there to our home-port is 1100nm, therefore in total about 7000nm are still to be covered; the remaining oil supply, based on consumption up until now, leads me to conclude that the only way to cover these huge distances is a reduction of our average speed. We need to keep an eye out in the future for a tanker that might fall into our hands; if we're lucky, it might have full tanks and perhaps we could pump some oil across to our boat. After all, we had to have enough fuel for a patrol that would last at least 110 days and possibly as many as 140...

Nor was oil fuel the only limit on U152's range;

On top of concerns about fuel, we also had a full crew to consider. Still, why shouldn't we be able to beat the existing record for the number of days at sea by a U-boat? Success in this will require luck. We have been supplied for 100 days, which provisions we could, if careful, stretch for another 20 days. We simply don't have the provisions for the three extra weeks of a patrol of the length being contemplated; the missing provisions must be obtained from steamers we stop...

On this particular mission, the fuel problem only got worse as a result of an unfortunate encounter with a British steamer:

On 24 September, towards evening, in hazy weather, an English steamer named *Alban* came into view. We immediately fired a few warning-shots around her in order to stop her. The steamer immediately returned our fire, began to steer a zigzag course, made smoke and escaped into the haze of the horizon because of her superior speed and because of a momentary breakdown of our oil motor. To our great distress, early the following morning, we discovered that our useless artillery attack of the day before had not been without serious consequences for us. As soon as it became light, we noticed to our considerable horror that in our wake, as far as our eyes could see, there lay a wide oil slick. The crime of it all was that during the night we had lost approximately 13,000 litres of valuable oil (a figure that was later determined to be closer to 18,000 litres), caused by the loosening of a valve in the oil bunker ventilation piping, which had in turn been caused by some damage to the sheet metal of the hull through wave action or perhaps due to the gunfire last evening. Needless to say, we repaired the damage as quickly as possible 'using available resources'.

It is important to note that despite propaganda to the contrary and the fact that the British had armed all merchant ships early in the war and had given them explicit instructions to fire on any submarine, U152 essentially followed prize rules when it encountered a potential target. Already on this mission, U152 had stopped and released unharmed a Norwegian steamer carrying relief supplies to Belgium and a Danish sailing ship carrying salt from Cadiz to the Faroes after their papers had been checked and were found to be in order.

The abortive attack on *Alban* on the 24th and another, equally unsuccessful, attack on an American tanker, *George Henry*, on the 29th, left Franz frustrated and embarrassed at the poor results of his boat's gunnery. Franz wrote after this second attack:

Somewhat repentant and unsatisfied with the outcome of the previous day's efforts and, as a former surface ship gunnery officer and veteran of the Skagerrak[6], particularly bemoaning our 116 shells fired harmlessly into the water, I wished the watch officer on the tower a good watch and a good night just before midnight. I went, still mostly clothed, to my bunk. As the gunnery officer of this U-cruiser, I tried to put the day's events in the best light; about the poor shooting today nothing could be said, but we would do better the next time. 'We would approach much closer to the enemy, hold our fire as long as possible and not start the attack too soon!'

Franz's continuing emphasis on gunnery as the primary means of sinking targets was anachronous at this point in the war. Most U-boat commanders had abandoned the use of the deck gun as being needlessly risky, exposing the boat to fatal damage from armed merchantmen and the increasingly numerous escort vessels. The institution of a convoy system in the North Atlantic by the British in mid-1917 had brought the heyday of the solitary U-boat to an end. No longer could a commander place his boat in a shipping lane and expect a steady stream of targets to pass his way. Convoys meant that chances of seeing a target dropped dramatically and, at the same time, that an attack on a target became far riskier, due to the massed gunnery of multiple targets and the presence of the convoy's escort vessels. By this time, if a U-boat was fortunate enough to find a convoy, the standard means of attack was the submerged torpedo attack.

A number of factors urged Franz to favour the gun as his primary weapon, despite the dismal showing so far in this patrol. His boat, U152, was really better suited for use as a gun platform. His boat had only two torpedo tubes, which severely limited his ability to attack while submerged. On the other hand, it had four deck guns, two of which were large 15cm (c.5.9in) guns, larger even than the weapons carried on contemporary destroyers, the most powerful adversary it was likely to meet. The power of his armament and the short, broad hull form, which gave U152 unusual stability (for a submarine), made Franz's boat more potent on the surface than submerged. Adding to the factors that favoured the use of his guns was Franz's concern to conserve his torpedoes for use after he reached his assigned patrol area and his already-documented awareness of the shortcomings of U152's underwater handling characteristics. But it certainly was Franz's training as a surface fleet gunnery officer that must have led to his almost total reliance on his guns as the primary means of attack.

Manning and firing the guns on U152 was an intricately choreographed dance that involved a significant portion of the boat's crew. (As merchant U-boats, the *Deutschland*s were designed to carry a crew of 56. When militarised, room had to found for an additional 20 crewmen, the torpedomen and the gunners who maintained and manned the boat's offensive weapons. This made the boats very crowded.)

When the guns were manned, a high percentage of the crew was involved directly or indirectly in aiming, firing, loading or supplying ammunition to the guns. Each gun crew was officially three men: aimer, layer and loader. The first of these was responsible for maintaining the correct azimuth and the second for maintaining elevation settings. The loader handled the gun's breech mechanism. He was responsible, during the firing cycle, for opening the breech after a round was fired, extracting the spent cartridge, receiving the fresh round from the ammunition handlers, ramming the new round home in the breech, closing the breech block, setting the trigger mechanism and, finally, firing the gun when the aimer and layer were ready. Overall command of the guns, which included selecting targets, deciding when and at what rate to open fire, was exercised by an officer. On most boats this would be the IIWO, the second watch officer, but on U152, it was Franz himself. But the actual decision as to when to pull the trigger had to be the responsibility of the gun crew itself, because, despite the superior stability of the ex-mercantile boats, they still rolled and pitched far more than the battleships on which Franz had previously served. Except in the calmest of waters, the boat, and the gun with it, moved in a three-dimensional dance that brought the gun back to the same position only once per cycle. The trick to accurate gunnery was always to fire the gun when it was at the same position in the cycle. The art of the gunner was to be able to refine the initial ranging shots, despite the movements of the boat, so that hits could be obtained quickly and then consistently.

Since the rounds came as all-up rounds, there was, in theory, no variability in the energy supplied to a shell. Therefore, to put a shell in the air at a precise point that intersected the target's location entailed varying the azimuth (for angular deflection) and elevation (for range). To be good at what they did, the aimer and layer needed constant practice, which unfortunately was a luxury not available to U-boatmen once the boat went to sea. This lack of practice led to some poor shooting, particularly early in the patrol, which accounts in part for Franz's frustration.

The initial rounds fired in an encounter came from the ready-use containers set into the deck-casing, known as the 'asparagus beds' (*Spargelbetten*). It was necessary to have at least a half-dozen rounds immediately available for each gun because getting ammunition up from below was a slow process to get started. There were no convenient mechanical lifts, such as surface ships had. The rounds had to fetched up from shell lockers under the main deck aft of the control room (where they occupied the bottom half of the former aft cargo hold). From there, shells were passed either forward or aft and up through the old cargo hatches near the bases of the fore and aft 15cm guns. These shells were so big and heavy (each 15cm round weighed 88lb) that manhandling them in the tight confines of a U-boat's interior and then up the narrow hatchways was demanding in the extreme.

A Typical and Fair Encounter

Since setting out from Kiel some 25 days earlier, U152 had had no successes; all targets encountered to date had either been legitimate neutrals or had escaped through a combination of superior speed and defensive firepower. On the morning of 30 September 1918, still in the mid-Atlantic en route to its assigned hunting grounds off the American coast, U152 found another target. The encounter that followed was about as 'typical' and as 'fair' as any such encounter could be:

The 30th of September 1918 began for me at 0550, which was about when I expected to be awakened by the watch officer, who was under standing orders to waken me at first light. As was usual for U-boat commanders, I wanted to be on the tower for those most critical minutes of the day. This time, I was awakened by the sudden shout: 'Rudder hard aport', which jerked me out of my sleep. The watch officer shouted this command to the helmsman inside the tower, who repeated it for the Control Room and it went the length of the boat, into my open cabin. In less than a minute I was on the tower, followed immediately by my orderly, who just a moment before had himself been asleep in his hammock next to my compartment and now was hurrying behind me with my jacket, scarf, gloves and binoculars. What was wrong? Despite the fact that the boat's interior is lit at night with very weak electric light, my eyes had some trouble adjusting to the faint light of early dawn, so I had some trouble sizing up the situation.

In this faint light, the IWO had just sighted a steamer at a bearing of approximately 285deg, about seven points to port, at a distance of approximately 2500–3000m on a parallel course. The steamer was painted very much like the one we chased yesterday, i.e. splinter camouflage, with patches of colour painted in a chequerboard pattern broken by stripes of other colours, so that in the low light, the bow and stern could hardly be distinguished and therefore the steamer's course was difficult to determine. The WO had made a somewhat premature and over-aggressive turn towards the steamer and, confused by the camouflage and low light, I briefly also believed the bow of the steamer was the stern and planned on continuing the turn to port. Once the stern of the steamer was on my starboard bow, I would begin a stern chase. Once this error, i.e., mistaking the bow and stern of the steamer, was discovered, it was no longer possible to stop the turn away from the target due to the strong turning momentum of the boat. At the same moment, we noticed also that the steamer was now turning to port towards us. Obviously, she had sighted us as well, and wanted to turn her broadside away from us before we had the chance to get off a torpedo-shot, or maybe she intended to ram us. Upon reaching the tower, I had ordered the crew immediately to battle stations for a possible artillery-fight, so the guns were already fully manned when we noticed the steamer turning towards us. One possible tactic offered to us was a quick dive and an attempt at an underwater attack, but I didn't give that option any serious consideration. An attempt to dive in this situation would certainly have been disastrous. With the surface of the sea glassy smooth, it normally takes a full 40 to 60 seconds to get U-152 completely submerged. In more normal weather like this morning, with a windstrength of 3 to 4, the effect of the sea and swell is such that it could take 2, 3, 4 or more minutes before the tower was underwater, time enough for the steamer to ram us in this situation.

The crew was as nimble as it had ever been. With unbelievable speed, the guncrews and the ammunition handlers were roused out of the deepest sleep and appeared on deck through the forward, aft and tower hatches, freed the guns from their tied-down positions, removed the tampions, retrieved the ready-use rounds out of the so-called 'asparagus-beds' set into the deck-casing, loaded the guns and aimed them at the designated target.[7] It was still so dark that the aiming marks on the gunsights could not be made out; despite being against the rules, I yelled from the tower down to the guncrews on deck to break out flashlights to let them aim their guns. The crew: 'Guns ready to fire!' Command: 'Range: 1200m; aiming point: the base of the funnel!' That was all our gunners were waiting for!...

U152, with full power on both engines, swung across the bow of the steamer and pulled clear, allowing us to open fire to starboard with both 15cm guns, this time without a warning shot! Still the steamer continued to turn towards us, with the obvious intent to ram. Both first shots were hits, one on the bridge of the steamer, where immediately a big fire appeared to break out. The steamer turned further to port; U152 likewise continued our run to port, slowly increasing the distance to the target. We continued to hit our adversary, which, having come under fire, began to lose way. Sometime between our second and fourth volleys, our adversary opened fire on us; his shots fell both long and short, but in very dangerous proximity of us and on a direct line toward us. The fire on the steamer, especially on the bridge, began to burn fiercely. It continued to grow, while as the steamer turned more and more to port, a so-called 'running gun battle' seemed to be developing on basically parallel, somewhat diverging, courses. This really wasn't good for us, because of the danger of enemy gunfire; the adversary shot well, with guns fore and aft.

Suddenly, we saw gun-flashes at considerable distance off past the bow of the steamer and then, shortly afterwards, in the same direction we sighted a vessel with 2 or 3 funnels, like those of a cruiser, heading towards us at high speed on a zigzag course. In view of the fact that the steamer was continuing a steady fire at us and on top of that there was now an oncoming cruiser at a range of approximately 2500m, it was clear we needed to break off the artillery skirmish and dive. The securing of the guns, the passing of those ammunition casings that had accumulated on deck into the ship (so that they wouldn't drift away when we dived and thus betray our position), the scrambling of the crew that was on-deck down the three hatches, the closing of the hatches and the actual diving of the boat was all done in a manner that made the officers proud. The crew responded to our obvious appreciation and went to underwater battle stations ready to go after the targets. Both wind and sea were increasing. It took a while to get the boat under control submerged because of the ammunition consumption. The restowing of the rounds we brought below again had altered our balance. A quick sweep with the periscope revealed the still burning steamer, which was showing no signs whatsoever of sinking. I attempted to set up a shot at the steamer, which was still circling to port, without any success. From my month-long experience as a teacher of several U-boat-command-trainees, I knew this kind of set-up was a typical classroom exercise. After a second, equally useless run-in toward the target, the steamer gradually straightened its course, settling on approximately 270deg, and started to steam off, leaving us behind. I looked at the clock; it was 0705. Determined not to let the steamer escape, I ordered the rapid blowing of all dive tanks. The boat surfaced rapidly, with the tower, bow and deck-casing out of the water and the compressed air throwing up huge whirlpools on both sides of the boat. The over-pressure in the boat threatened to burst our eardrums before I was able to open the tower hatch. As the first to climb out on the tower, I could see that besides the steamer, there was nothing to be seen. How quickly the gun crews emerged from the just-opened hatches and were again at their guns! No sooner was our tower out of the water than the steamer had opened fire on us again, starting with her stern-gun. At a range of 2500–3500m we returned fire, mixing in some so-called DZ shells, a type of shrapnel round, which, depending on the setting of their fuses, would explode just before hitting the ship. The decision to use this ammunition was arrived at with great reluctance, because I knew its disastrous effect at the target. And shooting at that target was as much like artillery practice as one could ever have wished. Just as it had been before diving, once again we were getting numerous hits on the hull and the superstructure of the steamer. Meanwhile, the enemy kept up a rapid fire with his 15.2cm guns, fortunately without hitting us; nevertheless his shells seemed to be continually exploding about our ears. A shell-splinter seriously injured the knee of our excel-lent forward gun captain; a different shot sent a shell splinter into the tower shell plating immediately beside my arm. I let the stern chase continue at a range of approximately 2500m, gradually taking a starboard and windward position, much to the relief of our gun captains, since the smoke from the steamer's fires had been impeding their visibility. As far as we could tell from our position aft of the steamer, she had no more lifeboats hanging from her davits.

At 0745, we could observe through our binoculars that the steamer's crew was gathering on the main deck of the steamer. Since the enemy had by now stopped firing, I ordered our fire to cease as well. The stern of the steamer was sinking noticeably deeper. Because I wanted to take a survivor on board to interrogate, I directed the U-boat to be brought closer to wreck, steering among the floating debris. Gradually, the steamer sank further and finally it sank stern-first into the depths, after having stood almost vertically out of the water. A gruesome sight! Our ammunition-consumption was 35 shots before diving and 48 after, for a total of 83 rounds!

So far, this had been pretty much a 'textbook' encounter between a U-boat and a steamer. If anything was unusual, it would perhaps be that such pure artillery attacks had become very rare so late in the war. Now that all steamers large enough to carry a gun were probably armed and all but the fastest trans-ports were steaming in convoys with strong escorts, the opportunity to slug it out on the surface with a steamer was rare indeed, and Franz must be considered extraordinarily brave or equally foolhardy for having taken his boat into such clear danger and for having fought an artillery duel with the steamer. It could just as easily have turned out quite differently.

In this instance, it was the U-boat that prevailed and Franz had the satisfaction of watching a large, juicy target slip under the waves. What he found as he closed on the wreckage of the steamer, however, would give him pause. The ocean was awash not only with the normal debris left by a sunken steamer, but was also full of desperate, struggling men. There is almost inevitably loss of life in the cruel struggle between submarine and target, and by no means is it always the 'target' that is the victim. By the end of September of 1918, as often as not, it was the U-boat that lost the encounter. None of this, however, prepared Franz for what he came across here.

The steamer that U152 sank was in fact a US naval vessel, USS *Ticonderoga*. Ironically, she was, before the war, a German freighter, the *Camilla Rickmers*, of 5130 GRT. The ship had been interned in the US since the start of the war, was taken over by the US Navy when the United States entered the war, and was now an armed military transport, manned by uniformed naval personnel. *Ticonderoga* had sailed from Norfolk, Virginia, with a full cargo of munitions and 231 officers, crew and troops en route to the Western Front. She had joined a convoy of 18 British and American ships which left New York on 22 September under escort by a single cruiser, which was in fact in the process of turning back to New York at the time U152 encountered *Ticonderoga* on the 30th.[8] *Ticonderoga* had become separated from the rest of the convoy during the previous night and was steaming at 8kt on a course that her captain believed would bring it within sight of the convoy again at first light on the 30th. Instead, she found U152.

The shelling by U152, particularly when, after resurfacing, Franz had decided to use shrapnel, caused devastation on board *Ticonderoga*. That type of round, designed to injure people rather than damage the ship's structure, could hardly have failed to wreak havoc on a target like *Ticonderoga*, packed with troops, protected at best by the thin steel structure of a freighter's upperworks. Exploding just above *Ticonderoga*'s deck, those explosions must have left the decks awash with the blood of dead and dying men.[9] Perhaps as seriously, the shrapnel demolished the freighter's lifeboats. However, it was the first few shots of standard armour-piercing rounds that really doomed the ship. The shot which started the fire on the bridge, so clearly seen from the U-boat, killed or injured the ship's senior officers and demolished the bridge, radio-shack and pilot-house. In the very first minutes of the engagement, *Ticonderoga* lost the ability to steer and to communicate with the rest of the convoy and its sole escort. More importantly, she lost the experienced commanders who could have directed the recovery from the initial damage. So the ship continued slowly circling to port, providing U152 a relatively easy target to hit while making the freighter's return fire more difficult, because of the constantly changing angle to the target. Had the escorting cruiser been aware of *Ticonderoga*'s plight and had it come to her aid at that point, the freighter would probably have survived. At worst, there would have been little further loss of life, even if the freighter had sunk, because the cruiser would have been available to pick up survivors and to put lifeboats into the water in the place of *Ticonderoga*'s own. But the escort sped back to base blithely ignorant of *Ticonderoga*'s agony and, even though gallant exertions by her crew managed to straighten the helm, the freighter no longer could manoeuvre and was once again an easy target for U152's gunners when the engagement turned into a classic stern chase.

The advantage was now entirely with the U-boat. *Ticonderoga* was damaged and the situation on board was increasingly chaotic. The freighter was an easy target, steaming a steady course. Only the increasingly thick smoke billowing out of the damaged ship caused the U-boat's gunners any problems, and a quick shift of quarter solved that problem. *Ticonderoga*'s return fire became increasingly ineffective. Even though the submarine was now on a steady bearing, its low profile and narrow silhouette, as seen end-on from the freighter, made it a tough target to hit. And, as the situation on board *Ticonderoga* deteriorated into chaos as the U-boat's shelling continued, any pretence of effective defensive fire evaporated and the firing from the freighter eventually ceased as it became clear that the ship was sinking.

Having determined, once *Ticonderoga* slipped beneath the waves, to attempt to bring on board a prisoner or two for interrogation, U152 approached the spot where the freighter had gone down. Franz was presented with an unexpected and extremely unpleasant scene:

> We were amidst a debris-field full of survivors from the steamer, many of them seriously injured, some wholly or partly in the water, others on various pieces of flotsam. This is the expected result of war at sea.

Stated bluntly, and there was no other way to state it, war killed men. War at sea is both kinder and crueller than most, especially when compared to the orchestrated carnage that land warfare became in the First World War. Kinder in that far fewer men died. Sinking a merchant target, even if none of the crew survived, would kill a few dozen men. Minuscule compared to the hundreds and even thousands killed daily in any one of a dozen desperate charges that might gain a few meaningless yards of dirt. Crueller, too, because the sentence of the sea was final. If a man was wounded on the ground and if he was lucky enough to be rescued and his wound wasn't too grave, he stood a good chance of recovery. On the sea, particularly in the frigid North Atlantic, unless there was time to launch lifeboats or, by great good fortune, there was a rescue vessel nearby, the sea would claim every man thrown into it. The cries of the wounded and the pleas of the drowning became normal, in a dreadful sort of way. A U-boatman, like any warrior, who couldn't steel himself against those sounds would soon go insane.

As part of his after-the-fact musings on the ironies and cruelties of war, Franz had the following thoughts on the 'fairness' of his encounter with *Ticonderoga*:

If ever a fight on the sea was 'fair', then it was this one. Certainly we had an advantage in our ability to dive, which always gave us the option to escape if, during the run-up to the battle or in the battle itself, we'd found ourselves facing superior enemy forces. We also had the ability to attack the enemy while submerged, though, in this case, our attempts to make such an attack failed. The timely diving of the U-boat in this engagement was solely a defensive measure, brought on by the appearance of the escort cruiser, which event most often gives the intended target a chance to run, to avoid becoming a victim of the submarine in a torpedo attack.

And don't forget that our enemy in this engagement, apart from its colourful camouflage, had the look of a peaceful merchant ship, but in fact was a warship of the US Navy, with a brave and well-trained crew and was a worthy opponent in this fight with an equal chance of winning.

Still, even the hardest of men sometimes encounters exceptional circumstances that open anew the nagging moral dilemma of war at sea. This was one such event:

The whole horror of war stood before our eyes, now that the fight had finished. While we were in the midst of the engagement, we had no idea, nor cared, to which nationality our heroic enemies might belong, we'd been too busy fighting for our lives, engaged in trying to sink the steamer while they tried their best to sink us; now, we saw to our great astonishment, that all survivors floundering in the water were dressed in uniforms, indeed in American uniforms, and we heard, from some of these survivors cries for help and rescue in our own mother tongue. German-Americans! 'How horrible and cruel is this war' was driven home to our hearts! What brought this horrible situation to pass? Did we sink a military hospital-ship? Regardless of how this happened, what could we possibly do to save these men from their inevitable destiny? So many of them were wounded that the water around us was coloured red! Could we take some aboard without dooming the rest of the survivors and endangering our own crew? Was it somehow possible to take all the survivors on board and to accommodate them, without putting our boat in danger? How could we do this, bring on board these survivors, many wounded and in need of medical care, when they'd have to stand around or lie on the deck because our own crew of 77 men already used every bit of free space, every corner, every angle? Our own crew lived and slept for weeks on end between ammunition-stacks, torpedoes and mines. In bad weather, the air inside the boat was often unbreathable for healthy persons, much less for wounded men. And then, which survivors should be brought on board? And how many? 5, 10, 20, 30, 40, 50, or was it to be more?

Clearly, duty required that Franz do nothing that would prevent him from carrying out his mission. He was sent to make war on the ships of his enemy and he had done just that. In many ways, the fact that the men floating in the water were wearing uniforms made his decision easier. Technically, merchant seamen weren't combatants, even when they manned ships flying the enemy's ensign, although the arming of merchantmen blurred the line separating combatants and non-combatants. (There was good reason behind the position that merchant crews were not combatants, namely that many of the men in fact weren't nationals of the warring countries. This was particularly true of the British merchant marine, in which a significant percentage of sailors were Indian or of other South Asian ethnicity – so many, in fact that a term existed, Lascar, to refer to them. Lascars did the dirty, difficult work on board British merchantmen. Without them, the ships wouldn't have moved.)

Standing orders for U-boat commanders called for the interrogation of selected survivors of sinkings to determine the particulars of the vessel just sunk (name, tonnage, cargo, destination, etc.), as well as any other useful information that might be volunteered. Experience showed that this kind of information was most likely to be obtained from officers, rather than crewmen, who, in most cases, simply didn't have this knowledge, whether or not they were willing to share it with the enemy. So Franz directed U152 to navigate into the debris field, nosing its way among the desperate survivors, looking for ship's officers. (It was left to the discretion of the U-boat's captain whether a survivor subjected to interrogation was kept on board after the questioning or returned to the water, in all likelihood to drown. Cases of both are documented.)

Through questioning of some of the survivors, we were able to identify the two senior surviving officers of the steamer and took them on board from a wrecked lifeboat, horribly overcrowded with injured men, the officers being barefoot, dressed in nightshirt, trousers and uniform jacket. This could only have been managed by the voluntary efforts of several U-boat crewmen who, with a rope fastened around their waists, jumped fully clothed into the water and swam both officers carefully back to the boat. They showed great appreciation for the chance to come on board. Both of them lost consciousness as they were carefully brought down through the front hatch. One of the two, the Second Engineer of the steamer, named Fulscher or Miller, seriously wounded with shell-splinters in his legs, was placed in the compartment of our LI, who graciously gave up part of his meagre space. Our excellent doctor operated on him there with success. The other, the First Officer of the steamer, with the other name, was undressed likewise, rubbed down and wrapped in warm woollen blankets and given a swallow of rum for fortification and as a sick-bed was given the sofa in our officer's mess, where until now, because of the general lack of room, the mess steward had bunked.

The care and consideration given the two American ship's officers was certainly admirable, but it was a very carefully, even cynically, calculated mercy, rationed out to two selected survivors. The two men Franz chose were the ones most likely to give him useful information. The decision not to rescue more men was reasonable and rational. Nevertheless, under similar circumstances, other commanders made different decisions (see Chapter 7: the *Laconia* incident).

Satisfied that he had selected the two most useful from among the many in the water, Franz ordered his boat to continue heading west:

With great regret, at 0945 I reluctantly gave the order: 'Both engines ahead full, continue on our assigned mission!'

U152 continued towards the American coast, as ordered. On 2 October, it sighted, but was unable to catch, a fast steamer sailing alone on a course towards Spain. Nine days later, still several hundred miles short of the American coast, the U-boat received orders directing it to head back east towards the vicinity of the Azores. Two days after that, now heading eastward, the U-boat lucked upon a cornucopia of unexpected plenty:

On 13 October, our American captives watched with great interest our pursuit of a big sailing ship, *Stifinder*, which we found to be carrying contraband from New York to Fremantle in Australia. At noon on Sunday, just before our frugal lunch, our lookout high above in the 'crow's nest' on the radio mast, sighted a tiny, gleaming white sail motionless on the horizon, which couldn't be seen from the tower. It was with pleasure that I received notification that the watch officer confirmed the sighting. The luckless victim was sighted only because, as we found out later, its captain had decided that morning to replace its old topmost sail, the royal on its main mast, and the new sail had shimmered bright white in the sun and had betrayed him. Had they not done this, our lookouts would probably never have sighted the ship. The luck we had in finding this target makes up for a lot of other potential victims we lost through bad luck. The crew of the sailing ship was put out in two excellent lifeboats, after we gave them their exact location and sailing directions to shore. We made sure both boats were well supplied with provisions. We supplemented our provisions from the sailing ship in a manner of which we Germans could only dare to dream: one big and two little live pigs, hundredweights of fresh potatoes and the best American wheat flour, butter, condensed milk, canned fruits, tobacco and other things in unimaginable quantities were taken on board. We took all the American food we could salvage, because the provisions we'd brought from Germany were, by now, mostly rotten.

Putting survivors into lifeboats, making sure they had adequate provisions and giving them an accurate current position and sailing directions to the nearest shore was the moral equivalent of rescuing the men. A competent crew could navigate a lifeboat many hundreds of miles on the open ocean, barring bad luck such as a severe storm, and many merchant crews saved themselves in this manner. *Stifinder's* crew was no exception.

This unexpected and very welcome bounty raised the spirits of the crew and left them eager to start hunting again south of the Azores. Not only had the encounter with *Stifinder* relieved their worries about provisions, but the redirection eastward had also eased, if not completely assuaged, the nagging worries about the fuel oil supply.

On the 15th, there was another frustrating encounter with a potential victim.

On 15 October, in very clear weather, we were forced to begin an attack on a steamer prematurely, at a range of about 8000m. The target turned off and our warning shot was answered by sustained fire from his stern gun. The resulting stern chase once again resulted in excessive ammunition consumption in less than ideal circumstances, due to a head sea, so that, when the range opened to 12,000m we broke off the attack, despite a good 'ranging' hit and excellent use of shrapnel. The SOS we intercepted identified our target as the *Messina* and said that their port lifeboat was shot up. They recommended that a nearby steamer not steer towards the south-west because a U-boat was in their way. Many other steamers also responded to the SOS. Meanwhile we resumed our pursuit of *Messina*. Out of the hazy horizon, a second steamer with a fat smokestack and high superstructure appeared and stopped near *Messina*. This new ship began steaming in circles, firing with broadside guns and then seemed to sight us and charged towards us at high speed. Because of the head sea and, further, because the previous stern chase had seriously depleted our electric batteries, to which must be added our concerns about the status of our diesels, I was led to abstain from an artillery duel with this new enemy, which I very soon concluded was a very well-armed auxiliary cruiser and which we soon noted was actually flying the English ensign from its gaff. Seeing this led me to determine that it was the perfect time to dive. The radio call-sign of this auxiliary cruiser was known to us, as an American radio station had recently transmitted a message to the *Arlington*. Our crash dive was the fastest we've ever achieved, because the auxiliary cruiser was headed right towards us at top speed and was firing at us steadily with several guns. In expectation of depth charges, we went immediately to considerable depth; we continued to dive until we reached a depth of 66m. The depth charges made their expected appearance. The feeling we each felt, as we waited there amidst all the rattling and banging and with detonations crashing over us and about us, was in no way agreeable! Soon, however, it was dusk and I took the boat up to attack depth and had a look around through the periscope. Nothing more could be seen of our enemies.

The reference to depleted batteries implies that, in the vain effort to close the gap on the fleeing *Messina*, U152 had resorted to the rarely used *zweimal AK* (twice flank speed – *AK = Ausser Kraft* = flank speed). By this point in the evolution of submarine design, all nations had settled on a common propulsion design paradigm for most submarines. This involved separate surface and submerged propulsion systems geared to common propeller shafts. The surface propulsion was generally diesel engines; the submerged propulsion was always electric motors driven by wet-cell storage batteries which had to be recharged after use by using the diesels to rotate the electric motors, which caused them to act as generators. The presence of two separate propulsion systems allowed a unique ability to boost the top speed of the boat when necessary. In cases when the normal top speed provided by the diesels, *AK*, wasn't quite enough, it was possible to bring the electric motors on-line at the same time, adding their power to that of the diesels. *Zweimal AK,* due to the cruel realities of hydrodynamics (which dictates that, as a general rule, the increase in speed obtained by adding more power falls off geometrically as speed increases), generally added little in terms of actual increase in speed. Adding the full output of the electric motors probably added, at the most, another knot to U152's nominal top speed of 12.4kt.

On Being Depth Charged

Until well into the Second World War, the depth charge was to remain the sole effective anti-submarine weapon available to defenders. When the First World War began, there was no such thing as anti-submarine warfare, and no weapons designed specifically to attack submarines existed in the naval arsenal. Passive, defensive measures were implemented, most particularly the massive mine barrages across the Dover Straits and later the Northern Barrage between Scotland and Norway and the mine barriers laid in the Otranto Straits. The initial mine barrages were intended to deter surface traffic, but the Royal Navy eventually realised that deep mines would endanger U-boats trying to slip through these narrow waters, and these measures took a steady toll of the unwary or the unlucky. But, as far as more active measures were concerned, the Royal Navy was inadequately prepared to locate the enemy or to attack a U-boat decisively once it was found. The problem of locating enemy submarines was not effectively solved by the Allies during the war. Sound location was tried. This involved simply dipping waterproof microphones into the water and hoping that the sound of a submarine would be heard. The limitations of this approach are obvious. Even though sound carries very well in water, there is always a lot of background noise present. Unless the submarine is especially noisy or very close, the chances of detecting it by emitted sound alone are slim.

The Germans very quickly deduced that sound was being used to track submerged U-boats and they developed silent-running disciplines which allowed U-boats to creep along in near total silence. The survivors of UB72 reported:

The previously ascertained silent running speed was 1.8 knots with both motors set to 100 revs. per minute, at which speed they were said to be hardly audible in the boat. The hydroplanes and steering gear were clutched into 'Hand'. Trimming was done by compressed air. It was not considered necessary to stop the gyro compass, which made very little noise and was not audible at either end of the boat. The depth maintained depended on circumstances and varied considerably. No watertight doors were closed.[10]

Even if a U-boat could be detected, that knowledge was of little use in precisely locating it. If a directional microphone was used, rotating the microphone might give a very crude bearing (actually two bearings 180deg apart), but could give no indication of exact distance or depth. Location became somewhat easier after the Royal Navy finally introduced convoying late in the war, forcing U-boats to approach within detection range of anti-submarine forces in order to find targets. But location alone was insufficient if there was no effective means of attacking a submerged U-boat once it was found.

(The problem of the accurate location of a submerged submarine was not solved until the development, between the wars, of ASDIC – known to Americans as sonar. Named for the Allied Submarine Detection Investigation Committee that sponsored the original research, starting in 1918, ASDIC is a system of active detection of objects underwater based on measuring the time delay between the generation of a short-duration sound pulse and its return after being reflected off an underwater object. ASDIC gave a precise range and bearing to a target, though it was not until 1944 that a version was introduced which, through a succession of angled sound bursts, could also determine depth. Another Second World War innovation was doppler sonar which, by measuring the change in frequency of the reflected pulse, could give information about the target's speed and even direction of motion. The similarity in operating principles, but not in underlying science or technology, to radar is obvious.)

No such means of attacking U-boats existed in the Royal Navy's arsenal at the outbreak of the war or even as late as the beginning of 1916. An incredible array of weapons, from the ill-conceived to the downright absurd, were tested before an effective weapon was found. Among the serious, but poorly thought-out, weapons actually deployed at one point or another were hand-thrown lance bombs and mortar-fired 3in bombs, both of which required that the weapon actually contact the submarine in order to detonate. There were no reported successes with either weapon. Others included several types of dragged mines, variously known as sweeps or paravanes, which, either by contact or by electrical discharge, were intended to be detonated at or near the target. Only one sinking was ever credited to this method.

It was not until the deployment of the Type D dropping charge, more commonly known as a depth charge, in the first few months of 1916, that a weapon was finally available to defenders which stood a chance of damaging a U-boat at depth. The idea behind the depth charge was amazingly simple and it had in fact first been proposed as early as 1911. The Type D consisted of 300lb of TNT packed into a simple steel barrel and detonated by a pressure-sensitive switch which would trip at a specified depth. These first depth charges were as dangerous to the attacker as the target. They were rolled off the stern of the attacker and would explode when they hit the pre-set depth, approximately 100ft. Unlike air, which compresses easily and thus absorbs the shock wave from an explosion in a short distance, water has virtually no compressibility and transmits the over-pressure created by the explosives with less dissipation over greater distances. (The physics of shock waves is complex, with such factors as the size and speed of the explosion, the density of the medium and its compressibility all playing a role. In general, regardless of the other factors, the energy in a shock wave dissipates radiply as it expands outward.)

A depth charge, therefore, did not need to be particularly close to its target in order to damage it. Because the hull of a submerged U-boat was already under stress from water pressure, a relatively minor amount of additional pressure, applied suddenly and unevenly to the hull, could cause sufficient damage to force it to the surface, where it was vulnerable to more conventional weapons. (It must also be remembered that welding, which allowed truly watertight joints between hull plates, didn't become common until just before the Second World War. All the U-boats of the First World War had riveted hulls, which were much more vulnerable to damage by depth charges.)

However, the very physics that made accuracy less important in dropping depth charges often made them as dangerous to the attacker as the attacked. The same over-pressure that endangered the submarine would burst to the surface immediately above the point of the explosion, producing a towering plume of water and explosive gases. A small or slow escort could be damaged by the depth charges it dropped. The immediate solution was to deploy a smaller depth charge, named the Type D*, with only 120lb of explosives. The longer-term solution was to revert to the larger charge, but provide a means of altering the sensitivity of the trigger switch in discrete steps, so that the charge could be set to detonate at 100, 150 or 200ft. By the end of the war, the depth choices had been extended to 300ft, as U-boat commanders learned that they could evade the danger by diving deeper.

How close a depth charge has to get to a target to damage it is also a matter of physics and is a function of the power of the explosion (itself a function of the size and type of the explosive charge) and its depth. In general, the deeper a submarine, the smaller the 'kill radius' from a given charge. During the Second World War, it was commonly understood by U-boatmen that the standard, surface-dropped depth charge (which had a 500lb charge), had a kill radius of approximately 300ft at a depth of 300ft. As depth increased, kill radius decreased in geometrical proportion, so that doubling depth quartered the effective kill radius. Knowledge of this fact led logically to the standard U-boat tactic when being depth charged, which was to dive deeper. The standard mid-war Type VII U-boat had a depth gauge calibrated to 200m (c.600ft). The 'official' maximum depth was 150m (c.450ft); the calculated crush depth of the hull was 250m (c.750ft). In comparison, the UBIII boats of the First World War had an official maximum depth of 70m. The official maximum depth was exceeded regularly by U-boats attempting to escape depth charging. Since the gauge stopped working at those depths, survivors could only estimate the depths they actually reached; but they believe that, in some extreme cases during the Second World War, they survived dives to 1000ft and beyond. Of course, it is impossible to know the exact depth at which a hull would fail. If the crew survived to talk about it later, then, obviously the hull withstood the pressure; if the hull failed, there were no survivors.

The experience of being depth charged is utterly unforgettable.[11] (Germans knew depth charges as *Wasserbomben*, always contracted, in the German manner, to *Wabos*.) Going to war in a submarine in those early days required uncommon bravery on the part of every crewman. Malfunctions were so common that every dive was an adventure. In this environment, the added danger of being depth charged could fill all but the stoutest heart with dread. Waiting in the cramped, dank confines of a narrow pressure hull, surrounded by a few dozen equally fearful men, the ears search desperately to pick up the soft clicking sound of a depth charge's pressure switch closing, to be followed a half-second later by the explosion of the charge. The louder the click, the closer the depth charge, the greater the danger. The explosion of a depth charge sent a 'hammer' of water smashing into the boat's hull. If the charge was close enough, that blow might be sufficient to breach the pressure hull. If that happened, the death of the entire crew was the only possible result. The only sign of their passing would most often be an oil slick and maybe some few items of flotsam that would escape the fractured hull. But such catastrophic failures were rare. The depth charge is a very inaccurate weapon, which explains why it soon became clear to the Royal Navy that it was necessary to drop a pattern of anywhere from three to five or even more charges. That way, the odds of a near miss increased dramatically. And a near miss was often just as good as a direct hit.

The shock wave generated by a near miss was powerful enough literally to shake a U-boat like a powerful earthquake. The warning click of the pressure switch closing was often a blessing because it might give the crew enough time to grab a handhold on something attached to the hull. Failing such a warning or handy object within reach, the jolt of the detonation was enough to send bodies flying. Men were thrown out of bunks and off chairs. Minor injuries, cuts, gashes, twisted joints and even broken bones were common. Then there were the flying rivets to deal with. The differential pressure put on various parts of the hull caused rivets to shear, often with a crack louder than that of a rifle being fired; and the loose ends were sometimes expelled with sufficient velocity to cause injuries remarkably similar to those produced by shrapnel. Flying rivets were often accompanied by high-pressure leaks as sea water forced itself through the loosened joints between hull sections. Small leaks could be stanched by forcing rags into the joints: major leaks required wooden balks hammered into place in an attempt to force the gap closed.

More distant misses could still cause serious damage. The pressure hull of a U-boat is pierced in multiple places by openings that let water, oil, air, exhaust, munitions, provisions and people in and out of the hull. Every such opening needed a hatch, flap or valve that allowed it to be closed before the boat dived, and flanges that attached the pipe or hatchway to the outer hull. Each of these attachments and closures was a potential weak point, particularly in the days before welding became common in U-boat construction. Every time the shock of a depth charge detonation hit the hull, these joints shifted against one another and sometimes they sprang leaks. Inside the hull, pipes ran through the overheads, carrying water and oil between tanks and bunkers. These had joints which could work loose under the pounding of a depth charge attack. For that reason, all piping inside the boat was fitted with frequent valving, so that the flow of the liquid could be shut off until repairs were made. The often repeated scene in submarine films of sudden jets of high-pressure water spurting across a compartment until an alert crewman shuts down the appropriate valve, is in fact pretty accurate. So are the scenes of glass shattering. Anything of glass, be it an instrument face, the 'bubbles' (liquid-filled glass levels used to indicate the boat's attitude) or the glass tubes of the manometer-type depth gauges, was liable to breakage during a depth charge attack and replacements had to be carried.

Even if a depth charge caused no internal damage or leakage, it could still doom a U-boat. U-boats of First World War vintage were riveted together, and the UBs and other small U-boats all carried their fuel oil in external saddle tanks. Therefore, a depth charge could easily start a leak without the knowledge of the crew inside the pressure hull, and a fuel oil leak was like a flashing arrow pointing towards the boat. A U-boat leaking oil could easily be tracked and, even if lost, readily found again. For example, the following extract from the report of the survivors of UB72:

On 7 May off Anglesey a dirigible dropped three bombs on her, but the explosions were some distance away. A few hours later a destroyer pursued her for two hours, dropping 23 depth charges in her neigh-bourhood, and making things very uncomfortable. When she was able to come to the surface later, it was discovered that the No. 2 port ballast tank, which was filled with oil fuel, was leaking, leaving a distinct and easily followed trail of oil. At dawn the next day, 8 May, another destroyer discovered this oil track and dropped 20 more depth charges, extin-guishing the lights and shaking the boat very badly. Another tank was started and the oil track was very distinct. The submarine was followed by trawlers during the whole day, but managed to shake them off in the evening. Just before nightfall five more depth charges were dropped by a P-boat.[12]

This problem of fuel leakage from external fuel tanks was considered a suffi-ciently serious problem that, when Germany began designing U-boats again between the wars, the boat that was intended to become the standard U-boat model, the Type VIIA, carried all its fuel oil inside the pressure hull.[13]

While the crew waited out a depth charge attack as best they could, the boat's officers had work to do. The captain, understandably enough, was responsible for figuring how to get his boat out of danger. That meant using every trick he knew. The first priority was to gain and maintain a tactical 'picture' of the boat's situation. How many attackers were there? Where were they? What resources did they have? How deep was the boat and how deep was the bottom? The only way of knowing anything about the world outside the pressure hull was by listening. By the beginning of the Second World War, U-boats were regularly fitted with sophisticated passive sound sensors, listening devices that, as the war progressed, allowed increasingly accurate location of sound sources. In the First World War, U-boats relied mostly on the sounds that reached the boat and could be heard with the unaided ear. This meant that they were aware of only the loudest sound sources. One such source was the screw noise of an attacker as it gained speed prior to dropping a pattern of depth charges.

The normal tactic employed in attacking a U-boat in the days before ASDIC was for an attacker to stop all engines and listen with its hydrophones in order to determine as far as possible the target's location and, once a satisfactory location was determined, to accelerate rapidly towards the target, since an attacker had to be moving at high speed to avoid damaging itself on the depth charges it dropped. If there were multiple attackers, they could co-ordinate the tasks of listening and attacking. As the attacker accelerated, the U-boat had a brief opportunity to attempt to evade the depth charges. The time lag between this acceleration and the explosion of the depth charges could be as much as several minutes, during which time a clever captain could change course and depth in an attempt to move the boat away from the attacker's aiming point.

Undoubtedly, the hardest part was the waiting. The responsibility for repairing the boat, plugging the leaks, fell on the bosun and his few mates, but when water was spurting, the entire crew got drafted into the bosun's force. Except for those moments of intense activity, however, the majority of the crew spent most of the time during a depth charge attack sitting on their hands, waiting. In the early days of depth charging, when anti-submarine vessels went to sea with just a few charges to drop, it was easy to wait out an attack, but the British soon realised that success in a depth charge attack could be statistically measured and the odds of success increased not only through dropping more charges at a time but in dropping multiple patterns of charges.

The Royal Navy gave the highest priority to the manufacture of adequate numbers of depth charges and, by 1918, the standard load was 35 depth charges. Combined with the steady increase in the number of patrol vessels and their concentration as convoy escorts, this meant that it was not uncommon by late in the war for a U-boat to be held underwater and subjected to depth charge attack for hours. These extended attacks were not only difficult to bear mentally for men forced to sit and wait, but were also hard on the men physically. As the minutes stretched into hours, the general overall fug inside the boat, a mixture of fuel oil, battery acid, cooking smells, rotting garbage and human body odour, only grew stronger. After some period of time, the need to relieve bladders and bowels had to be addressed. The state of technology of submarine toilets was such that, even during the Second World War, toilets could be flushed only at fairly shallow depths, generally no deeper than periscope depth. When a boat was held down at greater depths for extended periods, the only possible relief was provided by buckets. If a bucket tipped over, which could easily happen during depth charging, the reek of its contents added unpleasantly to the boat's overall smell.

Once a depth charge attack commenced, there was no way of telling how long it would last. Unless the U-boat was fortunate enough to be able to slip away, it survived a depth charge attack by waiting it out. When the attackers had dropped all their charges or had been tricked into thinking the U-boat had sunk or were called back to the convoy they were escorting or just plain got bored, they would steam off, allowing the U-boat the blessed relief of a quiet ocean and the opportunity to resurface to a clear horizon, open the hatches and vent the boat with fresh salt air. Sometimes, however, the depth charges did their work. Catastrophic destruction at depth was rare (though less rare in the Second World War than in the First). More often, depth charges did their job by one or more near misses, causing unstoppable leaks or other damage sufficient to force the commander to make the fateful decision to surface the boat. It was an admission of defeat. The choice to surface in the midst of one's attackers was made after all chance of escape was gone and the only real issue yet to be decided was whether any of the crew would survive.

Once on the surface in proximity to an escort, a U-boat had little chance of survival, because then it was a gun battle and U-boats almost always lost such battles with escorts. It wasn't because the escorts outgunned them. In fact, a *U-kreuzer* like U152 would be better armed than most escorts. Rather it was the fact that escorts were regular warships, manned by well-trained crews, so that, unlike the gun crews on merchant ships, they probably could shoot faster and straighter than the U-boat. U-boats, after all, were miserable gun platforms, rolling and pitching continually in all but the smoothest seas. But the real difference was in the comparative vulnerability of the antagonists. A U-boat and any escort could trade hits and the U-boat would always lose. One hit was generally all it took to disable a U-boat, certainly a guarantee that it would never dive again. So, when a U-boat surfaced, it might make an attempt to man guns and put up a fight, but generally, it took only a minute or two before the crew that could get out was abandoning the boat and praying that the crew of the escort was merciful.

And the End...

It was now mid-October 1918. U152 had been at sea since early September. Dramatic changes had taken place in Germany since the boat had sailed. When U152 left port, there still seemed to be some hope, however slight, that the war could be eventually won by Germany, or at least prolonged to the point that the Allies would accept a conclusion short of total German surrender. But the collapse of the German Army on the Western Front in the face of the Meuse–Argonne offensive in late September led directly to political collapse and revolution. As the situation at home deteriorated, U-boats at sea continued operations. The orders received on 11 October to turn east towards the Azores had been a direct result of naval command's expectation that the end of the war was approaching rapidly. None of this was expressed in the orders, but it probably took little in the way of reading between the lines for the import of the order to be clear. Eleven days later, all doubts were removed:

On 22 October, the birthday of the German Empress, we received a radio message from home, ordering us to begin the return leg of our mission immediately and, because of ongoing negotiations, no merchant ships were to be attacked, though we were still free to attack any warships we encountered. We were again in the middle of the ocean, in fact right in the middle of a line from Gibraltar to Norfolk. We set a course of NNW towards home.[14]

U152 headed north into steadily worsening weather and a dense concentration of potential targets, including at least two warships, but the boat was never able to obtain a favourable attack position and no attacks were launched. By 8 November, it was rounding the Faroes to the north in a full gale.

With thick clouds covering the sky, it wasn't possible to determine our position by day or at night. We watched our instruments and, not knowing where we actually were within 2°, we crossed almost the whole northern North Sea at night and closed the extensive English mine-barrage. God only knows what a miracle it was that we passed through the mines safely on the night of 10/11 November in heavy weather.

Once through the minefield, there was no obstacle to reaching home. The crew was informed of everything we had learned over the radio of events back home; prior to crossing the minefield I had restricted this information to only my officers. This U-boat's crew, all volunteers who had put in months and, in some cases, years of risking their lives in combat, didn't believe my words. Shaken to the depths of their souls, each man was left to his own thoughts – to deal with these events in his own way. We passed through the Skagerrak, the Kattegat and the Sound, the southern exit of which our German patrol boats had left unguarded. We were left to our own fate as we made our way, in the middle of November, into our home-port. We had been at sea almost 75 days.

By this time, the war was over. The Armistice signed on 11 November had ended the fighting. Kiel was in the hands of revolutionary councils of sailors who had taken over the fleet rather than sail their ships out on an ill-conceived plan to challenge the Grand Fleet one last time. When the two American captives applied for permission to be transported to England, their permissions, dated 19 November 1918, were signed by the Commander of the *Soldatenrat des UnterseekreuzerVerbande* (Soldiers Council of the U-Cruiser Association).

UB68

Foreshadowing

1918 was a disastrous year for the U-boat arm. The previous year had been one of great success, although, by the time it ended, the impact of the belated adoption of a convoy system had begun to reduce the success rate enjoyed by the U-boats. As the effectiveness of the convoy system improved throughout the first part of 1918, and fewer and fewer individual targets were to be found, it became clear to the thoughtful that new tactics were needed to reclaim the initiative in the battle to strangle Britain's seaborne lifeline. One man who was thinking about the problem was a very young Oberleutnant zur See named Karl Dönitz.

Dönitz had joined the Navy as a cadet in 1910 and had started the war as a Leutnant zur See on board SMS *Breslau*. When that light cruiser, along with the battlecruiser *Goeben*, was caught in the Mediterranean by the unexpected outbreak of war, she found refuge in the Turkish port at Constantinople. The ships were nominally purchased by Turkey, then a German ally, and Dönitz, again nominally, became an officer in the Turkish Navy. While not exactly idle in Turkish service, neither did the ships see important action, and an ambitious and patriotic officer like Dönitz was undoubtedly eager to get back to Germany and the main conflict. In December 1916, he requested and was granted transfer back to Germany and permission to attend U-boat officer's school. He was, by then, an Oberleutnant zur See and had gained the attention and approval of his superiors. Fresh out of school, he was given a choice assignment, as IWO to one of Germany's most successful U-boat commanders, KL Walter Forstmann in U39, operating out of the Austro-Hungarian naval base at Pola on the Adriatic.[1] He was given his first command, the small UCII-class minelayer, UC25, on 1 March 1918. Dönitz commanded this boat, operating out of Cattaro, until it went into dock there for a long overdue refit in August 1918 and Dönitz took over command of the bigger UBIII boat, UB68, at Pola on 1 September.[2]

In Pola, while working up his new command, Dönitz had a chance to sit down and talk with one of Germany's U-boat 'aces'. Korvettenkapitän Steinbauer had already successfully commanded two UBIII boats before taking over the *Mittel-U* series boat, U48.[3] As he and Dönitz talked, the topics of conversation included the increasing difficulty of finding targets, now that convoys were standard even in the Mediterranean, and the increasing dangers U-boats faced when actually attacking targets, because convoys not only concentrated the targets but also the defences. Steinbauer and Dönitz had some ideas on how to address those problems.[4] If a single U-boat was finding it increasingly hard to find targets, since they were concentrated in convoys, why not fight back with a concentration of U-boats? (U-boats not only were used to hunting alone, but their assigned operational areas were deliberately widely separated to reduce the chance of interference or even accidental fratricide.) Instead of hunting alone, why not co-ordinate the U-boat's search capabilities, organising two or more boats into a sweep line that would lie across the most heavily travelled sea lanes and, thus, vastly increase the odds that a sighting would be made? And, once a U-boat found a target, why not implement tactics that would increase the odds that an attack could be carried out and escape made despite the concentration of defenders?

Throughout much of the war, the standard U-boat tactic had been to search for targets on the surface in daylight. Once a target was found, the U-boat could submerge and attack by torpedo or give chase, using the gun or torpedoes, depending on the relative positions of attacker and target and the audacity of the U-boat's captain. The small size of a U-boat and the relative inexperience of a merchantman's lookouts made it likely that a target could be approached on the surface in daylight without detection. The implementation of a convoy system rendered this tactic obsolete, both because it was now far less likely that a U-boat would even find a target and because it was equally unlikely that a convoy could now be approached openly by day without being detected by the defensive screen. An alternative tactic evolved, in which a U-boat, once it found a target, would attempt to swing around the convoy at high speed on the surface, at a distance that made detection unlikely, get out ahead of it and submerge in its path, so that an underwater attack could be made. While this sounded good in theory, this tactic failed a high percentage of the time because convoys regularly zigzagged to foil exactly this kind of attack.

Dönitz and Steinbauer proposed a new tactic designed specifically for attacking convoys well-protected by escorts. Once a convoy was sighted, a U-boat would shadow it until dark and then approach the targets on the surface at night, when the U-boat's small size would render it all but undetectable even to the numerous escorts. Attack would then be made, using torpedoes, and the U-boat would submerge to evade the now-alerted defences. If by then more than one U-boat had found the convoy and simultaneous attacks could be made from several directions, so much the better. (In the First World War, there was no easy way for U-boats to communicate with each other or with home. Advances in radio technology between the wars made the concentration of multiple U-boats, once a convoy had been sighted, a practical possibility.)

The two men decided that they would try out these tactics on their next patrols, which were due to start at the end of September 1918. The plan was that the two U-boats, U48 and UB68, would rendezvous at a point 50nm south-east of Capo Passero, the south-eastern corner of Sicily, and there they would troll for one of the frequent convoys heading from the Suez Canal to Malta.

Dönitz thought at the time that this would be the first experiment in co-operative tactics between U-boats, but he was wrong. The problems facing the U-boat force in 1918 were pretty obvious and U-boat commanders, as a group, were fairly intelligent; so it is not surprising that one or both of these main ideas occurred more or less independently to others as well. In early May 1918, nine boats formed a search line across the Western Approaches in the Atlantic, but since there was no plan for any co-operation or concentration after a sighting was made, the experiment failed.

UB68 departed Pola at midday on 28 September, proceeding southward down the length of the Adriatic on the surface, although Dönitz took advantage of the opportunity to practise diving the boat several times a day. He had reason to be worried about his boat's stability underwater. The previous captain of UB68, OLzS von Heimburg, had asked to be relieved of command because he found his boat to be nearly unmanageable while submerged:

> Von Heimburg had himself transferred from UB68 in the summer of 1918 because of its underwater handling characteristics and constant diving trouble. As a result, the boat was overhauled at Pola in the summer of 1918. The refit included strengthening of the pressure hull, reballasting, and replacement of the 10.5cm deck gun by a 8.8cm. The boat's test-runs under water went reasonably well, but, significantly, according to the LI, it never handled as well as UB50, on which he had previously been LI. Particularly noticeable was sluggishness of handling at high speed, especially when the planes were set at more than 8–10deg.
>
> From the beginning, crossing the Ionian Sea, there was noticeable difficulty in handling the boat in a seaway or in any swell. The boat always was heavy and could be maintained at periscope depth only with constant effort. The normal daily trim test dive was extended therefore into a half-hour-long practice dive for training in depth-keeping.[5]

Furthermore, Dönitz was well aware that his wasn't the only boat in its 'series' to suffer handling problems. The entire run of six UBIII hulls, starting with UB66, all built by Germaniawerft, Kiel, had suffered from similar problems and Dönitz knew that four of the six had already been lost without a trace. It is hard enough sailing out to meet a determined enemy, knowing that the only way to succeed is to put yourself in mortal danger, without having to worry about the reliability of your own boat. (At the time he was writing this account, Dönitz didn't know the fate of the four boats. In fact, of those four, the RN could account for the sinking of three of them and those sinkings were unrelated to handling problems.)

Despite these concerns, the boat continued heading to war. UB68 passed the Otranto Barrage on the surface at night.[6] Along the way, they had sighted a bale of cork floating in the water and the boat stopped to recover this prize, lashing it to the deck forward. UB68 arrived at the rendezvous point on the evening of 3 October 1918 and waited for U48 to show up. (U48 never made the rendezvous, having been delayed by mechanical troubles.) Dönitz was still waiting at 0100 the next morning when a small 'smudge' was sighted on the south-eastern horizon, which proved to be a barrage balloon tethered to a destroyer escorting a convoy headed from Port Said to Malta, exactly the kind of target Dönitz had hoped for.[7] UB68 remained stopped on the surface as a convoy of six merchantmen in two columns of three, shepherded by an indeterminate number of active escorts, approached from the east. Once the targets were close enough, Dönitz flooded tanks so that the U-boat's decks were awash, guided his boat into a position inside the escort screen and prepared to fire torpedoes at the first ship of the near column. Then, without warning, the convoy zigzagged towards the U-boat and suddenly the steamer that a moment before had been a target was now steaming directly towards UB68, threatening to slice the boat in two. Only quick thinking and quick manoeuvring enabled UB68 to turn out of the path of the oncoming steamer and scrape past its stern. Now between the two columns of the convoy, but still undetected, Dönitz again set up a firing solution, this time on a large freighter in the middle of the farther column. The target steamed steadily this time and Dönitz fired a single torpedo, being rewarded by a massive explosion and a brilliantly illuminated column of water alongside the target.[8] He had no time to admire his handiwork or set up another target, because UB68 was immediately sighted and charged by one of the escorting sloops. The boat slipped beneath the surface and headed deep in anticipation of a depth charging, but the expected attack never came, probably due to the proximity of the convoy's merchantmen, and when UB68 surfaced again a half-hour later, the convoy had passed to the west.

Not content with a single probable sinking, Dönitz set out in pursuit of the convoy. Almost immediately he came upon a 2000GRT steamer dead in the water behind the convoy. He set up and fired two torpedoes at a range of less than 300m, but, incredibly, they both missed. (The explanation for the misses was simple enough. Dönitz was informed the next day that his target had been a Spanish steamer that had lost its screw. It was returning empty to Malta and thus had less than half the draft of a normal steamer. Both torpedoes had passed harmlessly under the target.)

Unwilling to waste more torpedoes or time on the straggler, Dönitz broke off the attack and continued in pursuit of the convoy. He performed a classic 'end around' manoeuvre, steering his boat around the convoy at the limit of visibility and taking up a position in its path. Because dawn was now fast breaking, the boat submerged and waited for the convoy to steam into range. He was just setting up a shot on the centre steamer in the near line when UB68 lost trim, apparently spontaneously, and took on a 10deg angle towards the stern. Given the boat's history of problems with longitudinal stability, this came as no shock, but the timing was certainly inconvenient. The boat had been at periscope depth, which was 12.5m. At 8.5m, the net-cutter at the bow would break water and give away the U-boat's presence. The periscope was quickly retracted and both motors were stopped. Dönitz instructed the LI to pump some water out of the bilge and to stabilise the boat at 20m. Theoretically, this left the boat slightly bow-heavy, but, by running both motors ahead half, dynamic stability was achieved. Satisfied that the boat was now again under control, Dönitz ordered periscope depth once more.

His satisfaction was premature because, as the boat passed through 15m, it again developed a 10deg aftward angle and started to slip downward aft first. This time pumping water out of the bilge didn't restore stability. They next tried using the trim pump to flush water out of the aft compensating tank, but that too failed to halt the aftward slide. Dönitz then ordered full ahead, but that only slowed the boat's descent; it didn't stop it. When the depth hit 60m, Dönitz ordered the systematic blowing of the boat's dive tanks, starting at the stern. Despite this, the boat plunged another 20m before it stopped and started back up again. It wasn't sinking any more, but the basic problem still hadn't been solved. It remained tilted down 10deg by the stern and the motors were still straining at full speed. As it passed through the 40m mark going up, Dönitz attempted to gain control of his boat, ordering the helm 10deg over to port in an attempt to steer the boat away from the convoy. For maybe 45sec, the boat seemed to respond, even levelling off momentarily, then it tilted suddenly down by the bow and started plunging again. Except, this time they were heading down much faster, in part due to the motors still churning full ahead, and the tilt was now 50deg downward, which caused crewmen to lose footing, loose equipment to fly towards the lower bulkheads, hitting crewmen and knocking out a number of the electric lights, and battery acid to spill over the tops of cells, generating chlorine gas.

This plunge was far more serious than the previous two, given its angle and its speed, so orders followed one another rapidly. First, Dönitz ordered motors stopped and then set to full back. The rudder was ordered hard aport, again in the hope that the plunge would be slowed. Finally, he ordered all tanks blown, the last, desperate measure. Despite all this, the boat continued down a while longer. Several loud bangs were heard aft and the Chief Machinist, Meinke, was sent to investigate. Word quickly came back that two seals had failed and water was pouring in aft.[9] Despite this leakage, the boat still dropped bow first. Dönitz and his IWO, Müssen, in the boat's conning tower, watched the depth gauge by flashlight as it crept down past 100m. (Remember that a UBIII's rated maximum depth was 70m and, unlike the welded boats of the Second World War, dives past that depth were known to be dangerous.) Finally, at 102m, the needle on the depth gauge quivered, stopped and began rapidly to unwind. The boat was shooting upward, stern-first, like a cork.

Out of the Frying Pan . . .

There was no possible way of halting the upward movement of the boat. Within seconds, UB68 broached stern-first and settled on the surface in a bow-down attitude. No sooner had they broken the surface than Dönitz opened the conning tower hatch and went up to get a quick look around. What he found was about as bad as could be. UB68 had resurfaced right in the middle of the convoy. Two Flower class sloops were closing and firing and the merchantmen were turning away to bring their stern guns to bear. Already shells were splashing in the water. The closer sloop was only 800m away, point-blank range for its 12pdr (7.9cm) guns. Dönitz dropped back into the conning tower, reclosed the hatch and ordered a crash dive, but the LI reported that there was no more compressed air in the tanks. Stopping the two preceding plunges by the boat had depleted the supply. So desperate was the situation that Dönitz again ordered a dive and again the LI reported the lack of compressed air, this time reporting that the boat was apparently holed aft because it was taking on water rapidly.

At last, there remained no other options. Dönitz had no choice but to order that the boat be abandoned. For the last time, he opened the hatch and climbed out onto the tower. The helmsman came up next and the two positioned themselves on either side of the hatch, grabbing men as they emerged and pulling them through the narrow opening as quickly as possible. The first men out were ordered onto the foredeck to free the small raft stored under the deck-casing just forward of the gun. The next up were told to cut loose the cork bale strapped to the foredeck and begin distributing sheets of cork to each man before he jumped into the water. (They all had standard issue life jackets, but the cork gave added buoyancy.) The raft was dropped alongside and all non-swimmers were ordered into it.

Quickly, efficiently, men came up out of the boat and into the water. OL Müssen was positioned on the foredeck, making sure the men got overboard and away from the boat. By now a half-dozen guns were shooting at the boat at short range; shells were continually landing around it and some were hitting. The LI stayed in the control room, urging the last men up the ladders and out of the hatch. A seaman began to drown off the starboard side. Müssen jumped in and pulled him around to the raft. Dönitz yelled orders down into the boat and the LI carried them out. Because men were coming through the hatch coughing from chlorine gas, he ordered the ventilation fans shut down. And, finally, when the last men came up, he ordered the seacocks opened so that the boat would sink. That last order proved unnecessary, because the boat was already sinking rapidly. The LI was halfway out of the hatch and Dönitz reaching down to grab him when the swell washed over the tower and carried Dönitz away from the sinking boat. Before he could look back, UB68 was gone.

In the water, the crew now faced a new batch of problems and Dönitz at once set about establishing order among the crew. Because he had been dressed to take up position on the conning tower, he now found himself trying to swim in leather trousers and jacket and heavy sea boots. Weighed down by this garb, he was having trouble keeping his head above water, so his first act was to kick off the boots and discard the rest of his outer clothing. Fortunately the Mediterranean is a relatively warm sea, even in October, so he and his men had no need to fear the inexorable onset of numbing cold that would have faced them in the North Atlantic. Now unencumbered and swimming easily, he swam over to the raft and made sure that the poorest swimmers were on it and stronger men were moved into the water. Although they were surrounded by ships, those ships belonged to the enemy they had just minutes before been trying to sink; there was absolutely no assurance that they would be rescued by their intended victims. Dönitz became concerned that the men might drift apart or become dispirited as they floated in the water, so he swam around the group, herding them towards the sloop HMS *Snapdragon*, which had stopped nearby and was indeed putting out boats with the obvious intention of rescuing his men. He noticed that the LI was nowhere to be seen and called out for him. The swell was such that, in the water, visibility was a few yards in any direction. One of the petty officers, Machinist Barwitz, yelled back that he'd seen the LI in the water earlier and assumed he was just straggling behind the main mass of swimmers. Those thoughts got pushed aside as *Snapdragon's* boats approached and one by one the men were picked up.

As they assembled on *Snapdragon's* deck, Dönitz noted with pride that the men were sombre and silent. Now that they were prisoners, he was sure the British would try to interrogate them and extract what useful information they could. His crew was in good spirits and showed no inclination to co-operate with their captors. Some of the crew were missing, but most had been rescued and were safe.[10] He knew that shortly they would be led below and most likely separated into small groups. Before that could happen, Dönitz gathered his men and spoke to them briefly of their lost boat and mates and then led them in three cheers for the Kaiser. A moment later, *Snapdragon*'s captain took Dönitz by the arm, led him to his cabin and had a warm bath drawn for his prisoner. It was only then that Dönitz became aware that he had given the pep talk to his crew, leading them in their final hurrahs clad only in a shirt, underpants and one sock. The captain's orderly laid out a set of the captain's tennis whites for Dönitz to put on after his bath and it was in this natty attire that he was delivered, along with the rest of his crew, to the POW camp at Verdale on Malta.[11]

Time to Think

At the camp on Malta and later as he served in a variety of capacities in the rump *Reichsmarine* that the Versailles Treaty allowed a defeated Germany, Dönitz thought long and hard about why the U-boat offensive had failed to strangle Britain when, in 1917, it had appeared to be close to success. He certainly wasn't alone in considering this, but the fact that he was the man selected in 1935 to lead the reconstituted and still illegal U-boat arm made his opinions on the subject count more than most. He reflected at length about the strategy, tactics and equipment necessary to beat the English if it came to that again. He thought hard on the subject because he, like most Germans, believed that the issue hadn't been decided at Compiègne or Versailles, and Hitler certainly encouraged Germans in that belief. Dönitz was certain that another test of arms with the British was inevitable.

Concerning strategy, he concluded that the only valid use of U-boats was in unrestricted commerce warfare against the lifeblood of the British Isles, its merchant fleet. Civilised prize rules applied to another day, when merchantmen were not armed or gathered into convoys. U-boats had to attack without warning and leave survivors to their fate. Convoys could only be located by sweep lines of many U-boats and their concentrated escorts over-come by a similar concentration of multiple U-boats into a wolf-pack. The maturing of radio technology and the powerful encryption provided by the Enigma machine allowed the shore-based commander of U-boats to direct the movement of his boats across the ocean like a chess master.

Once a wolf-pack gathered around a convoy, control of the battle would devolve from Dönitz on shore to the individual commanders on the scene. In Dönitz's conception of wolf-pack tactics, there would be no local commander of the pack once the attack began. The first U-boat to sight a convoy would serve as a beacon, broadcasting a homing signal to the rest of the pack, but, after the pack had gathered, each commander would use his own initiative to attack when and where he could. When enough boats had gathered, their sheer numbers should allow them to overwhelm the convoy's escort. Those escorts would always keep some of the attackers from getting close; but if there were enough, a few would slip through and attack the merchantmen. The preferred method of attack was at night and on the surface.

Ultimately, in Dönitz's opinion, the U-boats of the First World War had been defeated because there were not enough of them to carry out the kind of tactics he envisioned. Dönitz carefully calculated the tonnage of shipping he might need to sink to bring Britain to its knees and then worked from there to deduce the number of boats he would require to accomplish this task. His calculations told him that he needed 300 U-boats to win the next war. To get that extraordinary number of boats, he would forego building the huge and wasteful *U-Kreuzer* types and would limit the number of big ocean-going *Mittel-U* boats built. Instead he would concentrate on the smaller, more easily built boats of the UBIII type, boats designed from the beginning for mass-production. Of course, his new boats would be better built than the likes of UB68. He planned to design and build boats of the Type VII and Type IX series, respectively the successors of the UBIII and *Mittel-U* boats of the previous war. And he hoped he would have enough time to build enough of these boats to win the next war. Unfortunately, Hitler, who had promised him repeatedly that there would be no war with England until 1946 at the earliest, invaded Poland and precipitated war in September 1939. Dönitz had only 57 U-boats at his disposal and, of those, only 26 were his preferred Types VII or IX.

— 6 —
U47

Tweaking the Lion's Tail

The Second World War started too soon. There simply were not enough U-boats to wage the methodical war of attrition which Karl Dönitz had devised to defeat the British in this, round two, of the barely interrupted struggle to determine whether Germany would be allowed to dominate Europe. Certainly, those boats that were available were achieving tremendous successes. Only days after the war started, U29, one of the few Type VII boats available, found and sank the large aircraft carrier HMS *Courageous* which was on anti-submarine patrol in the Western Approaches. This success was a major coup, a clear demonstration that no ship in the Royal Navy was safe from attack, but to Dönitz it was hardly more than a distraction from the battle he knew he had to fight and win in order to defeat Britain. Sinking warships was always good, especially high-profile units such as *Courageous*, but it did little to affect the real battle, which was the Tonnage War, the campaign to strangle Britain's seaborne lifelines. Dönitz recognized, unfortunately, that he had too few U-boats to wage a decisive campaign against the British merchant fleet, certainly not enough to allow the use of the co-operative pack tactics he had thought so hard about between the wars. So single dramatic acts had to suffice. Yet Dönitz knew he was settling for pinpricks when he should have been striking sledgehammer blows.

One single act had already brought Dönitz into trouble with Hitler. No sooner had the war begun when U30 encountered and sank the passenger liner SS *Athenia*, apparently believing her to be an armed merchant cruiser. The loss of life was appalling. Worst of all, almost 20 per cent of the dead were Americans, and Hitler had specifically ordered that prize rules were to be followed, fearing that an American entry into the new war would be as disastrous for Germany as it had been 25 years earlier. British propagandists had a field day with this sinking, resurrecting all the images of the barbarous Hun that had been the standard fare of the daily press in the previous war. Hitler ordered total denial of the incident. Goebbels dutifully claimed publicly that the British had manufactured the entire incident, sinking *Athenia* themselves, so that they would have an atrocity to blame on the Germans. KL Lemp's log was altered to expunge any reference to the liner. Few outside Germany believed the official denial. Hitler seethed. Dönitz needed a counterstroke to assuage Hitler's anger and to raise the stock of the U-boat weapon again. Fortunately, he had a plan.

Everyone in Germany knew about Scapa Flow. It is a deep-water harbour in the Orkney Islands immediately north of Scotland, large enough to hold a fleet comfortably – exactly as it did throughout most of the First World War. Britain's Grand Fleet sat in residence at Scapa Flow, ideally positioned at the western end of the narrows between Britain and Norway and at the northern end of the North Sea, able to block the movement of German ships out to the Atlantic and to swoop down on any fleet movement by the Germans into the North Sea. That would have been reason enough for any German to hate the place, but Scapa Flow was also the site where, after the war was over, the surrendered German High Seas Fleet was interned and where, on 21 June 1919, it was scuttled to prevent what was believed to be certain capture by the British. U-boatmen knew the place as well. During the First World War, two U-boats had tried to break into Scapa Flow to wreak what havoc they could. Both failed to get in. Ironically, the fleet they intended to attack had not even been there.

Scapa Flow is surrounded by a ring of islands and is accessible by seven entrances: Hoy and Burra Sounds on the west, Hoxa Sound to the south, and four smaller passageways (Water Sound and the three branches of Holm Sound) to the east. The three entrances to the west and south are large and easily navigable and were guarded by nets and picket boats. The widest, most easily navigated channel was Hoxa Sound, which outlets due south into the Pentland Firth, the body of water that separates the Orkneys from Scotland proper, famous for its furious rip tides. It was this channel which the Royal Navy used to enter and exit Scapa Flow, and it was here that U18 and UB116 were sunk trying to break in during the First World War.[1] The four eastern entrances were narrow and given to fierce tides and, during the course of the First World War, had been further plugged by blockships.[2] Despite this, Dönitz had reason to believe that Scapa Flow was vulnerable to attack through one of those eastern entrances. He had recent aerial photography which showed that the blockships, at least in the northernmost of the entrances, Kirk Sound, had either been misaligned when put in place or they had shifted in the currents over the last 25 years, because they no longer fully blocked the entrance. A brave and resourceful captain, commanding one of his newest, most capable boats, might just be able to slip in and out by that route. Fortunately, he had the perfect man and boat to do the job.

The boat was U47, one of his newest boats. It had been in service less than a year. U47 was a Type VIIB, meaning that it was an improved version of the boat that Dönitz had originally conceived a few years earlier as his ideal wolf-pack boat. But a boat is only steel; it is only as good as its crew and a crew most often reflects the personality of its commander. U47's real strength was KL Gunther Prien. If it were possible to create the perfect U-boat commander out of the best personality traits available, Dönitz probably would have created Prien. He was still young, just 31 years old, but old enough to have 15 years of sea-going experience behind him, including four years as an officer in Dönitz's elite pre-war U-boat arm. But it was really his personality that made him so ideal. He was brave, resourceful, quick-thinking, dedicated and extremely patriotic. He had a simple, uncomplicated soul, not given to pondering his place in the universe. Among the short list of pleasures that gave meaning to his life was commanding U47. When Dönitz called Prien into his office on 1 October and explained to him his idea that a U-boat just might be able to slip in and out of Scapa Flow through Kirk Sound, he knew he had his man. He told Prien to take 48 hours to think about it, but Prien only took a day and that was mainly for show. He had clearly decided right there in Dönitz's office that this was too great a challenge to pass up.

Slipping in

U47 left port on 8 October 1939. The passage to the Orkneys was deliberately done at a leisurely pace. The boat surfaced only at night. During the day it settled on the bottom to wait out the daylight hours. Arriving at Kirk Sound undetected was far more important than getting there quickly. Anyway, the plan was for U47 to arrive at Scapa Flow on the night of the new moon, when the harbour would be at its darkest and the tides best timed for passage in and out. On the night of 13–14 October, both periods of slack-water came during the long hours of dark. Unfortunately, the fact that it was new moon also meant that the tides would be at their strongest. Should U47 get in during the slack-water period soon after dusk, as was the plan, and then be unable to wait until the next, almost 12 hours later, it would face a fearsome ebb tide through the sounds towards the east.

Up until the daylight hours on Friday, 13 October, only Prien, among U47's crew, knew exactly where they were headed. Dönitz had decreed absolute secrecy and Prien had told no one, not even his own crew, the purpose of this strange mission. Of course, the men were suspicious, because, so far, every-thing had happened backwards. Instead of hunting for targets as they crossed the North Sea, they had done everything possible to avoid the enemy. It didn't take a genius to figure out that this was no typical patrol. Now, with the boat resting quietly at a depth of 90m on the sea-bed just east of the Orkneys, Prien assembled his crew and explained where they were headed. He was too smart to try to play down the dangers. Every crewman knew of the fates of U18 and UB116. Prien simply told his men that their mission was to sink as many British warships as possible and get out again if they could. They would surface again at dusk and make the final run-in.

At 1600, the crew were roused; not that it took much to get them going.[3] Few had slept much during the long day. Life on a U-boat is hard enough when there are duties to occupy your time. At its best, a U-boat is a tiny cylinder of steel sent out into the cold sea to do battle with an equally determined enemy. Life inside that confined space was perhaps at its hardest when there was nothing to do and so much to think about. A U-boatman had to be able to detach himself from the palpable dangers involved in fighting under the surface of the sea, to come to terms with the ever present possibility of a cold, watery death. Each man on board had made his own deal with God or the devil or fate: as long as he didn't have to think about it. But the long days that U47 had spent resting on the sea-bed gave a man lots of time to think.

Now, moreover, there was something very specific to think about. Scapa Flow! Sure, everyone knew about the two boats from the first war that had tried to get in and failed; but that wasn't really what rested heavily on the mind. After all, a man had to have faith that *BdU* wouldn't send them on a suicide mission and *der Alte* wouldn't throw his life away along with those of his crew.[4] No, as the men lay in their bunks or tried to find some comfortable position on the deck-plates between the torpedoes, unable to sleep, listening to the shallow breathing of 40 other men similarly occupied, it was simply fear of the unknown. Each man wanted, more than anything else, for the long day to be over. Thank God, it was finally time to move and eat and make an end of this nightmare of waiting.

Despite the fact that it was four in the afternoon, the *Kombüse* was cooking up breakfast. Since they were just a few days out of port, there still were fresh eggs, the bacon wasn't yet rancid and the bread hadn't taken on the green colour of penicillin, so the food was welcome indeed to the grateful crew. (*Kombüse* was a slang term for the boat's cook. Any crew was lucky if it had a cook who could produce decent-tasting fare in the cramped galley, with its miniature two-burner electric stove, especially after the boat had been out a month or more and the only ingredients left were canned bread, canned kraut and very old sausage, all of which tasted basically of diesel oil and mould. This was especially true late in the war when *Bratlingspulver*, a soy-based filler that was essentially tasteless, had replaced a significant proportion of the meat in the sausage.)

The crew was given an hour to eat and perform what few ablutions were possible on a submerged U-boat. Then, at 1700, the work started in earnest. The LI was put in charge of rigging detonating charges throughout the boat, in case they got trapped inside the harbour. The Lords were put to work hoisting two reserve torpedoes into rapid-load position behind tubes I and II.

(Lords [*Pairs*] was a slang term used to refer to the ratings on a U-boat, the men who did the hard work on a boat. Most of the crew was made up of officers or technical petty officers. That left only about a third of the complement to move torpedoes, stand lookout, man the guns, etc.) Normally spare torpedoes were stowed on the deck of the forward torpedo compartment. There was a loading rail that could be moved from side to side to line up with the left or right tubes. Moving the torpedoes into rapid-load position meant raising them from the deck and suspending them, by chains, in place right behind the loading rail. In this position, they were in the way of any normal activity in the torpedo room, but the assumption was that they would be loaded into the tubes before the crew's next chance to rest.

The work was completed at 1915 and the boat was surfaced. They were still some miles offshore, so the next four hours were spent closing the Orkneys from the south-east. The first land sighted was the coast of Mainland, the largest of the islands. At the south-eastern corner of the island is a promontory called Rose Ness. South of that headland is the opening into Holm Sound, which was U47's target. That bay runs several miles to the north-west between Mainland and the island of Burray. At its farther end, it is split into three channels by two islands: Lamb Holm to the north and Glims Holm to the south. In 1939, all three channels were at least partially closed by blockships sunk there during the First World War. The southernmost of the three, the channel between Burray and Glims Holm, was completely blocked. So was the middle channel, known as Skerry Sound, between Glims Holm and Lamb Holm. It was the northern channel, Kirk Sound, where Dönitz found navigable channels in his aerial photography. Three blockships had been sunk here, but, if they ever had completely blocked the channel, they no longer did so. Now, they were positioned some distance west of the narrowest point of Kirk Sound and there were at least three discernible channels, one on either side of the northern blockship and one between the southern blockship and the shore of Lamb Holm.

The existence of these channels wasn't a secret. They were well known to local fishermen who used them to enter and exit Scapa Flow. In fact, the Royal Navy was 'officially' aware of the gaps in the defences at Kirk Sound. When *Royal Oak* arrived at Scapa just before the outbreak of war, one of her officers, a submariner putting in his time on a surface unit, had surveyed the harbour's defences and had reported in writing that he was certain that he could navigate a small submarine through Kirk Sound. *Royal Oak*'s navigator made an independent examination of the channel and came to the same conclusion.[5] Even before then, the Navy had designated an old steamer as a fourth blockship for Kirk Sound, but, in a supreme irony, the intended blockship was sunk by a U-boat on its way north. Still, there was no feeling that the harbour was particularly vulnerable, because the known channels were extremely narrow and were considered passable by the local boatmen only a few hours a day, when the tide was at or near slack-water. At other times, the tides roared through Kirk Sound at a speed that should discourage any but the most foolhardy from attempting a passage. Prien was aware of the tidal conditions in Kirk Sound and knew that if he arrived at the channel before midnight, he had a good chance of finding relatively gentle currents through the narrows. Getting out again, he realised, might be a different matter.

The night was basically calm. There was a light breeze from the north-north-east. The sky was overlaid with a veil of high clouds, thin enough for a magnificent display of Northern Lights to illuminate the whole northern horizon. The thin clouds tended to diffuse the light of the aurora, bathing the entire sky in a flat pale glow that made it extremely difficult to distinguish objects.

> The view is utterly strange. On shore all is dark, while high in the sky the Northern Lights are flickering, so that the bay, enclosed by quite high hills, is lit directly from overhead.[6]

Approaching Rose Ness, a few minutes after 2300, Prien sighted a steamer heading towards him and quickly dived in the path of the oncoming ship. Once submerged and stabilised at periscope depth, he searched for the steamer and found no trace of the ship. His sound devices also picked up no trace of the steamer.[7] British records show no record of a ship there at that time, and this may well have been the case. Given the strangeness of the lighting conditions, the relative inexperience of all involved (Prien and his crew were only on their second war patrol) and the stress (composed of equal parts fear of the unknown and pressure to succeed), it is understandable that Prien might have seen a ship which wasn't there. This wouldn't be the only time that night that Prien would see ships that weren't there.

When Prien brought U47 to the surface again at 2331, no activity of any kind was visible on the surface. The steamer, if it had ever been there, was long gone. The boat was trimmed decks awash. (By taking water into its dive tanks or blowing it out again, a submarine dives or surfaces. However, there were more choices available to a captain apart from flooding or blowing all tanks. By partially flooding tanks, the amount of the boat showing above the surface could be carefully controlled. In situations when remaining undetected was critical, a captain could opt to trim the boat so that the decks were awash and only the tower showed above the surface.)

This was a calculated risk. It made the boat less visible and allowed faster dives, but it increased the boat's draft as it headed into the narrow channels.

Greater draft increased both the risk of grounding on a shoal and the boat's susceptibility to the swirling currents ahead. Now clear of Rose Ness, Holm Sound opened before him. As he rounded the headland and headed north-west intending to stay close to the northern shore, he could clearly see block-ships off to the left and, supposing himself to already be well into Kirk Sound, ordered a change of course to due west. The navigator, at his chart table in the control room, reported to Prien that, according to his calculations, the turn had been made too soon. They couldn't be in Kirk Sound yet. At almost the same time, Prien realised his error. He had mistaken Skerry Sound for Kirk Sound. He ordered an immediate turn north and then north-north-east to get around Lamb Holm and once again close under the northern shore of Main-land. Finally, well clear of the island and back in the intended channel, he turned the boat again to the west and then slightly south of west.

Now in the main current, U47 quickly approached the blockships. The orig-inal plan had called for U47 to attempt to pass through Kirk Sound at or soon after the slack water period shortly after dark. However, it was now midnight and U47 was heading into a strong current flowing out of the harbour. Never-theless Prien intended to pass between the northern and central blockships. The middle ship was clearly visible due west of his position. He again altered course, a few degrees more to the north, so that he would make the gap with a comfortable clearance of 15m. But now the increasing ebb tide took a hand and, caught by an eddy, U47's bow kept swinging to starboard. Out of the gloom, Prien saw that an anchor chain stretched out from the northern block-ship and that, if the boat's swing continued, U47 might get trapped between chain and ship. Only quick action could prevent disaster. Port motor full stop! Starboard motor ahead slow! Hard port rudder! Blow all tanks! The bow rose out of the water and slowly swung to port, just clearing the anchor chain. The boat scraped along the chain, pressed against it by the increasing momentum turning it to port. The aft propeller guard seemed to catch on the chain. For agonising moments the boat hung on the chain and then it came free with a sudden jerk and surged forward. A quick turn to the south-west in order to clear Skaildaquoy Point, the headland close by the tiny town of St Mary's that marked the exit from Kirk Sound, and then the vast expanse of Scapa Flow opened up before Prien's eyes. They'd made it! They were in the Royal Navy's main harbour with a full load of torpedoes. And, as far as Prien could tell at first glance, the harbour was absolutely empty!

Empty... Well, Almost Empty!
Incredibly, all major units of the Royal Navy, with the sole exception of *Royal Oak*, which was too slow to keep up with normal fleet operations and was consequently treated as a special case, had been moved to another anchorage

on the night of 12 October, less than two days before Prien's arrival. During the day of the 12th, the Germans had flown a photo-reconnaissance mission over the harbour and had returned with a photograph showing the lower harbour full of the main units of the Home Fleet. In the north-eastern corner, well separated from the others, were two big ships, easily identifiable as *Royal Oak* and, to her north, *Repulse*. This information was relayed to U47 by urgent radio message. Thus Prien expected a full harbour and the disappointment at being confronted by an empty anchorage must have been palpable.

Having come this far and risked this much, it certainly was worthwhile to double check. Maybe the fleet had moved to a different part of the harbour or maybe the odd light just made it appear that it wasn't there. The only way to find out for sure was to head into the harbour. Prien turned U47 west-south-west, and held that heading as long as he dared. He knew that the farther he went into the anchorage, the more visible he would be to the guardships at the Hoxa Sound entrance, the main channel in and out of the harbour. But he had to see if there were any ships in the large bay formed at the western side of the Flow between Cava, Rysa, Fara and Flotta Islands. The fleet, if it was in, would be there. Halfway across the harbour and it was painfully obvious that there were no ships hiding to the west. The only hope was that *Royal Oak* and *Repulse* might still be in the north-east corner, near Scapa Pier. Prien swung the boat in a wide turn to port and headed back towards Kirk Sound. A few minutes later, he changed course to north-east and then, when what appeared to be two large ships came into view, he turned again, this time past north to 340deg. Here, at last, were targets worthy of the risk of breaking into Scapa Flow. Plainly visible, anchored directly north of him, with no apparent activity, was the old battleship *Royal Oak*. Farther to the north, with only its bow visible beyond the nearer ship, Prien identified the equally old battle-cruiser *Repulse*. (This can only have been a case of poor visibility in confusing light leading Prien to see what he expected to see. In fact, there was only one major ship there that night, the unfortunate *Royal Oak*. *Repulse* had been in approximately the position where Prien claimed to have seen her, as radio reports had led him to expect, but in fact she had sailed the night before. Prien also claimed to have sighted destroyers anchored between the two big ships and the shore to the east. They were not there either.)

Regardless of the discrepancy between what Prien saw and what really was there, U47 now approached the target from the south and prepared to fire three torpedoes. The range was 3000m. Depth was set at 7.5m. The magnetic detonators were switched off, leaving the standard contact pistol. (The Germans had developed a sophisticated, super-secret magnetic detonator for torpedoes before the war. In theory, it was simpler and more effective to use a magnetic pistol and run torpedoes deeper so that they passed under targets and exploded directly below them, than to try to guess the draft of a target and hope that the torpedo's depth-keeping was accurate. In practice, the detonator was hyper-sensitive and generally unreliable, causing U-boat captains regularly to turn off that feature and rely on the standard contact pistol. Later in the war, when the bugs had been worked out of the system, use of the magnetic pistol increased.)

One torpedo was aimed at the bow of *Repulse*, which was thought to be protruding beyond the nearer target, *Royal Oak*. The other two were aimed at the broad beam of the nearer ship. Tubes I, II and IV were fired at 0058. Three-and-a-half minutes later, a low-order detonation was heard as the first torpedo hit what Prien believed was the bow of *Repulse*. The torpedo in Tube IV was a tube-runner, getting caught in the tube. The other missed. (In fact, the first torpedo hit *Royal Oak* well forward on her starboard side, causing some minor flooding in her bow compartments. The explosion was relatively weak and the resulting shock so mild that many on board slept through the first hit; the officers and men who were aware of the explosion reacted in an incredibly confused and desultory manner. The assumption was that a small, and not particularly consequential, internal explosion had taken place, probably in the paint locker, and, since there appeared to be no fire and any resultant flooding was minor, there seemed to be no reason to rouse the crew in the middle of the night. The thought that a U-boat might be in Scapa Flow firing torpedoes seems not to have occurred to *Royal Oak*'s officers.)

As soon as the torpedoes were fired, U47 began a sweeping turn to starboard. When the aft torpedo tube came to bear, a fourth torpedo was fired at *Royal Oak*. It also missed. U47 continued towards the south-east for another ten minutes while the Lords struggled to reload the two upper forward torpedo tubes. At about 0112, the boat turned and headed north again. At 0122, the three remaining torpedoes (the two new reloads in the forward upper tubes and the one as-yet unfired torpedo from Tube III in the forward lower bank) were fired at *Royal Oak*. At least two of the three appeared to hit the battleship.[8] One definitely hit alongside 'B' turret, about a third of the way aft, on the starboard side. Perhaps 15 seconds later there was a single or double detonation alongside the mainmast, which tore open the hull in way of the No. 1 boiler room. In the process, it opened up the main oil tank on the starboard side, causing the thick layer of oil on the water which made swimming so hard for many survivors. This explosion alone, regardless of the others, was almost certainly enough to sink the ship. There was a third detonation in one of the after magazines which ignited cordite charges there and sent fire raging through the accommodation spaces alongside and aft of the after turrets. It is unclear whether a separate torpedo hit caused this or whether it was a secondary effect of the hit alongside the mainmast. It is likely that the magazine which ignited was one of the secondary armament magazines and not the aft magazine for the main 15in guns. Had that magazine exploded, the ship would have been torn apart.

As it was, *Royal Oak* was doomed. The ship immediately began listing to the starboard and in less than 20 minutes she had turned turtle and slipped beneath the surface of the harbour. Of the approximately 1200 men on board the battleship that night, more than 800 died, either trapped in the sinking ship or succumbing to the cold water and the thick scum of oil on its surface. Most of the survivors were taken on board *Daisy II*, a drifter which had been tied up on the battleship's port side and had only just avoided being dragged under when *Royal Oak* sank. A few managed to swim to shore and several others were picked up, hours later, by boats arriving from HMS *Pegasus*, which had been moored two miles away to the west. One survivor missed the boats coming from *Pegasus* and swam all the way to the seaplane carrier, being pulled out of the water three hours after the battleship sank.

To the men on U47, the explosions from that last spread of torpedoes seemed to light up the harbour and were followed by a flurry of activity. The destroyers Prien had noted inshore of the battleship were observed to come to life and begin sweeping the area with searchlights. Several automobiles were seen on a road parallel to the coast, barely 200m from the U-boat, heading south from Scapa Pier towards St Mary's. Prien was certain that U47 had been seen because one car appeared to point its headlamps right at the boat, stop, turn around and head off in the other direction. (None of this activity, however, actually happened. As noted already, there were no destroyers near *Royal Oak* or anywhere else in the harbour that night. Moreover, the road from Kirkwall to St Mary's runs well inshore, so that Prien couldn't have seen headlamps, even if there had been vehicles on the road. In fact, there were very few cars on Mainland and none were driving towards St Mary's that night.) Prien thought it was prudent to head back towards open water. He still had five spare torpedoes, but all tubes were empty (except Tube IV with its tube-runner) and none of the spares was in position to be loaded easily. It would take hours of work to get even one tube ready to fire. The torpedo in Tube IV could be pushed out manually or brought into the boat and checked for malfunction. Neither was an easy task. Nevertheless, he could have opted to put his boat on the bottom, reload tubes during the day and resume the attack on what he believed to be the damaged *Repulse* the next night; but he had every reason to assume that *Repulse* would be moved, if possible, or otherwise heavily defended. This would all depend on himself not being found by sonar and attacked in the intervening hours. In the circumstances, no one faulted him for deciding that he had done what he could and that escape was the best option.

With both engines ahead half, U47 headed south-east back towards Skail-daquoy Point and the western entrance to Kirk Sound. The tide was still ebbing, slack-water was still several hours off, but now the strength of the tide was much reduced. Of prime concern, however, was the fact that there would now be much less water under the hull. He had barely scraped through the middle channel with deeper water. Now, he opted to try the channel between the southern blockship and Lamb Holm, because his charts showed the deepest water there. Standing well to the south of the entrance, almost into the middle of Skerry Sound, Prien then swung the boat to east-north-east, both engines now slow, letting the current carry him along. However, close into the shore of Lamb Holm, the boat got caught in a backwash and seemed to stand still in relation to shore. Increasing power to half speed, then three-quarters and finally full speed, the boat just cleared the blockship; then up ahead there appeared a jetty projecting from Lamb Holm out into the sound. For a moment it looked as if the boat might not clear the jetty, but a sharp swing to port and then back again to starboard and U47 was around the jetty. Another turn to starboard a few minutes later and the boat was clear of Lamb Holm and heading out into Holm Sound and then the Fair Isle Channel. Open water!

Home Again

For U47, a hero's welcome awaited. The British, not wanting to be caught in the position of acknowledging Nazi claims, announced the sinking even before Prien had a chance to radio Dönitz. Having been deprived of the chance to astound the world with the news of this incredible feat, the Germans nevertheless understood that *Royal Oak*'s sinking was a propaganda coup of unprecedented proportions and made preparations to play up the event for all it was worth. The boat entered Kiel to the accompaniment of brass bands and lined decks. After formal greetings by Dönitz and every available admiral, Prien and the crew were flown to Berlin and fêted again, this time by Hitler himself. Within days, an account of the sinking, attributed to Prien, was in print and selling out in German bookstores. This hastily crafted account was based on U47's log and Prien's recollections, so it included all the errors he had made that night, such as believing he'd seen and torpedoed *Repulse*, that there had been destroyers present inshore of *Royal Oak* and that he'd seen car headlamps onshore. It also added a number of new errors, which had no basis in U47's log. For example, it told the exciting story of U47 being pursued by one of the non-existent destroyers. According to the popular account, one of the British destroyers spotted U47 and gave chase at high speed. The destroyer closed on U47 as it tried desperately to make its escape, firing shells which landed around the U-boat but, miraculously, failed to hit.

Finally, as the U-boat attempted to fight its way out through the narrow passage into Kirk Sound, the destroyer pulled within a few hundred yards and then, as if suddenly struck blind, seemed to lose sight of its target, stumble around Skerry Sound for a few minutes and then turn back into Scapa Flow where it joined the other destroyers, dropping depth charges at random into the murky waters of the harbour. The whole story was fictitious. There were no destroyers, no pursuit and no depth charges were dropped in Scapa Flow that night.

The story, particularly as told in Prien's book, was so fantastic in parts, that some have called into question whether U47 ever penetrated Scapa Flow at all that night.[9] Most of the arguments point towards the factual inaccuracies in Prien's log and in the subsequent popular account. Many of these inaccuracies have been pointed out already. Some, however, should be specifically addressed. In particular, such inaccuracies point out the frailty of human memory, especially when the person involved was engaged in most dangerous adventure of his life. For example, Prien described the night as being brightly lit by the Northern Lights, while *Royal Oak*'s survivors universally recall how dark it was that night. This, as with many of the inconsistencies between Prien's account and the historical view of the event 60 years later, can be explained by the natural subjectivity of the observations made by men in the heat of combat, especially at night, in cold water, with a ship sinking around them. Add to this a certain amount of 'relativity'. Prien wanted the harbour dark, so any amount of light was too much; the survivors of *Royal Oak* and their would-be rescuers wanted it bright, so the dimly illuminated night struck them as pitch black.

The most difficult inconsistency to explain away is the orientation of *Royal Oak*'s wreck relative to U47's reported position and to the shore. The hull of *Royal Oak* now lies in a north-south orientation, while Prien's account indicates that the battleship was oriented east-west, with her starboard side facing south, towards the U-boat. For Prien to have seen his target's open starboard side would seem to require him to have been east of the battleship, firing west. But there was only a half-mile of open water between *Royal Oak* and the shore. Prien specifically states that he was two miles from his target when he fired his torpedoes. The only credible explanation, short of assuming Prien was never there, is that the battleship's orientation was somewhere between east-west and north-south, allowing Prien the impression that the ship was broadside to him, and still permitting the wreck the reasonable chance to settle into a position parallel to the coast.

Critics have used these inconsistencies to make the case that Prien was never in Scapa Flow and that *Royal Oak* sank due to sabotage. According to this hypothesis, the Royal Navy announced that the cause of *Royal Oak*'s sinking was a U-boat before they had explicit evidence that this was the case. Later they maintained the story, despite evidence to the contrary, for propaganda reasons. (According to this theory, admitting a sinking by U-boat was far less damaging to public morale than the acknowledgement of sabotage, which would have been disastrous.) The Germans, according to this line of reasoning, were only too willing to go along with the RN line, because it protected their saboteurs and did wonders for the image of their U-boat arm.

For this argument to be believable, however, requires the acceptance of an extraordinary conspiracy to bury the truth, all the more so because it presumes the co-operation of enemies (and, later, former enemies) during and after the war, up to the present day. Much of the official British documentation on the sinking, in particular the divers' reports describing the wreck, is still covered by the Official Secrets Act. The wreck itself is off-limits to sport divers, being a memorial site (much like USS *Arizona* at Pearl Harbor), although, in 1957, the Royal Navy proposed raising and disposing of the wreck, only to be inundated with protests from the families of crewmen who died when *Royal Oak* sank.

A good many of the crew of U47 died during the war. Both Prien and his IWO, Endrass, were casualties. But a number of crewmen who were on U47 that night survived, and it strains credulity to believe that they would maintain a fiction concerning that mission, as some claim it to have been, for all the years since the war's end.

Beyond the propaganda value of the sinking, and the horrendous loss of life, U47's sortie into Scapa Flow did absolutely nothing to change the outcome of the war. The Royal Navy lost an old battleship, one for which it really had little use, and, more importantly, over 800 fine, experienced sailors. But, beyond that, *Royal Oak*'s sinking changed no plans and altered no strategies, in terms of how the British thought they might win the war. On the German side, besides the marvellous propaganda value of the event and the consequent reinstatement of Dönitz in Hitler's favour, the strategic position remained unchanged. Dönitz still had too few U-boats with which to fight the merciless campaign to deny Britain the means to fight the war or even feed its population.

Interlude
U556

Cruel Irony

The U-boat service attracted strong personalities. After all, it was a special breed of sailor who chose to take a tiny steel tube and deliberately dive it beneath the waves. Many of the officers who volunteered to join Dönitz, particularly those who signed up before the war, were the kind to make a lasting impression. The U-boat service provided a home for men who would have had a hard time fitting into the more rigid structure of the surface fleet. This was particularly true of KL Herbert 'Parsifal' Wohlfarth.[1]

Wohlfarth, whose nickname recalled a knight from Arthurian legend (Parsifal is the German rendering of Percival), known for his outstanding bravery and honesty, was quite a character. For one thing, he had a reputation for always being well dressed and groomed, even at the end of a month-long patrol. Even more, he was renowned for an irreverent sense of humour: nobody and nothing were too sacred to be the target of his barbs. Even after hostilities began, he continued to play pranks and generally to make light of the very serious business of waging war. Like all U-boat commanders, Wohlfarth was a young man, yet with solid experience of captaining submarines.

He joined the U-boat service in 1937 and served as watch officer on U16 during 1938–39. Prior to taking over the new U556 in January 1941, he had commanded U14 (October 1939–April 1940) and U137 (June 1940–December 1940). it was while working up his new boat in January 1941 that Wohlfarth encountered a target worthy of his humour. He was taking U556 out of the Blohm & Voss yard in Hamburg on one of its acceptance trials, when he crossed paths with another, somewhat larger product of the same yard, the battleship *Bismarck*. Wohlfarth, unable to resist the opportunity, had his radioman signal to *Bismarck*:

Captain-to-Captain: What a nice boat you have!

The impertinence was twofold. Not only did Wohlfarth, a mere Kapitänleutnant, have the temerity to address *Bismarck*'s commander, Kapitän zur See Ernst Lindemann, as an equal, but he also had the effrontery to refer to *Bismarck* as a 'boat' and not a 'ship', a sure insult to anyone in the surface navy.[2] Needless to say, *Bismarck*'s reply was more than a bit testy:

What boat, skipper?

The question was one that a superior officer would make of a junior, before putting him on report. Wohlfarth, unimpressed and oblivious to the implied threat, responded:

I can do this. Can you?

And promptly crash-dived U556 right in the path of the oncoming leviathan.

The incident merely added to Wohlfarth's lustre in the U-boat service, where irreverence plus skill made a winning combination. To patch up any wounded feelings among *Bismarck*'s officers, Wohlfarth hosted them at a dinner a few weeks later, just before U556 left for the Baltic to continue training. At that occasion, 'Parsifal' presented *Bismarck* with a hand-drawn certificate, declaring U556 to be *Bismarck*'s godfather and taking on the task of protecting its godchild under all circumstances. It was all meant in lighthearted good humour and *Bismarck*'s officers took it as such. The certificate read as follows:

SPONSORSHIP CERTIFICATE

We, U556 (500t), declare before Neptune, ruler of the oceans, seas, lakes, rivers, creeks, ponds and rills, that we will stand by our big brother, the battleship *Bismarck* (42,000t), everyday, on the water, under the water, on land and even in the air.
Hamburg, 28 January 1941,

(Signed) The commander and crew of U556

Even more irreverent than the text were the drawings that graced the top and bottom of the certificate. The one at the top showed a stick figure knight, 'Parsifal' himself, waving a sword and swatting down aircraft (including one that looks suspiciously like a Swordfish), while, with a big thumb, he pushes away a torpedo. The drawing at the bottom shows a U-boat, obviously U556, towing the battleship. It was all meant to be funny. Little did anyone there that night realise how cruelly ironic it would all be just four months later.

Frustration

On 1 May 1941, U556, ready for action, sailed from Kiel on its way to the Atlantic. For a first patrol in a new boat with a new crew, Wohlfarth had spectacular success. He hadn't even reached the open ocean when, barely six days out of Kiel, U556 encountered and sank a fishing trawler by gunfire near the Faroes. [3] On 8 May, U94 and later U110 found a large outbound convoy east of Cape Farewell, the southern tip of Greenland, headed south-east. U556 homed in on U110's beacon and found the convoy, OB.318, in the early morning of the 10th. Three U-boats, U94 (Kuppisch), U110 (Lemp) and U201 (Schnee) had already attacked and had sunk six steamers. Wohlfarth attacked the convoy three separate times on the 10th. The first attack was on two steamers which he claimed to have sunk, although, in fact, one wasn't hit and the other, though badly damaged, limped into Reykjavik. The second attack, near dawn, was more successful, sinking a British steamer. The combined attacks had been so devastating to the convoy that it was ordered to disperse and the remaining merchantmen told to make their way to their North American destinations as best they could. After trailing the remnants of the convoy all day, U556 attacked again after sundown on the 10th and sank another steamer, the last victim from that unfortunate convoy.[4]

The next convoy, this time eastbound HX.126, was also sighted first by U94 in the afternoon of the 19th. This time U556 was close by and was able to attack after sundown on the 20th. Wohlfarth reported sinking three motorships, two of them big tankers, juicy prizes indeed. In fact, the biggest of them was only damaged, but the other two sank, giving U556 a respectable score for the patrol.[5] Wohlfarth reported that he had expended all his torpedoes and U556 was ordered to make course for Lorient.

That should have been the end of the story, but while U556 was fighting the hard, day-by-day struggle for control of the North Atlantic, another, far more famous battle was taking place over the same patch of water. U556's godchild, the huge battleship *Bismarck*, had left Bergen heading north, accompanied by the heavy cruiser *Prinz Eugen*, on the 21st. The plan was for the two ships to break into the North Atlantic and there wreak as much havoc as they could to the Trans-Atlantic convoy routes before they ran low on supplies and headed towards the French coast. (A number of German supply ships were at sea south of Greenland and had been regularly supplying U-boats with extra fuel and provisions. The plan was for *Bismarck* and *Prinz Eugen* to extend their mission as much as possible by resupplying from these ships, but some consumables, particularly ammunition for the main guns, couldn't be resupplied at sea and their depletion would eventually force the ships back to port.)

By the early hours of the 24th, the two German ships were passing between Iceland and Greenland, and were being trailed by British cruisers and closed by a major force composed of *Prince of Wales* and *Hood*. The well-known gun-battle followed in which *Hood* blew up and the German ships subsequently shook off the trailing cruisers and effectively disappeared into the North Atlantic, exactly as planned. The only problem was that *Bismarck* hadn't escaped the engagement on the 24th unscathed. She had received a hit in the bow under the waterline, suffering some minor flooding, nothing to cause concern. However, that hit had ruptured the bow oil tank, causing a serious loss of fuel oil and reducing her range to the extent that the planned commerce warfare in the Atlantic had to be abandoned. She had just enough fuel to make St-Nazaire, the only French port with a large enough dry-dock. *Prinz Eugen* was detached to carry on with the planned raid; *Bismarck* changed course towards France.

Bismarck's sortie had, so far, not required any assistance from the U-boats at sea, but now, heading directly back towards the pursuing forces of the Royal Navy, she needed all the help she could get. On the 24th, Dönitz received a request for all available U-boats to concentrate south of Greenland in order to attack any Royal Navy units still shadowing *Bismarck*. U556 was far to the east of the proposed gathering and was out of torpedoes, but, despite this, it represented another set of eyes available to search for the British and so it was included in the order to form the patrol line. By the next morning, *Bismarck* had changed course to the south-east and the patrol group, five U-boats including U-556, was switched rapidly into a position on a line between the south-western corner of Ireland and Cap Ortegal at the north-western corner of Spain. Thus, *Bismarck*, the U-boats and several detachments of Royal Navy ships spent 25 May and most of the 26th converging on a point south-west of Ireland. For much of that time, the British had only a very general idea of *Bismarck's* whereabouts. They had guessed correctly that *Bismarck* was headed towards France, but they had lost track of her exact position. For much of this time the closest RN force was made up of the battleships *King George V* and *Rodney*, paralleling *Bismarck's* course slightly to the north and about 150nm behind. Another RN task group, Force H, made up of *Renown* and *Ark Royal*, was approaching from the south. Still, unless they got lucky, *Bismarck's* lead on her pursuers would prove sufficient and she would slip through to France.

That lucky break came at 1030 on the 26th, when a Catalina search plane from Loch Erne, Northern Ireland, sighted *Bismarck*. That was enough. Soon after that, carrier aircraft from *Ark Royal* took over from the Catalina and then the light cruiser *Sheffield* established radar contact and *Bismarck's* position was firmly established. However, it still wasn't clear whether the British could slow down *Bismarck* sufficiently to allow the trailing heavy units to bring her to bay. The only hope the British had was 15 fragile Swordfish torpedo bombers on *Ark Royal's* deck.

Sometimes the fates of ships are linked in the strangest of ways. It had seemed pure coincidence that U556 and *Bismarck* had crossed paths back in January, and Wohlfarth's adoption of the battleship, with its elaborate promise of protection against enemies in the air and on the water, had certainly been a pure lark; but now, in the cruellest of ironies, it became U556's fate to witness *Bismarck's* demise and be unable to do anything about it. According to U556's log, at 1948 on the 26th, *Renown* and then *Ark Royal* came out of the mist in front of the startled lookouts on the U-boat's bridge. U556 dived and Wohlfarth literally screamed in frustration as the two ships crossed in front of his empty torpedo tubes. He knew they were chasing *Bismarck*. He watched impotently as aircraft launched and recovered on *Ark Royal*'s wildly pitching deck. If only he'd had a few torpedoes! If only... According to witnesses, Wohlfarth broke down in his rage and anger. He recovered in time to send a message to Dönitz at 2010 reporting his contact, in the hope that one of the other boats in the area might be able to attack the British and somehow save *Bismarck*. (In fact, U556 sighted Force H after the second and critical attack had been launched by *Ark Royal*, so even had U556 had torpedoes and been able to sink the aircraft carrier, *Bismarck* still would have been doomed.)

U556 trailed Force H , maintaining visual contact until 2035 and sound contact until 2240. It then continued south-east, following the trail of the British forces, sending beacon signals for other boats to home in on. At 0300 and again at 0340 and 0430, U556 reported seeing gunflashes at a distance of 15nm, south-west of her position.[6] (U73 actually sighted *Bismarck* soon after midnight and tracked her for over two hours before losing sight of her again.) This was *Bismarck* fighting off the night-time attack by British destroyers. At 0700, U556 received orders to close with *Bismarck* and attempt to retrieve her logbooks. However silly this order may have seemed, Wohlfarth attempted to comply, heading off in the direction of the last-seen gunfire. By noon, having not sighted *Bismarck* or any other ships, Wohlfarth reported that his fuel situation required a direct return to port; U556 was relieved of this duty and U74 was ordered to continue looking for *Bismarck*. By now, however, *Bismarck* had gone down and the search was futile. (*Bismarck* sank at 1036, north-west of where U556 had been looking.) In fact, the mission to recover *Bismarck*'s logs may have cost German lives. Two British warships were stopped at the site of *Bismarck*'s sinking, picking up survivors, when they detected U74's presence. Taking the prudent course, they left the scene, leaving an unknown number of survivors still in the water. U74 picked up three of them. The next day, a German trawler picked up two more. The rest perished in the cold Atlantic water.

U556 didn't long outlast its godson. It reached Lorient on 30 May and immediately prepared for its second patrol. It put out to sea again on 19 June. On the 27th, in operation against convoy HX.133, Wohlfarth attempted a surface attack, but was detected, attacked and eventually destroyed. Five of the crew lost their lives. 'Parsifal' Wohlfarth and 39 of his officers and crew survived to live out the war in a British POW camp.

U156

The *Laconia* Incident

The rules were certainly well understood by everyone. A U-boat, even a big Type IXC like U156, had no extra room to take on survivors. Everyone knew that U-boats existed to sink enemy ships and there were men on those ships who would end up in the water. Even if you wanted to, you couldn't rescue them all; and trying to save a few could be a fatal mistake. Increasingly, even here in the South Atlantic, aircraft could appear at any time and they didn't care whether you were rescuing survivors or not: they attacked without asking any questions. But occasionally, something would happen to upset all those well-understood rules.

U156, ably commanded by KK Werner Hartenstein, had two very successful patrols in the Caribbean under its belt, and was now part of the *Eisbär* group en route to Capetown. This group, which left Lorient in mid-August 1942, was composed of three other big, long-ranging Type IX boats besides U156: U68 (Merten), U504 (Poske) and U172 (Emmermann). It also included U459, the first of the Type XIV supply U-boats known popularly as *Milchkühe. Gruppe Eisbär's* assignment was to attack the rich concentration of shipping that was believed to round the Cape of Good Hope near Capetown, on its way to or from the Indian Ocean. In order to achieve the maximum surprise, and therefore the best results, the four attack boats were told that south of 5deg south of the equator they were to refrain from attacking any but the most valuable of targets, until they had resupplied from U459 off the African coast and had reached Capetown with full tanks and a full load of torpedoes.[1]

On the way south, the *Eisbär* group was deployed against the northbound convoy SL.119 as it approached the latitude of Spain on its way towards the British isles. Only one sinking resulted: U156 came across a straggler from the convoy and dispatched it on 27 August.[2] The group was withdrawn again without further successes and ordered to resume course towards Capetown. The boats stayed in a sweep line until they reached the Cape Verde Islands and were then ordered to disperse and proceed to Capetown independently. On 12 September, as they approached the line at 5deg south beyond which they were to avoid attacking enemy shipping, Hartenstein found another target. Line or no line, this one was too tempting to pass up.

U156 was less than 200nm south of Cape Palmas on the coast of Liberia, the point at which the African coast, after sloping south-east from Dakar, turns slightly north of east and heads towards Lagos. The U-boat was on the surface, making cruising speed, approximately 12kt, on a course towards the south-south-east. The wind was moderate and from almost straight ahead. The sea was nearly calm and, under scattered clouds, visibility was average. At 1137, a lookout sighted a smoke plume on the horizon of the port quarter. Because they were still just north of the 5deg line, Hartenstein turned U156 around and took off in pursuit of the source of the smoke.[3] By mid-afternoon they were close enough to determine that the smoke was coming from a single, large steamer, which was zigzagging around a base course of 290deg. Checking the recognition books, Hartenstein guessed that he was chasing an old colonial service steamer of about 7000GRT, one of those ships built before the first war to carry passengers and cargo between Britain's various African colonies and the home islands. U156 stayed on the surface, maintaining a discreet distance to avoid being detected, waiting until nightfall before moving in. Shortly after 2100, Hartenstein judged it to be dark enough and began his run in towards the target. An hour later, he was in position and ready to fire. Based on the target's estimated size, he decided on a spread of two torpedoes.

The set-up was absolutely 'by the book'. With the IWO sighting through the UZO (*Überwasserzieloptik* – Surface Targeting Sight) on the bridge, the data was fed down to the navigator, whose battle station was at the attack computer mounted on the after bulkhead of the conning tower. Target bearing was fed directly to the computer from the UZO. Hartenstein shouted the rest of the information down the open tower hatch. (The information required by the attack computer was target range, target bearing – supplied by the UZO – target angle on the bow, target speed, target length, torpedo speed and torpedo depth. Angle on the bow is the angle between the target bearing and the target's course, measured in degrees from the target's bow. The attack computer was a mechanical analogue device, similar to, but much more sophisticated than, a mechanical adding machine. All information not supplied automatically to the computer was entered by means of a set of knobs on the computer face.) When the computer had ground out a solution and fed it to the torpedoes, the ready lights on the torpedo control board in the control room switched from red to green. The rating who manned the board shouted this information up to the navigator, who, in turn, relayed it up through the hatch to the captain: 'Tubes I and III ready'. If the target set-up had changed – a not uncommon occurrence in the several minutes it took for the attack computer to work out a solution and the torpedoes to be set – changed data would be shouted down to the navigator and a new solution computed. If, as happened this time, the target maintained a steady course, the captain would shout, as Hartenstein did: 'Fire tubes I and III'. The firing buttons for the appropriate tubes were pressed on the torpedo control panel. Proper firing was acknowledged when the green light went out.

The attack computer had calculated a running time of just over three minutes. The officers and lookouts on the tower each made their own personal wish or prayer for success as the torpedoes sped on their way. For three minutes, there was nothing to do but wait and stare out into the darkness, hoping for a dull explosion and a waterspout and, perhaps, the flash of secondary explosions and the red glare of fire, all of which would indicate success. Then again, nothing might happen. The torpedoes might miss and speed off past the target until they ran out of electrical power and sank. This time, however, they didn't miss. The first torpedo hit the target amidships. The second detonation was heard, but not seen, so Hartenstein wasn't able to record where it hit. The steamer drifted slowly to a stop and began to settle, but showed no signs of sinking rapidly. Hartenstein, surprised that two torpedoes were insufficient to destroy the target, commented in his log: 'Steamer must be considerably bigger than estimated.'

As the tower watch on U156 watched with fascination, the steamer continued to slowly settle on an even keel. It might have been going more slowly that Hartenstein would have wished, but the ship was indeed sinking. In good order, the steamer's lifeboats were loaded and lowered, and they pulled away into the lee of the sinking ship. First on the 600m band and then on the 25m band, the two standard frequencies for distress signals, the steamer radioed: 'SSS SSS 04 34S 11 25W LACONIA TORPEDOED'.[4] The U-boat's radioman attempted, without success, to jam the broadcasts because it would give away the presence of U156. The message did resolve one issue in Hartenstein's mind. The steamer was the Cunard White Star liner, RMS *Laconia*, based at Liverpool. A quick glance at the recognition books explained why the steamer was taking so long to sink. She was, at 19,695GRT, indeed much bigger than he'd estimated. Nevertheless, she continued to settle and, about an hour after the attack, she slipped beneath the waves.

Short-term Consequences

It had been, until now, entirely routine. The steamer was gone and the passengers and crew seemed to have got safely away in the ship's boats. U156 was about to resume its prior course when, through a trick of the wind, the tower watch heard cries in Italian for help from the water. This was entirely unexpected and warranted investigation. Creeping cautiously towards the source of the shouts, Hartenstein was horrified to find what appeared to be hundreds of Italians in the sea. Suddenly, he was faced with the same horrible set of choices as had faced Marschall 24 years earlier (see

Chapter 3), the only difference being that these men weren't enemy soldiers but were obviously allies. Like Marschall, Hartenstein had to decide whether to leave these men to their fate or attempt to pick some or all of them out of the water.

Hartenstein never hesitated. He immediately ordered his off-duty crew on deck and began pulling as many of the survivors out of the water as he could. Very soon the story they told to his crew cleared up the mystery of why so many men remained in the water long after *Laconia*'s lifeboats had pulled away and why they all spoke Italian. *Laconia*, it transpired, was carrying a crew of over 400 and, as passengers, almost 300 British servicemen and 80 British civilians, including women and children. But the primary 'cargo' in *Laconia* was 1800 Italian POWs, guarded by 103 Polish soldiers. According to the Italians, when the torpedoes hit, the Polish guards had locked down the compartments where they were held and, later, when the prisoners had been released and had made their way onto the deck, the British soldiers had held them back at gunpoint, preventing them from boarding the lifeboats as they were being loaded. So, the Italians had ended up in the water, while most of the British passengers and crew and the Polish guards had taken to the lifeboats.

Hartenstein was in a quandary. Even with the best will in the world, he couldn't rescue 1800 men from the water. At 0125 on the 13th, he radioed Dönitz for instructions:

> Sunk by Hartenstein, British Laconia, Qu FF7721, 310deg. Unfortunately with 1500 Italian POWs. 90 fished out of the water so far. . . Request orders.[5]

Dönitz approved Hartenstein's actions so far and immediately ordered the remaining *Eisbär* boats to come to U156's aid, as well as two boats which had been operating off Freetown.[6] He also passed a request along to the commander of the Italian submarine flotilla based at Bordeaux, asking that *Cappellini*, which was operating in the vicinity, also join in the rescue. As soon as word of the rescue was reported to Naval High Command, diplomatic efforts were begun to request aid from Vichy French warships based at Dakar. So, as the early morning hours of the 13th passed, assistance for U156 was being organised, but it would still be long hours before the first of it arrived. At 0437, Hartenstein reported again:

> . . . Have on board 193 men, including 21 British. Hundreds of survivors are drifting with only a life jacket. Propose diplomatic neutralisation of the site. Radio watch reveals unknown steamer in vicinity.[7]

Hartenstein was requesting the naval equivalent of a local cease-fire. He wanted to 'neutralise' the site of the sinking so that he could continue his rescue operations without fear of attack. As dawn approached, knowing that *Laconia* had radioed her location before sinking, and understandably fearing that Allied aircraft would search for survivors and would attack any U-boat on the scene, he radioed twice in uncoded English on both the 25m and 600m bands:

> If any ship will assist the crew of the shipwrecked Laconia, I will not attack her, provided I am not attacked by ship or air force. I picked up 193 men. 4 52 s 11 26 w. (signed) German submarine.[8]

U156 spent the day of the 13th, while awaiting reinforcements, moving survivors around between the water, the U-boat's deck and the various lifeboats, in an attempt to get as many men out of the water as possible. By nightfall, places for 100 men had been found in the various lifeboats which gathered around the U-boat, while the total of survivors on board U156 was reduced by 31. Late that night, Hartenstein received a radio message from Dönitz explaining that Hitler wanted the Capetown operation to resume as soon as possible; therefore U156 was to turn over all survivors as soon as U506, U507 and *Cappellini* arrived. The crew of U156 continued the work of hunting for survivors and finding places for them out of the water. At 0209 on the 14th, Hartenstein radioed to Dönitz, for the first time, a full description of the disaster on his hands:

> Estimate about 1500 survivors in about 22 big, completely full boats and many little rafts . . . over 400 fished out of the water. 200 distributed among the boats. So far, no steamers or aircraft.[9]

At 0245, Hartenstein received a long message from Dönitz, explaining that Vichy ships were on their way, setting up recognition procedures and fixing the rendezvous point some 70nm north-east of U156's and the survivor's current location. The remaining three *Eisbär* boats and the *Milchkuh*, if they had not yet taken on survivors (and they hadn't), were ordered to leave the rescue to Hartenstein, the two Freetown boats, *Cappellini* and the Vichy ships, and were immediately to resume their former course to Capetown. U156, in order to reach the rendezvous point as rapidly as possible, abandoned the lifeboats with great reluctance and started at high speed towards the north. All the while, Hartenstein attempted, without immediate success, to get a message through to Dönitz requesting that the rendezvous point be moved southward to where the lifeboats actually were. Dönitz finally replied later in the day, ordering Hartenstein to return to the site of the sinking and, as per his request, relocating the rendezvous point to the south. U159 (Witte), which was moving south with the intent of patrolling off the Congo delta, was ordered to proceed southward at slow speed so that, if necessary, it could replace U156 in the *Eisbär* group. U156 reversed course at 1347, but hadn't reached the lifeboats at nightfall and, therefore, lay to at 2100 so as not to overshoot the survivors in the dark.

At dawn the next day, 15 September, U156 began searching again for the lifeboats. At 1107, the first help finally arrived in the form of U506 from Freetown. Hartenstein gratefully turned over 132 Italian survivors to Würdemann, which still left his deck cluttered with 131, evenly split between Italians and British, including a number of women. The transfer took two hours and then, just after 1300, the two boats together continued searching for the remaining survivors. Three hours later they sighted a large cluster of lifeboats, some of the 22 boats U156 had left behind a day and a half earlier. The rest of the boats had drifted away during the intervening hours. Gradually more boats were sighted and brought back into the group. U156 launched its own lifeboat, filled it with provisions and moved some of the survivors still on board into that boat, which was kept tied to the U-boat's stern. (Type IXCs, like U156, had a small lifeboat stowed aft under the deck plates of the deck-casing. It was difficult to extract and launch from its stowage location, which explains why the operation of launching it and stocking it with supplies took several hours on the afternoon of the 15th.)

One by one, the lifeboats were inspected, the weakest of the survivors taken on board for rest and a hot meal, their places being taken in the boats by other survivors who'd had a chance to recuperate on board, and the rest of the survivors given water and food. Hartenstein had received word that a second *Milchkuh*, U460 (Schnoor), was on its way with orders to resupply U156 after the rescue was completed, so he felt no compunction about stripping his larder and water supply to provision the lifeboats. Another stray lifeboat was found at nightfall and tied to U156's own boat, so the U-boat was now towing two lifeboats towards the rendezvous point. Just before midnight, however, the U-boats lay to again.

By the next morning, now more than three days since the sinking, Hartenstein realised that there simply was no way to gather all the lifeboats together again. The only boats which hadn't drifted off towards the north-west overnight were the two that had been tied to the U-boat's stern. Mid-morning, a group of three lifeboats was found and then a fourth, which was taken in tow, and then an abandoned boat, which was also tied into U156's towline, now four boats long. For three days, Hartenstein had been able to proceed as best he could with the rescue without interference from or even, as far as he knew, detection by Allied forces, but at 1125, that idyllic state came to an end. A large, four-engine bomber with American markings, a B-24 Liberator, appeared from the north-east and flew overhead. Hartenstein had known that this had to happen sooner or later and had crafted a Red Cross flag from a piece of white cloth 2m square. This was draped over the side of the tower facing the oncoming aircraft. The plane doubled back, passed directly over the U-boat a second time and then circled for a few minutes. Hartenstein tried sending a message to the American by signal lamp, asking if it had any rescue ships in sight. The aircraft then resumed its course to the south-west, only to reappear from that direction a half-hour later, overfly U156 one more time and then continue on towards the north-east.

Shortly after 1230, another American Liberator appeared, passed low over the U-boat and dropped two bombs with delay fuses which exploded off the boat's bow. The reaction was one of incredulity and outrage, especially among the survivors, but the U-boat was under attack and had to take measures to defend itself. How could the American pilot fail to recognise that the U-boat he was attacking had a deckful of people and four lifeboats in tow? The towline to the four towed lifeboats was still being untied when the bomber approached again and dropped a bomb directly in the middle of the towed boats, overturning one of them. On another pass, the bomber dropped four more bombs, all of which missed. The aircraft then began circling again, seemingly out of bombs, but certainly homing other attackers to the scene. Hartenstein took advantage of the lull in the attack to complete the casting-off of the towed boats, giving him more freedom to manoeuvre. The lull was all too brief. Just minutes later, the Liberator approached again, dropping two more bombs. One of these exploded directly under the U-boat amidships. Reports of leaks in the bow as well as the Control Room finally forced Hartenstein's hand. He immediately ordered the 55 remaining British survivors still on-board, including all five women, into the water. He had intended to take the 55 remaining Italians into the boat somehow, but reports that chlorine gas was leaking from damaged battery cells decided that issue. He had no breathing gear for the Italians. They too were put overboard.

The Liberator finally seemed to have exhausted its bomb supply and flew off. U156 now had a breather, a break of unknown duration, to attempt to stop the leaks and to make sure that all the people put into the water found space in a lifeboat. A thorough recheck of the hull showed that, except for some minor leakage at the cold water intake ports for both diesels, the hull was sound and there were no serious leaks. At 1345, more than an hour after the Liberator had departed, Hartenstein glanced over the survivors one last time, wished them the best of luck, submerged and set course due west. After trimming the boat, the crew then took a detailed inventory of the damage. Both periscopes were out of order: the sky periscope couldn't be raised and the attack periscope's traverse mechanism was inoperative. The radio direction finder, sound locator and plumb gauge were all non-functional. All in all, the damage was serious but not critical. Maybe with more time, repairs could be made. The boat surfaced at dark and continued due west on the surface. Watch was kept all night with the radar detector; no signals were detected. Hartenstein reported the incident to Dönitz at 2304. Not too surprisingly, the reply was an order to break off all rescue attempts, complete repairs as soon as possible and report back when ready to resume operations.

Longer-term Consequences

U506 and U507, which had been over the horizon at the time of the attack on U156, continued the rescue operation. An air attack was also made the following morning on U506, which escaped by diving with 142 survivors on board. At noon, U507 was also attacked. The increasing presence of Allied aircraft was making this business of rescuing survivors decidedly unhealthy. Nevertheless, the two U-boats carried on, rendezvousing with three Vichy French warships on the 17th, handing over their survivors and then happily setting course for Freetown to finish operations there.[10] The Italian submarine *Cappellini* never met up with the German U-boats, but it rescued 42 survivors and turned them over to the French warships on the 18th. U156 did not rejoin the rescue effort. It did, however, resume operations, not returning to France until the middle of November.

In all, the rescue effort had probably saved several hundred lives, if not more. Of the original complement of 829 British soldiers, family and crew, 588 were eventually rescued. Of 103 Polish guards, 73 survived. Of approximately 1800 Italian POWs, 450 made it. It is hard to estimate how many of the British and Poles would have survived had U156 not initiated its rescue effort. The majority had taken to the lifeboats at the time of the sinking and most of the lifeboats were eventually found by the Vichy warships. The weather throughout was remarkably benign, with mild temperatures, little wind and only mild swells on the ocean. Nevertheless, the lifeboats drifted apart and were discovered spread over more than 20nm of water. Some were never found, the occupants, one presumes, eventually dying of hunger, thirst or exposure. Had U156 not started the operation and, as a consequence, the three Vichy warships had not arrived on the scene, then most, if not all, of the survivors in the lifeboats would probably have suffered the same fate. As for the Italians, there is no question that Hartenstein's efforts saved all of those who eventually survived.

On the 17th, having had time enough to regret his initial permission to conduct the rescue operation, Dönitz radioed the now-famous *Laconia* Order to all boats. It read:

1924/17.9

1. All attempts to rescue the crews of sunken ships will cease forthwith. This prohibition applies equally to the picking up of men in the water and putting them aboard a lifeboat, to the righting of capsized lifeboats and to the supply of food and water. Such activities are a contradiction of the primary object of war, namely, the destruction of enemy ships and their crews.

2. The order for the seizure of Commanding Officers and Chief Engineers remains in force.

3. Survivors are only to be picked up in cases when their interrogation would be of value to the U-boat.

4. Be severe. Remember that in his bombing attacks on German cities the enemy has no regard for women and children.[11]

After the war, Dönitz was brought before the Nuremberg court on charges that included the accusation that, with the *Laconia* Order, he had directed his U-boat commanders to kill survivors. The court concluded that the evidence was insufficient to convict on that count, but did criticise Dönitz for the ambiguity of the order, which didn't explicitly state that survivors were *not* to be killed.

U156 was sunk on its next patrol, going down with all hands, including Hartenstein. The other boats which participated did not last much longer, both U506 and U507 being lost in 1943. The Italian submarine *Cappellini* had the most interesting fate of them all. In 1943, *Cappellini* was converted to a transport for carrying war materials between Europe and Japan.[12] At the conclusion of its first trip to the east in this configuration in September 1943, *Cappellini* was interned by the Japanese at Sabang, because the Italians had meanwhile surrendered to the Allies. The Japanese handed the boat over to the Germans, who renamed it UIT24 and rearmed it with a German 105mm gun. It was seized again by the Japanese after Germany's surrender, renamed I503, surrendered to the Americans at Kobe and finally scuttled by the Allies after the war.

The American bomber pilot who attacked U156 was a Lt Harden, flying a B-24 Liberator of the 343rd BS, which was stopping over at Ascension Island on its way to Africa. The pilot reported the Red Cross flag and the presence of survivors on board and in boats to the commander of the 1st Composite Squadron based at Ascension, Capt. R. C. Richardson. Richardson ordered Harden to attack despite these indications, because he concluded that a U-boat was an ongoing threat and should be attacked whenever possible, regardless of circumstances. Richardson later achieved the rank of general in the USAF.

An Extreme Solution

Most submariners, of all nations, accepted the brutality of submarine warfare and went about the business of sinking enemy ships. A few took the logic of this warfare somewhat further than the rest. The most extreme example on record was that of the American, LCDR Dudley W. 'Mush' Morton, CO of USS *Waboo*. At the beginning of 1943, Morton took over *Waboo* just before its third patrol. The boat had gone through two lacklustre patrols, and Morton was determined to infuse *Waboo* with a new, more aggressive spirit. His energy and daring were rewarded with luck. On 26 January, *Waboo* encountered a small Japanese convoy carrying troops and supplies to the army on New Guinea. During the course of the day, Morton sank two freighters, a tanker and a troop transport. After sinking the troop transport, *Waboo* surfaced in the midst of approximately 20 small boats of various types (open boats, landing craft, motor launches, etc.). These had apparently been carried on the transport's deck for the purpose of landing the troops when the convoy arrived at its destination. They were now being used as lifeboats by those troops who had managed to get off the transport as it was sinking. The transport had been carrying a full division of soldiers, nearly 10,000 men, to New Guinea. Morton had no qualms about doing what he thought was necessary:

> We surfaced to charge batteries and destroy the estimated twenty troop boats now in the water. These boats were of many types, scows, motor launches, cabin cruisers and other nondescript varieties. At 1315 made battle surface and manned all guns. Fired 4in gun at largest scow loaded with troops. Although all troops in this boat apparently jumped in the water, our fire was returned by small calibre machine guns. We then opened fire with everything we had.[13]

It is not known how many Japanese soldiers and other survivors were killed, but by the time *Waboo* set off in pursuit of two other steamers, which had been fleeing while *Waboo* was shooting up the survivors, an hour had passed. None of the various lifeboats was left intact, and there were no longer any signs of life in the water.

There is one recorded case of a U-boat similarly shooting at survivors in the water. U852, under KL Eck, sank the Greek steamer *Peleus* on 13 March 1944 off the west coast of Africa. A number of U-boats had recently been lost to air attacks in that area and Eck, deciding that floating wreckage from the sinking would put his boat at risk, attempted to sink the wreckage, including the rafts upon which the survivors were floating. U852 continued around the Cape of Good Hope to its assigned operating area in the Indian Ocean, all the while being tracked by HF/DF fixes. The boat was located and attacked by RAF

Wellingtons.[14] After being damaged to the point where diving was no longer possible, Eck opted to beach the boat on the Somali coast, where 59 of the crew, including Eck, were captured. After the war, Eck and four others were put on trial for the murder of the crew of *Peleus*. Eck's defence, that he acted to protect his boat, was rejected by a British court-martial, as was the claim of the other defendants that they were just following orders. Eck and two other officers were sentenced to death and were shot on 30 November 1945. He was the only U-boat commander to be executed for war crimes.

The reaction in the American chain of command to Morton's actions was almost universally supportive. Morton's justification for shooting the survivors, that these were Japanese soldiers and, if they made land, would continue to fight and kill Allied soldiers, was accepted and approved. His job was to defeat the enemy and that necessarily included killing enemy soldiers when he had the opportunity. His immediate superior, the CO of Submarine Squadron 10, wrote an official commendation and recommended Morton for a medal as a result of this patrol. His boss, Acting COMSUBPAC J. H. Brown, wrote:

> This patrol speaks for itself, and the judgment and decisions displayed by the Commanding Officer were sound.[15]

It might have been interesting to hear Morton's comments on Eck's actions, but neither he nor *Wahoo* survived the war. Morton and *Wahoo* were lost to a Japanese air attack on 11 October 1943 while attempting to exit from the Sea of Japan after a very successful patrol.

Interlude
U185

The Birth of a U-boat

By mid-war, U-boats were being built in unprecedented numbers. Manning these boats and getting them ready to join the fight in the Atlantic had become a tightly orchestrated dance involving a rigid sequence of steps. Before the war, U-boats had been hand-crafted and their crews slowly polished to a fine state of readiness for war. By the middle of 1942, these niceties were a thing of the past. U-boats were being mass-produced and their crews had to be trained as well as possible in the few short months between a boat's commissioning and its first war patrol. As more and more boats were being lost in the remorseless battle in the Atlantic, fewer and fewer veterans, particularly among the chiefs and the junior officers, were available to season an otherwise green crew.

U185 was just another of those boats. It was work number UW1021, a big Type IX under construction at the Deschimag Seebeck yard at Bremerhaven.[1] The boat was launched in March 1942. During the next two months, the crew reported for the *Baubelehrung*, a process whereby the men gathered in specific sequence to observe the completion of the boat and learn its components as they were assembled. As a rule, the first to arrive was the LI (*Leitender Ingenieur*), the boat's chief engineer. On most boats he was a Leutnant or Oberleutnant in the Engineering Corps, which comprised technical officers, entirely distinct from the line officers who commanded the boat. Then came the rest of the officers and the chiefs, particularly the *Maschinisten* in charge of the diesels and the electric motors. Finally, in the last days before the scheduled commissioning, the remaining petty officers and the ratings collected in Bremerhaven. In order for them to get to know one another and come together as a crew, they were all quartered in the same rooming house, the *Lloydheim* on Hemmstrasse.

On 12 June 1942, U185 was commissioned and officially handed over by the yard to the *Kriegsmarine*. The ceremony was brief and dignified. The crew, in their dress uniforms, assembled on the aft deck-casing facing the pier. The new commanding officer, KL August Maus of the 1934 Naval Academy class, stood on the *Wintergarten*, the gun platform built into the aft end of the tower structure, facing aft. Dignitaries from the yard, naval representatives and distinguished naval officers stood on the pier. The best-known officer present was KK Nicolai 'Niko' Claussen, whose new boat was just a few days away from commissioning at the same yard. Niko Claussen was one of the U-boat 'aces', the rapidly vanishing breed of officers who had been in U-boats since before the war and who had been the beneficiaries of the *Fette Jahre*, the period roughly between July 1940 and the end of 1941, when the few U-boats available had achieved incredible successes. (*Fette Jahre* – literally the 'fat years', figuratively the 'happy times'.) He had taken over Hartmann's U37 in 1940 and had commanded that boat until it was withdrawn from service to become a training boat. Claussen had then commissioned U129 and commanded that boat with great success until turning it over to a new captain (KK Hans Witt) in May 1942. Now he was waiting to take U182, a superlong-range *U-Kreuzer*, designed for operations far beyond a U-boat's, even U185's, normal radius. Claussen's presence at the commissioning added a special dignity to the ceremony – which came in handy when, during the climax of the proceedings, the raising of the German naval ensign at the aft end of the boat, it was discovered that the flag was being raised upside-down.

Afterwards, everyone got a good laugh at the expense of the bosun. The crew and some of the yard workers retired to the *Lloydheim* for a dinner and then the party moved on to a favourite seaman's tavern known as the *U-boots Mutti*. (*Mutti* is common German slang for 'mother'.) At a separate dinner, the officers of U185 were hosted by Deschimag officials and were presented with engraved pocket knives and framed photographs of the boat. It was good that the officers and crew had a chance to enjoy themselves, because the real work of turning steel into a U-boat now began in earnest. By the evening of the 15th, three days later, U185 was ready to begin its trials. The boat exited the lock into the Wesermünde and tied up at the pier waiting for escort to Kiel. At 0500 the next morning, U185 departed in company with a large minesweeper, heading for Brunsbüttel and the western entrance to the Kiel Canal. The boat and its escort arrived at Kiel on the evening of the 18th and tied up at the *Tirpitzufer*. The next morning, UAK trials began.

The *Ubootsabnahmekommando* (UAK – U-boat Inspectorate) was responsible for determining that a new or repaired boat was fit to be accepted into the fleet. For a week and a half, U185 would head out of the harbour into the Kieler Förde to methodically test each of the boat's sub-systems. The boat ran speed and endurance trials, dived to its rated depth, fired torpedoes and each of its guns and tested the radios, sound gear, and the GEMA (FuMO 29) radar set fixed to the front of the tower. Only a few days passed before the crew began to see that there was a pattern to the timing of the trials. It was quickly evident that the boat would always head out first thing in the morning and then start back to port before 1100. After it tied up at the UAK pier, ten or more UAK workers would come on board and partake of the lunch served up by the boat's cook, even taking home the left-overs, if there were any. When they departed, generally around 1400, the boat would resume the trials sequence. There were as many as 15 other U-boats in Kiel at the time, all going through the UAK trials process and all following the same pattern of lunchtime activity. By this time in the war, the civilian population in Germany was beginning to feel the pinch of food shortages, so the actions of the UAK workers were understandable. In general, the crew of U185 didn't enjoy their time in Kiel. For the first two nights they were put up in a naval barracks at Kiel-Wick, but then they were transferred to the accommodations ship *Ubena*, which they described as decrepit and into which crews were crammed 'like Chinese coolies'. Many of the crew took leave of *Ubena* at night and slept back on board their own boat.

To everyone's relief, the UAK trials passed without any problems and, on 30 June, the boat was accepted into the U-boat fleet. The next morning, it was cleared to head east into the Baltic for more trials and intensive training. The first of these were conducted by the *Torpedoerprobungskommando* (TEK – Torpedo Inspectorate). U185 arrived at Danzig in the late afternoon of the same day, only to find the harbour facilities so crowded with other U-boats that it was ordered to double back to Kiel and await further instructions. After 24 hours back at Kiel, orders came through to proceed instead to Gotenhafen and carry out its TEK trials there. (Both Danzig and Gotenhafen were port cities on the Gulf of Danzig in what was then East Prussia. Now in Poland, they are known as Gdansk and Gdynia respectively.) The TEK trials, which started the next morning, lasted six days. Each day the boat would pick up nine practice torpedoes from the supply ship *Pontos* and, once the torpedoes were stowed to TEK's satisfaction, leave harbour for practice firings that would begin during the afternoon and continue past dark. Five of the torpedoes were fired during daylight and the remainder after nightfall. The target was a torpedo recovery boat. At the completion of the TEK trials on 9 July, Maus was informed that the boat had performed well and was cleared to proceed to Danzig and more torpedo training. During the six days U185 had remained at Gotenhafen, there had been air raids by both British and Russian bombers. One of the RAF aircraft was shot down by another U-boat in the harbour. Both raids, particularly the Russian, caused considerable damage in town, but none of the boats in the harbour were harmed.

U185 next headed back to Danzig for its *Komandantenschiessen* (commander's test shots). There were at least 25 other boats in port undergoing the same training. While the TEK trials had tested the crew's proficiency at torpedo handling, these exercises were intended to train the men, particularly the commander, to shoot well. Accuracy was the goal. Over the next two weeks, Maus fired off over 200 torpedoes in practice attacks day and night. Torpedoes were loaded twice daily, gruelling labour for the crew. When this training was completed on 24 July, a Friday, the boat was given orders to tie up at the Danziger-Werft dock on the following Monday morning. That gave them a whole weekend off. The crew were allowed ashore at Zoppot, a resort town a few miles up the coast from Danzig; they were permitted on the beach, but were prohibited from entering the town itself.

U185 was in the yard's hands from 27 July until 2 August. The major work done was the repair of its exhaust manifold and valves. It was then supposed to take part in a round of tactical exercises, but there were so many boats present that U185 was ordered back once more to Gotenhafen for gunnery training. The tactical exercises would have to be fitted in later. The training was just one morning spent firing off 25 or more rounds from each of the boat's three guns: the 10.5cm main gun on the foredeck, the 3.7cm on the after deck and the 2cm in the *Wintergarten*. Then, on 4 August, U185 departed Gotenhafen for Hela and AGRU-Front training. Hela is at the tip of the long, narrow Hela Peninsula, which partially encloses the Gulf of Danzig. (The town is also now Polish and known as Hel.) AGRU-Front (*Ausbildungsgruppe-Front* – Combat Training Group) was the organisation responsible for assimilating the lessons learned from actual combat and passing this hard-won wisdom along to new boats. Towards the end of this two-weeks' course, which involved nine or ten boats, Admiral von Friedeburg, Dönitz's second-in-command in charge of all training operations, came on board U185 at Hela for a two-hour visit, lavishing praise on the boat and its progress. At least two days of this training had to be cancelled because Russian submarines had been detected operating in the Baltic just offshore.

On 20 August 1942, U185 entered the Oderwerke yard at Stettin (today Polish Szczecin) for another round of repairs. The GEMA set was repaired, the pair of temporary life-rafts which were carried on deck during training were removed and the boat was inspected thoroughly end to end and all defects rectified. The repairs to the GEMA set on both sides had been necessitated because dipole elements had come loose during the gunnery exercise. (The GEMA set was an early, metric wave, radar set characterised by a fixed antenna installation which curved around the front of a U-boat's tower structure. It worked by switching send and receive functions from side-to-side. It was notoriously inaccurate in its locations and, as shown by this experience of U185's, prone to antenna damage.) The crew noted that even here, in Stettin, the dockyard workers were mostly French and Russian; by now, all but the most essential or the most disabled German men of military age had been drafted into the *Wehrmacht*. When U185 was released from the Oderwerke yard on 6 September, it was ordered back to Gotenhafen to carry out the tactical exercises which had been missed earlier.

Arriving there the next day, U185 immediately joined nine other boats in practice attacks on a convoy. The school was run by KK Reinhard 'Teddi' Suhren, another of the surviving U-boat aces. Suhren's career in U-boats had started, like most of the aces, before the war. He had been IWO under three commanders in U48, the most successful boat of the war, playing so important a role on that boat that he became the first watch officer, as opposed to commander, to be awarded the Knight's Cross. Later he commanded U564 so successfully that before he was posted to the command of the 2nd ULD (*Ubootslehrdivision* – U-boat Training Division) in 1942, he became one of only five U-boatmen to receive the oak leaves and swords to the Knight's Cross.

Suhren made every attempt to make the exercise as realistic as possible. No more training during the day and resting in harbour at night. The boats left Gotenhafen and stayed out seven days, practising attacks day and night. The convoy consisted of a German freighter, a captured Russian steamer and the depot ship *Wilhelm Bauer*. The escort was made up of three torpedo recovery ships, three Norwegian torpedo boats and a pair of old minesweepers. The convoy ran between Memel and the Danish island of Bornholm. The realism of the training was such that the escorts dropped depth charges when they detected a U-boat. After the first week, the boats returned to Gotenhafen for a half-day of rest for the crews and classroom instruction for the captains. Then it was out again for three more days of training, this time with aircraft patrolling overhead to add to the realism.

Completing the tactical exercises on the 16th, U185 returned to Stettin for its final dockyard repair and maintenance prior to leaving for the front. The boat was in the hands of Oderwerke for over a month, not departing until 20 October. Besides a general overhaul of all systems, work done during this yard period included the removal of the rotating foredeck hydrophone and the rebuilding of both the inner and outer exhaust valves, because these had been found to be a perennial source of leaks. That interval in port was too long for some members of U185's crew. Seven men each received five days in the brig when they were caught smuggling food off the boat. The IIWO, LzS Rogovski, was commandeered by the local flotilla command for shore duty. He was replaced by the bosun, Oberbootsmann Loos, who was already an officer candidate and was commissioned shortly thereafter.

Released from the yard, U185 made fast to the naval pier in Stettin and took on provisions for its first operational patrol. This included food for 10 weeks, 24 torpedoes (eight G7as in the deck storage tubes and 16 G7es inside, 11 forward and five aft), 248m^3 of fuel oil and ammunition for its guns (4000rds of 2cm, 200rds of 3.7cm and 90rds of 10.5cm, 50 HE and 40 incendiary). The boat then returned to Hela for three more days of AGRU-Front training to make up for those missed earlier. Finally, on the 24th, the boat was back in Kiel. There, its MG34 standard machine guns were replaced by MG15s. At 0600 on 26 October 1942, U185 left Kiel en route to the Atlantic and the war.

U167

A Typical Boat

By late 1942, new boats were joining the U-boat fleet at the rate of 20 or more per month. U167 was one of those new boats. It was an improved model of the long-range U-boat type, a Type IXC/40. The improvements in the 'C/40' model over the standard Type IXC were incremental and completely internal. Externally, they were indistinguishable. There was little else about U167 that would distinguish it from the 20 other boats which were also commissioned in July 1942. True, most of these were the utilitarian Type VIIC, not the longer-legged Type IX, but they all shared many characteristics. Unlike earlier in the war, these boats weren't manned by seasoned veterans. One by one the old guys, old in experience only, were dying in the increasingly hostile North Atlantic; or the lucky few were promoted to command jobs on shore or even positions on Dönitz's staff. Prien was dead. U47 had been lost with all hands while attacking a convoy back in March 1941. Lemp, Endrass, Schepke and Hartenstein were dead too. Kretschmer had been captured and was sitting in a POW camp in Canada, as were Wohlfarth and von Tiesenhausen. A few others, like Lehmann-Willenbrock, Zapp, Kals, Suhren and Schulz had been given flotilla commands and were no longer taking boats out to sea. Now, in the lists the missing, there were few names that anyone recognised.

There was no reason for anyone to recognise the name of KK Kurt Sturm. Prior to taking over U167 just before its second patrol, he had commanded U410, a Type VIIC, for a year. His tenure in command of U410 had been utterly undistinguished. His sole success in that boat had been delivering the *coup de grâce* to an already damaged steamer straggling behind convoy SC.104 in October 1942. (It was the German practice, when two or more boats were involved in the sinking of a target, to 'credit' the kill to the boat that first damaged the victim, rather than the one that ended it all. Thus, U410 received no credit for finishing off the steamer originally damaged by another boat, probably U221.) The highlight of his several patrols in command of U410 had been the rescue of 80 survivors from the German blockade runner *Rhakotis*, on 1 and 2 January 1943. His comparatively high rank and relatively advanced age for a U-boat commander meant that, prior to being assigned to U410, his command experience would certainly have been with the surface fleet. (Sturm had graduated from the Naval Academy in 1925, indicating that he was at least

40 years old in 1943. That would have made him five and possibly even ten or fifteen years older than the typical U-boat commander.) In 1942, with the virtual cessation of surface fleet activity that followed the sinking of *Bismarck*, and the simultaneous increase in the launching of new U-boats, a number of mid-level surface fleet officers transferred to the U-boat arm and were given commands with little or no submarine experience. Which is not to say that Kurt Sturm was a poor commander. His lack of success to date could have been due to many causes. It was undeniably getting harder everyday to find targets and to attack them once found. The account of his first patrol in U167 shows him to have been tough and resourceful. Just not very lucky.

A Typical Patrol

U167 had been commissioned by KL Neubert in July 1942, worked up and taken on patrol. During that voyage, a crewman was lost overboard and Neubert was wounded. There were no sinkings. Neubert's wounds were of such gravity that he was relieved by Sturm on 8 February 1943. When U167 left Saint-Nazaire on its second patrol on 27 February 1943, the primary concern of the Germans was the rapidly deteriorating situation in North Africa. After the Torch landings the previous November, the advances by the Americans pushing east and the British pushing west through Libya were compressing the remaining Axis forces into a shrinking pocket in Tunisia. All attempts to date to help the beleaguered forces still in North Africa by attacking the supply convoys known to be sailing regularly from the east coast of the US to the Mediterranean had failed because the convoys hadn't even been sighted.[1] As a last resort, Dönitz decided to deploy sentry boats off the exits from the harbours at Boston, New York, etc., to watch for and report on departing convoys. U167 was assigned this duty and was initially ordered to head for an assembly point north-west of the Azores, where, along with a number of other long-range boats, it would head for the American coast. Before it got to the assembly point, the situation had changed and U167 was ordered to make best speed towards Sector DF15, south-west of the Azores, where it would join four other big boats in *Gruppe Unverzagt*. (The other boats in *Unverzagt*, all Type IXCs, were U513 [Rüggeberg], U515 [Henke], U130 [Keller] and U172 [Emmermann]. Groups, such as *Unverzagt*, formed into patrol lines and then, swarming around convoys, were the wolf-packs [*Rudels*] envisioned by Dönitz back in 1918. These groups were given names that invoked the spirit of a wild animal or some notable characteristic of a warrior. *Unverzagt* means 'undaunted'.)

B-Dienst, the German signals intelligence service (equivalent to the British GCHQ or the post-war American NSA), had found a large, slow convoy, UGS.6, heading towards Gibraltar. U130 and U513 sighted the convoy on 11 March, but U130 was sunk by the defenders the next day and contact was lost. U167 got close enough to see mastheads, but was driven off by the numerous radar-equipped defenders. U513 re-established contact with the convoy on the 13th and the four remaining *Unverzagt* boats, along with boats from the *Wohlgemut* line, attacked for the next five nights with minimal success. The following was typical, describing U167's attempted attacks on the 15th and 16th:

> I make contact and move in. Problems with the closely spaced and numerous screening destroyers. My first night attack failed, because I was located and forced away by a destroyer, and subsequently lost contact when the convoy zigzagged. By day I have again gained contact and I move in once again. During the second night attack, I was located by the destroyers operating not far off, despite it being a relatively dark night. I take in the FuMB as soon as I have the screen in sight. (*Funkmessbeobachter* – FuMB – radar detector.) As I am somewhat ahead of the destroyer (it is right aft), perhaps 1500m away and heading 30–40 off, I reduced speed on the boat. I use the opportunity for a stern-shot, set at about 1200m, heading 60. The shot misses, probably the speed had been under-estimated. The destroyer had either heard the torpedoes or had located me again with his sound gear; in any case, he turned on heading zero and ran at high speed straight at me. He can't have seen the U-boat given the visibility and range. At 600m, I submerged; the destroyer overran the diving position, spent only a short while searching and dropped several widely spaced depth charges. Almost immediately, another destroyer of the side escort came and overran me. After resurfacing, no contact.[2]

(The reference to 'taking in the FuMB' indicates that the earliest radar detectors deployed on U-boats didn't have a permanently installed antenna. They used a jury-rigged wooden affair known as a *Biskayakreuz* [Biscay Cross]. The cable leading down to the FuMB 1 [*Metox*] set in the radio compartment ran through the tower hatch, something which U-boatmen detested, since the antenna would have to be taken in and the hatchway cleared before a boat could dive. Anything that interfered with or slowed down the diving process was a danger. There are numerous stories of boats diving with the *Metox* cable jammed in the tower hatch, preventing the hatch from closing. In that case, the boat had no choice but to resurface, if it could, despite the danger which had forced it to dive in the first place. There is no way of knowing how many boats were lost to this cause. Fear of the problem led commanders, such as Sturm, to take in the FuMB whenever a known danger was present that might require a crash dive. Later FuMB installations used a permanently mounted antenna.)

Also increasingly typical was the problem U167 encountered when it submerged. A major leak developed around the port exhaust vent and its control linkage. As the war progressed, the initial quality of U-boats as they came from the yard declined. More boats were being built in less time by an increasingly overworked labour force. More defects were being found which needed repair before the UAK would accept a boat from the yard. (*Ubootsab-nahmekommando* [UAK], the U-boat Inspectorate, was responsible for determining that a boat was fit for service after construction or repair.) More defects were slipping through, not being discovered until the boat was actually on patrol. To make matters worse, the bulk of the work carried out on U-boats between patrols in French ports was done by conscripted French labourers. Earlier in the war, there had been few problems with these workers, because the defeat of France had been so total and the Axis looked to be invincible; but by early 1943, a spirit of resistance was beginning to appear among the French and the first cases of deliberate sabotage of U-boats by shipyard workers were being reported. Regardless of the cause, the leak had to be repaired and U167 withdrew until the defect could be corrected. U-boatmen were resourceful souls and the reseating of the exhaust vent and the repacking of its linkage were accomplished before dawn. Before dawn on the 17th, U167 had found the convoy again and, since it was getting light quickly, executed a classic 'end around' manoeuvre, getting ahead of the convoy while staying at the very limit of visual range. At dusk, with visibility fading, the boat began to approach closer to the convoy.

The attack on USG.6 so far had been an almost total failure. Worse than that, the reasons for the failure pointed ominously towards a future of ever-diminishing success rates. As many as nine boats, commanded by experienced captains, were in on the attack, but only three sinkings had been reported by the 16th. Nearly every attack had been thwarted by the aggressive tactics of the escorts. Despite the calm weather, the dark nights and the almost total lack of air cover, the escorts' radar repeatedly allowed them to home in on the attacking U-boats as much as 15nm from the convoy's edge. Few of the attackers got closer than 10nm from the convoy. Reluctantly, Dönitz concluded that the standard U-boat tactic, attacking on the surface at night, had become unproductive. He had no choice but to order his commanders to resort to older tactics:

> I submerge to attack and make my approach under water at high speed, far enough to get in position for a shot. The convoy is arranged in several columns, so that there are always perhaps 6–7 steamers over-

lapping. In the increasing twilight, I plan a four-shot spread; in the bow tubes I have: 1 T3, 3 FATs.[3] I am allowed to shoot the FATs, because the rapidly diminishing visibility will allow the track to be seen only in the immediate vicinity. Also, because it is still quite early in the evening, no other U-boats on the surface are likely to be in the danger-zone. (Author's note: *Flächenabsuchender Torpedo* [FAT] – shallow searching torpedo. This was the first of the anti-convoy torpedoes produced by the Germans, designed to require less careful set-up. Once fired, the torpedo would begin to run a zigzag course. The idea was that, given the density of shipping in a convoy, the torpedo would be likely to hit something. Because many U-boats might be attacking at the same time, Dönitz feared that FATs might present as big a danger to other U-boats, so a series of 'FAT Rules' were promulgated, requiring, among other things, that a U-boat firing FATs had to send a warning message on the medium-band, which would warn off all other boats for a half-hour. In theory, the steam-powered G7a torpedo on which the original FAT was based had a maximum endurance of 15min, after which it would sink. Dönitz was just being cautious when he established the half-hour warning period. Also, because the FAT was G7a-based, and these torpedoes left a visible bubble trail, FATs could only be fired at night.)

I begin the final approach, a shot at a column of perhaps 6–7 large steamers, which appear to overlap in the periscope. Target is a modern freighter, rated 8000 BRT.[4] Heading 80, range about 3500m. The boat is directly in the path of a flanking destroyer and I must dive deep immediately after the shot. The nearest destroyer, somewhat outside and behind me, has zigzagged back straight at me. About 3–4 minutes after the shot, a loud explosion was heard. Shortly after, the sound compartment reports distinct sinking sounds, bulkheads collapsing and so on. Meanwhile, the nearest destroyer passes above us at high speed and drops the first pattern of depth charges, with more soon to follow. *Wabos* don't come close, no serious danger.

About 4 minutes after the first one, we heard two more explosions further off than the first. Since another boat had not shot simultaneously, I must have got two more hits. The explosions must have been heard and reported by other boats. 'Bargsten' (U-512) reported the next day, that he, at the same position, encountered a big steamer lying dead in the water and sank it. That must have been the result of one of the two last torpedo hits, which were, in fact, by FAT.[5] After a lengthy *Wabo*- and sound-pursuit, I surfaced and reloaded. The convoy is out of sight.[6]

This attack appeared to have been successful. But it was exactly the kind of attack that Dönitz's tactics had hoped to avoid. His experiences from the First World War of attacking from a submerged position had convinced him that the surface attack at night was by far a better idea, and for three and a half years it had worked well. But against numerous radar-equipped defenders, the night no longer offered any concealment. The U-boat war was beginning to change and not in Germany's favour.

The next night U167 again approached the convoy, but was held at bay by the escorts, and on the 19th, with the convoy nearing Gibraltar, the attack was called off. Altogether, the attack on USG.6 had netted four sinkings, meagre pickings for the effort expended and the loss of U130. After the pack was dispersed, U167 headed west, away from land and land-based aircraft. A new group was being formed to attack convoy RS.3, outbound from Rabat to Freetown. Not as well protected as USG.6, U167 was able to get in position for a submerged attack during the daylight hours of the 28th. This attack netted a good hit, followed once again by the sounds of a ship sinking. The sounds are utterly distinctive: bulkheads collapsing under irresistible pressure and, finally, the sharp report of a boiler bursting as cold seawater meets hot steam. This time they were right.[7] U167 had indeed sunk one of the three merchantmen U-boats claimed from RS.3. As before, the attack was called off when they got too close to land and this group was also dispersed. U167 was assigned a new patrol area in the narrow passage between the Canary Islands and the Moroccan coast.

A Very Untypical Ending

The new patrol area proved to be a problem from the moment U167 arrived. The Canaries were Spanish territory and therefore not only neutral but sympathetic to the Germans. However, the islands lay right off the coast of Morocco, recently liberated by the Americans, and were under continual air-cover from bases on the African mainland. Almost from the moment U167 arrived off the southern coast of Gran Canaria, aircraft warnings from the FuMB came every few hours.

> By day, dived in front of an aeroplane which approached unnoticed, below water evaded a fishing trawler. Overnight, submerged three times due to aircraft, every time the same steady-tone, loudness 2–3 and 3. Search-tone not heard.[8]

We are apparently under continual air-pursuit. Because of the aerial coverage, I submerge during the day while heading further towards west, surfacing towards dusk and heading back in towards land ... That night, had to dive in front of aircraft five times. It was the same after short periods as after longer periods under water (½ up to 2 hours); I would get a zT shortly after surfacing (detecting a steady-tone at loudness 2–3 and 3 and zT quickly becoming louder), often while still blowing out the dive tanks ... battery and air-supply slowly are being depleted.[9]

After surfacing, I report by radio message the continual air-pursuit. The planned and drafted radio message was not sent, because, before I completed the tuning of the transmitter to the band of the new wave, I have been forced under water.[10]

The continual harassment by aircraft was beginning to take its toll. Even though, so far, there had been no attacks, the effect of repeatedly finding an aircraft overhead, often within minutes of surfacing, was cumulative. Physically, the men were wearing down and the boat, as noted, was unable to stay on the surface long enough to recharge batteries and refill the compressed air flasks. Even more critical was the psychological feeling of being hunted continually over several days. Prudence required a U-boat to dive when an aircraft was detected, particularly when the steady tone on the *Metox* and the increasing volume of that tone indicated that the U-boat had been located and the aircraft was approaching. But, eventually, the feeling of being hounded made men defiant. After a while, men wanted to fight back: a normal reaction, but, in this case, extremely dangerous. At noon on the 5th, U167 was approached by yet another aircraft, this one coming in out of the sun at about 600m. Sturm ordered the 2cm and the machine guns manned, but the 2cm jammed almost immediately and the smaller guns were ineffective in stopping the attacker. Once the aircraft passed overhead, Sturm sounded the alarm, ordered the rudder hard over and took the boat deep. Bombs fell close, but, besides a good shaking, the boat was undamaged.[11]

Surfaced in the afternoon. Because there is a thin veil of high clouds in the sun sector and, in the south through the south-west a bank of cirrocumulus has gathered, I let the FuMB be brought out. Boat is now south-east of Gran Canaria. About 2 hours after surfacing, an aeroplane appears out the sun at about 3000m and 6–800m altitude heading straight for the boat. Location had not been heard. Didn't dive, went to AK and hard to port to offer a smaller target, the approaching machine is at 200° bearing. Simultaneously I ordered: '2cm and machine guns clear, fire at will!' The fire from the 2cm passes about 1m too high. The machine gun fire cannot be observed. The aircraft holds steady, pressing its attack. From about 50-100m altitude 3 bombs were dropped. The boat had just started responding to the rudder and had turned, at the most, 2–3deg. The enemy, a big two-engine machine, also shot at us with his on-board weapons. The IWO at the port Flak-MG received a grazing shot in the face and a wound in the back. As the aircraft passes over the boat, I order 'Alarm!' As the bridge-watch dives into the tower, the bombs go off: A water-column 3m off the stern on the port side. The second 3m off the starboard side even with the diesels. The third perhaps 10–15m on the starboard in line with the forecastle. The disturbances in the water made the dive take a relatively long time, yet the bombs dropped on the second pass fell comparatively far off.[12]

But the damage was done. U167's luck had run out. Immediately damage reports came to Sturm in the control room from the aft end of the boat. There were numerous leaks in the pressure hull right aft. The aft end cap, a solid piece of steel, milled into a hemispherical shape and housing the two after torpedo tubes, was torn in two places above Tube V. There was another leak at a weld seam in the motor room and the diesel installation hatch was leaking at a rivet joint. The electrical air compressor appeared to be seriously damaged and had broken loose from its mountings. The Junkers diesel-powered compressor had also come loose from its wooden supports and was hanging from the overhead. Half of the compressed air flasks appeared to be losing pressure. Other lesser damage was reported, but it would have to wait. The leaks and the loss of compressed air represented an immediate danger to the boat.

In order to reduce the leakage rate and ease the pressure on the hull, Sturm brought the boat back up to 60m. Despite this, the water continued coming aft at the rate of more than 2.5t/hr. While leakage at that rate wasn't critical, it would, if unstopped and if the water was allowed to accumulate aft, soon cause the boat to lose trim and become unmanageable. A plan was improvised to pump the water in the aft bilges by hand into the compensating tanks and then use the electric pumps there to get the water out of the boat. That would work and prevent the leakage becoming a threat to the boat's survival. At least, it would work as long as the electrical power held up.

Sturm, like it or not, had bumped heads with some of the cold realities of U-boat warfare. When a U-boat was submerged, its ability to stay down was limited by a number of resources. One was oxygen, but since U167 had only been down a few hours, that wasn't yet an issue. The others were electric power and compressed air. Without those in adequate quantities, a submerged U-boat wouldn't be able to move or regain the surface, and it was exactly those resources which Sturm now realised were insufficient. His original plan had been to remain submerged for the rest of that day and all of the next, using the time to repair what defects could be repaired, and then to surface the boat after dark on the 6th, when the airborne pursuit would have declared victory and gone home. Then he would make good his escape on the surface. That plan, however, was quickly discarded. Given the state of the compressed air reserves (enough to surface the boat twice without refilling the available flasks) and the batteries (perhaps enough to power the boat for the required time, but only at the most conservative consumption levels), this idea was not practical. Equally important was Sturm's concern that most of the crew would have to be idle for more than 24 hours under this plan, a hard thing to ask. Sturm therefore devised a more aggressive plan for saving the boat. Needless to say, it was also more risky.

The new plan called for the boat to head towards shore underwater for the remaining daylight hours, arriving close under the rugged southern coast of Gran Canaria at nightfall. If all went well, the boat would surface and move in as close to the coast as possible, thereby hiding from airborne pursuit by remaining in the 'shadow' of the coastal cliffs. The boat would hug the coast heading west and then, when it rounded the southernmost tip of the island, continue up along its western side. During these hours it would recharge batteries and, assuming one of the compressors was repaired, refill air tanks, and submerge again at dawn, heading away from the islands towards the south-west. The main advantage of this plan was that it would put the boat where the airborne pursuit least expected it, close in to the island, and there-fore might enable it to pass the night on the surface without being detected. At least, that was Sturm's hope.

At first, this plan looked as if it might just work. Late in the afternoon, the machinists got the electrical compressor repaired and, using wooden beams to force it back into position against the port side of the pressure hull, stabilised it to the point that an attempt was made to get it started. But it still proved insufficiently stable and steel straps were added in order to hold it in place when it was activated. With these straps, the electrical compressor was ready to run. Had there been sufficient charge left in the batteries, Sturm would have started it up while the boat was still submerged, but the remaining electrical power was dwindling by the minute. It would have to wait until the boat surfaced.

Just before 2200 on the 5th, Sturm ordered the boat surfaced. To everyone's distress, it took only ten minutes for the U-boat to be located once more by enemy aircraft. Sturm ordered the boat down again.

Now they were in a pickle. There had been no chance to make any notice-able progress on recharging the batteries or the air flasks. Now there was only air enough to surface the boat one more time, and the charge left on the batteries could propel the boat at the most economical speed for only a few hours. Sturm's options had now been reduced to two and neither was particularly attractive. The first was to take the boat up and make the best possible speed on the surface away from land, ignoring all aircraft detections, hoping that the gods would smile, their luck would hold and the inevitable attacks would miss. But he would only be able to use one engine for propulsion, so full speed wouldn't be available; the other engine would have to be dedicated to recharging the batteries and running the electrical compressor in the shortest possible time. The second option was to accept the fact that the boat was doomed and try his best to save his crew and render the boat and its secret materials unsalvageable by the Allies. If that option were taken, he would head the boat in towards shore as far as he could until it grounded at periscope depth. He would then surface for the last time, disembark all but a skeleton crew and head the boat at full speed out to deep water where it would be scuttled with explosive charges.

It took very little thought for Sturm to conclude that the first option had no chance of succeeding. It was absolutely certain, given recent experience, that U167 would be found and attacked soon after it surfaced and repeatedly thereafter. In all likelihood, the boat wouldn't last long. It would probably be sunk while still in relatively shallow water, making its salvage by the Allies a real possibility. Also, every mile the boat did cover away from land reduced the chance that any crewmen lucky enough to get away from the sinking boat would reach safety.

The second option seemed to have no negatives, other than the fact that it meant accepting the loss of the boat as a *fait accompli*. Most of the crew should be able to swim to shore from the drop-off point. Once ashore they would fall into the friendly hands of the Spanish authorities and would likely be repatriated in good time. The boat, if it avoided being sunk long enough to reach deep water, would be completely demolished. Further, its chances of surviving long enough would be enhanced by the fact that it could use both engines for propulsion. Sturm wanted to be sure he wasn't missing any options, so he called his officers together, explained his decision and the reasoning behind it and asked if they could offer any alternatives. None could and Sturm's decision to save the crew and scuttle the boat was accepted without demur.

That decision made, there was much to do and not a lot of time left if the plan were to be carried out, if possible, before dawn. The radio operator was given orders to send an emergency message to U-boat Command in France as soon as the boat broke surface. The rotors for the *Schlüssel M* were to be removed at Sturm's command so that they could be thrown overboard.[13] All other secret materials were gathered into weighted canvas bags, so that they could also be tossed overboard just before the ship was abandoned. The torpedoes in the bow tubes, including all the remaining FATs on board, were fired off towards deep water, to prevent their inspection if the boat was salvaged. Tube VI contained a T3, another new torpedo, which Sturm would also have liked to fire off, but the outer door was jammed by the damage aft, so that proved impossible to accomplish.[14] Tube V contained a standard G7e, about which he had no concerns.

As soon as the boat scraped bottom at the 12m line, Sturm surfaced the boat and began the evacuation of the crew. The IWO and ship's doctor went overboard with the crew to provide leadership and aid in the water and, once they'd reached shore, on land. A quick look around showed that they were further offshore than Sturm had planned, still some four miles away, in a location where the charts showed a depth of over 30m. However, there was no more time to manoeuvre the boat around the shoal it had obviously encountered. The men all had life-jackets and should be able to negotiate the four miles to shore without difficulty. The only worry was a strong current running parallel to the coast from right to left. Off to their left was a headland with a lighthouse. Sturm warned them that they had to make shore before they got carried past the lighthouse, because beyond that was open ocean. He recommended they swim straight for land. The current should carry them ashore near the lighthouse.

That done, Sturm ordered the engines back slow, so that he could clear the area where his men were swimming before turning the boat and heading at high speed for deep water. The only men left on board now, besides himself, were the LI, the IIWO, the chief diesel machinist, one machinist's mate, one control room mate, a control room rating and most of his helmsmen, who took up lookout duties on the tower. The bags of secret materials were brought up to the tower, but would not be thrown overboard until they reached deeper water. It soon became clear that the boat wouldn't stay afloat long enough for that to happen. Without the crew constantly pumping water out of the aft bilges, the boat rapidly took on water aft.

At first, the boat remained on an even keel. We tried several times to shut the galley hatch, but it wouldn't seal. After several minutes, the boat began to sink somewhat deeper aft. I stop one engine and order that the Ventilation I vents be opened around the boat, to prevent the boat from settling aft too quickly. The engine room notified me that no more air was available for manoeuvring.[15] The boat slowly sank deeper aft. As the upper deck is awash, I tossed the secret materials over the side and ordered all unnecessary men off the boat. The engines wouldn't be needed any more. The water now stood about 1m above the upper deck and the boat was now quickly sinking; only the LI and I were left on board. I ordered the LI off the boat. The LI had opened all ventilation ducts (first those forward, then the amidships and aft simultaneously), before he came to the tower. The LI and I go overboard, as the water rose 1m over the tower. With slight aft-heaviness, the boat, with running diesels, went to the deep (down by the stern by about 5 degrees). The tower hatch was completely open. All ventilation ducts for crew spaces and the running diesels were completely open. The forward torpedo-cells were flooded, the deployed explosive charges seem to have ignited in one place.[16]

U167 hadn't lasted long after the crew had disembarked. It sank only a half-mile further out to sea, in approximately 50m of water.

Because the boat sank so close to the shore, Sturm and the rest of the skeleton crew were picked up by Spanish fishing boats, as was the rest of the crew. The fisherman put them ashore at the nearest port, where they were interned by Spanish soldiers and transported by minesweeper to the capital city, Las Palmas, that same afternoon. They resided in relative comfort in Las Palmas on the interned German steamer, *Corrientes*, until the 14th, when they were picked up by U455 (Scheibe) and returned to France and the war.[17] The entire crew were kept intact after their return, taking over U547, another Type IXC/40, which was completing at Deutsche Werft, Hamburg. Sturm commanded U547 for two patrols, after which it was taken over by OLzS Heinrich Niemeyer. U167 was salvaged after the war, raised in 1951 by a Spanish company and used briefly as a film set before being sold for scrap.

Interlude

U66

An Unexpected Stop

After its fifth patrol, U66's popular commander, Richard Zapp, was replaced by KL Friedrich 'Fritz' Markworth. Zapp had been very successful, but Markworth was competent and personable. The big Type IXC had success on his first patrol, sinking eight ships in the Caribbean, including a large tanker, and laying a minefield which damaged an American Coast Guard cutter and two PT boats. All in all, a good patrol. They had left Lorient in late June 1942 and, towards the end of August, they had met up with a *Milchkuh* to take on enough fuel and food to make it back to France.[1] The presence of *Milchkühe* allowed the extension of patrols, such as this one, far beyond the normal limits that consumables put on a boat's endurance. There were three main items whose consumption limited the length of a patrol: fuel, food and weapons (specifically torpedoes). In the early days of the war, when U-boats found plenty of targets near the British Isles, boats would fire off their torpedoes and return home with food and fuel to spare; but now, in late 1942, easy targets were scarcer and farther away and boats would, under normal circumstances, be forced to turn back by lack of food or fuel long before their torpedoes were expended. The presence of *Milchkühe* near the main combat zones made multi-month patrols, such as U66 was completing, a common occurrence.

Thus, late in August, U66 met U462 at one of the designated refuelling points and took on what was supposed to be 25m³ of fuel, just enough to get back to Lorient, and two weeks of additional provisions. Boats were expected to get from *Milchkühe* only what they needed. The supply boats were big, but even they had very limited capacity and keeping demands to a minimum extended their usefulness. It was only after U66 had left the *Milchkuh* far behind that it was discovered that sea water had leaked into the supply boat's oil tanks, and U66 had, in fact, received only between 16 and 18m³ of oil. That was not enough to get back to France. Of course, this wasn't the first time that a U-boat out at sea had found itself short on fuel, and there were contingency plans in place to handle just these situations. If there happened to be another *Milchkuh* close by, the boat could always top up again, but that wasn't a preferred solution. Every drop of fuel on board a *Milchkuh* was intended to go somewhere, and unscheduled refuellings simply meant that someone else would have to be shorted later. Anyway, there weren't a lot of *Milchkühe* at the best of times. The odds of finding one near by in

Above: A crude beginning for the legendary terror of the seas. The vaunted German *Ubootwaffe*, which dominated two wars, started with the miniscule U1, seen in 1906 during its initial, electric power only, acceptance trials. Had the boat been using its not-yet-fitted Körting engine, a long plume of dense white smoke would have obscured the ensign flying at its stern. (NPC)

Right: U9 at sea in 1918. This is four years after its brief moment of glory under Weddigen's command. Since April 1916, it had been a school boat based at Kiel, too old and slow for combat operations. (NHC)

Nord

U9 gefeuert

↑ 8⁵⁰ ausgelassen

7¹⁰
1500m

350m 7⁵⁵

1000m 8²⁰
500m 8³⁵

I

III
Panzerkreuzer

II
Panzerkreuzer

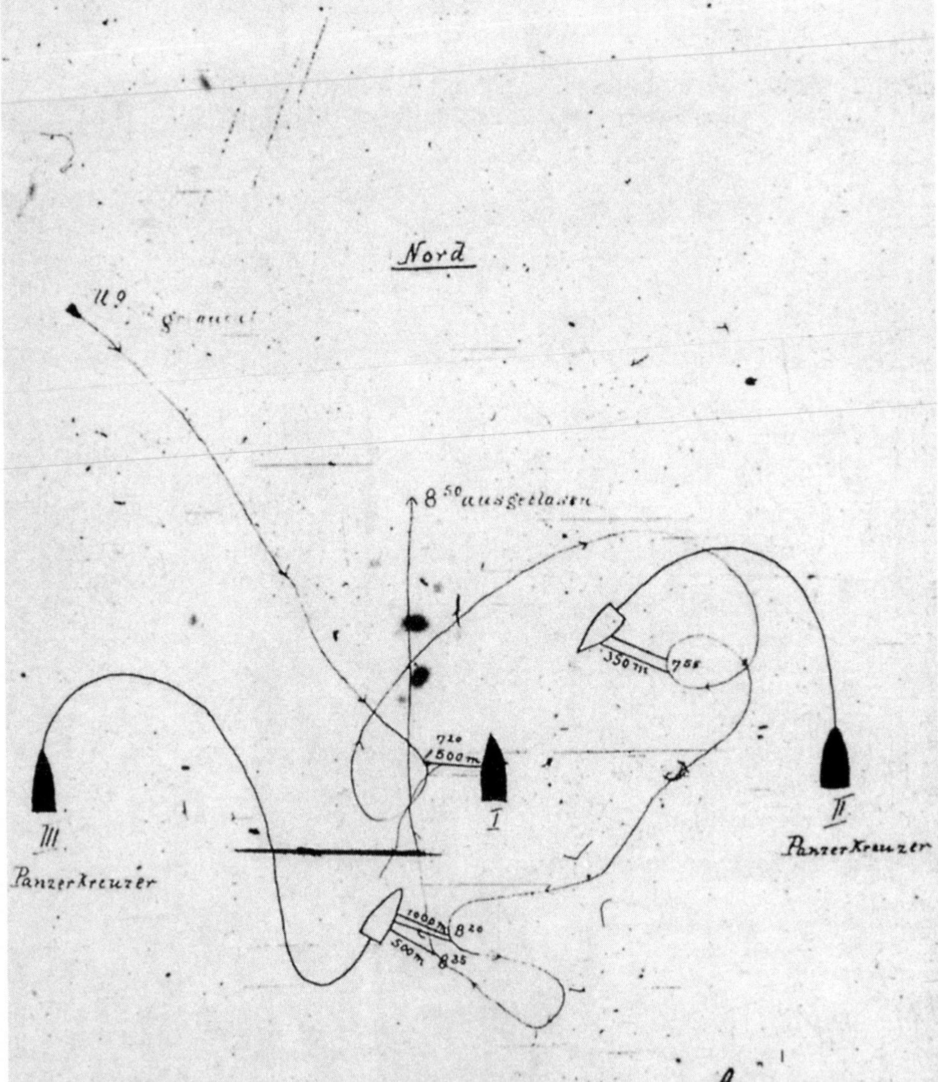

Left: Weddigen included a hand-drawn chart of the sinking of HMS *Aboukir* (labelled 'I' in the chart), HMS *Hogue* ('II') and HMS *Cressy* ('III') in his log entry for 22 November 1914. Never again would warships act so recklessly in the presence of a possible U-boat threat. (NARS)

Top: UC15, the last of the UCI series boats, is seen under rather unusual circumstances. First, it was actually in Austro-Hungarian service at the time this photo was taken. A number of UC boats were temporarily transferred to Austro-Hungary and were given new names, but they retained their German crews and eventually reverted back to the German Navy. UC15 was known as U19 in Austro-Hungarian service – hence the number on the tower and the red-white-red ensign. Second, its six mineshafts have been each been filled with a pair of watertight storage containers. A number of the Austro-Hungarian UCs were used temporarily to transport supplies. (Albrecht)

Above: *U-Deutschland* on its less successful second, and last, commercial voyage, seen at New London, Ct, in November 1916. Note the extremely bulbous lines of the hull, designed to give it a large interior space for cargo. (NHC)

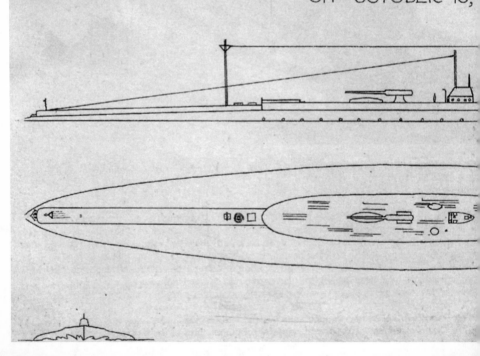

SUBMARINE WHICH CAPTURED NORWE

ON OCTOBER 13,

Above: Part of the reason for the failure of *Deutschland's* second commercial voyage was that it came immediately on the heels of U53's raid off the American coast. Although there was absolutely nothing illegal or unusual about what Rose's boat did, it nevertheless brought home the inherent brutality of submarine warfare to the Americans and did a great deal to sway public opinion away from the German cause. Here U53 pulls into the port of Newport, RI, on 7 October 1916 to hand over survivors from some of its victims to the American authorities. The fact that this was an unusually humanitarian act in the course of a U-boat's patrol was lost in the outrage over the sinkings so close to the American coast.

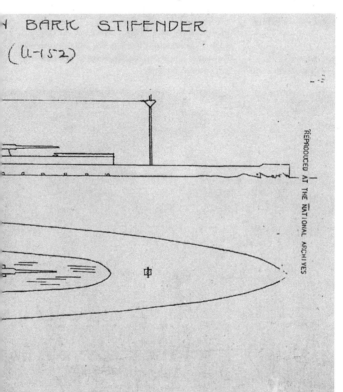

Left: When survivors of a U-boat attack were picked up, they were, if possible, interviewed by Naval Intelligence to glean whatever information possible about the attacker. In this case, *Stifinder's* crew was picked up and a sketch was put together, like a police sketch, showing the reported appearance of the U-boat. As with most police sketches, this one is accurate in some details and not in others. The bulbous shape of the boat's hull is accurately portrayed. The number of guns is wrong. These boats actually carried four deck guns, two forward and two aft, but that kind of error is understandable. The notation that the attacker was U152 was pencilled in later, after the war. (NARS)

Above: U153, the close sister of U152, is seen surrendered at Brest in late 1918. Note the extravagant width of the saddle-tanks, which caused these boats to have such poor handling characteristics.

Below: Between the wars, when Germany started building U-boats again in the 1930s, the first two flotillas were named after heroes of the *U-bootwaffe* from the First World War. The first flotilla was named after Otto Weddigen; the second after Reinhold Saltzwedel. This photo shows two young crewmen on U37, an early Type IX boat, during the period between the wars. Their cap bands read *U-bootsflottille Saltzwedel*. (ECPA)

When the image of a U-boat commander is called to mind, it will always be that of Gunther Prien. A man of great courage and initiative, but of very narrow focus, he was ideally suited to the task of taking a slender steel cylinder to sea and directing it against the enemy. (ECPA)

Left: The well-known shot of Prien being greeted by Admiral Saalwachter upon his return from sinking HMS *Royal Oak* in Scapa Flow. More elaborate greetings followed, including a trip to Berlin and dinner with Hitler.

Below: A less well-known photo of the same ceremony, taken a few minutes before the previous, when U47 was just coming alongside the quay in the harbour lock at Wilhelmshaven, 17 October 1939.

Left: Another photograph of U47 docking after a patrol, this time in November 1940 at Lorient. This was at the height of the good times for U-boat warfare, when a few boats under skilled, experienced commanders like Prien were achieving enormous successes against weakly guarded convoys. Note the 'Bull of Scapa Flow' insignia, thought up by Prien's then IWO, Engelbert Endrass, as U47 was returning to Germany after sinking *Royal Oak*. It is by far the best known U-boat insignia, so popular at the time that it was adopted as the insignia of the 7th Flotilla, to which U47 belonged. Note also the hand-carved and elaborately painted decoration atop the commander's flagstaff. (BAK)

Above: Prien on 20 February 1941. Note how the strain of a year and a half of continual warfare has aged him. Less than a month later, he and U47 would be lost in an attack on convoy OB.293. The exact circumstances of the sinking are unclear. However, the loss of Prien, and also of Schepke and Kretschmer within a few weeks of each other, marked the beginning of the end of the good times for U-boatmen. (BAK)

Herbert 'Parsifal' Wohlfarth, commander of U556, receiving his Knight's Cross personally from Dönitz.

Right: While working up U556 in January 1941, Wohlfarth encountered and 'adopted' the giant battleship *Bismarck* as his boat's 'big brother'. The hand-drawn adoption certificate included a promise to defend the battleship against all enemies, including those in the air.

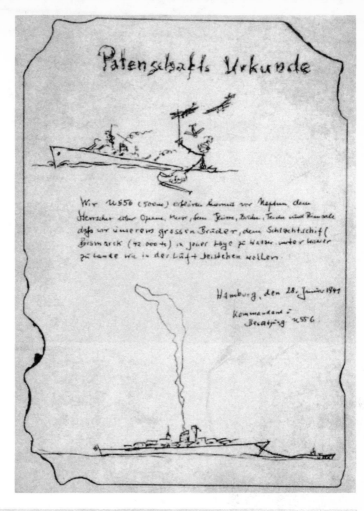

Below: Not many months later, Wohlfarth and U556 were witness to *Bismarck*'s destruction. Out of torpedoes and low on fuel, they were unable to do more than watch from a distance the sinking of their adopted big brother, 27 May 1941.

Top left and left: Three days later, Wohlfarth brought U556 into Lorient, victory banners flying and a claim of 49,900 tons painted on the front of the tower along with the stick figure representing *Parsifal*. Note the elaborate camouflage with stripes of dark grey over the lighter grey of the hull. This was U556's last homecoming. It was lost on its next patrol; Wohlfarth and most of the crew survived. (BAK)

Above: Neutrality markings allowed ships registered in neutral countries to trade with both sides in the World Wars, at least theoretically. According to prize law, a neutral ship could be sunk only if it was carrying contraband, and ascertaining that fact required stopping the boat and examining its papers. This freighter, SS *Lehigh*, shows off textbook neutrality markings, showing the US flag, the ship's name and nationality.

Above: Both sides regularly used false neutrality markings in an attempt to camouflage their combatants. The American steamer SS *Prairie*, seen in the company of U107 and another U-boat (U105) in the foreground, is actually the *Kriegsmarine* supply ship *Nordmark*, 3 May 1941. (BAK)

Below: U156 enters Lorient at the conclusion of a patrol. Another long-range Type IXC is in the foreground, U506. These two boats would later both participate in the '*Laconia* Affair'.

The spoils of war sometimes take unusual form. After one patrol, U156 came home carrying rubber tires which had been pulled from the flotsam left by a sinking victim. Note also the perforated metal housing for the dipole antenna elements of a fixed-antenna GEMA radar set. The antenna elements themselves, however, appear to be missing.

Left: Werner Hartenstein, U156's commander, contemplates a congratulatory cigar after being decorated with the *Deutsches Kreuz in Gold*, the German Gold Cross, on 17 March 1942. This was a rarely awarded decoration, given only for exceptional valour. The award, a large gold starburst with a black-and-white swastika medallion in the centre, can just be seen behind his hand.

Above: On 15 September 1942, three days after sinking *Laconia*, U156 handed over 132 of the survivors to U506. That boat is seen here with its deckload of survivors from the Vichy French rescue ships two days later.

Below: A U-boat joins the Navy. U109, a Type IXB, is commissioned on 5 December 1940, with the raising of the flag for the first time. (Hirschfeld)

Left: The *Indienststellung* (commissioning) of U185 took place on 12 June 1942. It was witnessed by, among others, KK Nicolai 'Niko' Claussen, former commander of U37 and U129. He is seen here in command of that latter boat as it entered Lorient on Christmas Day, 1941. (BAK)

Below: The advent of Allied airborne radar caused the Germans to add new electronics to their boats. This typical Type IX has a GEMA radar antenna behind the panel at the front of its tower and the crude wooden cross antenna for its *Metox* radar detector up above. This antenna had to be taken inside whenever the boat dived. It was easily broken, but, it was also very easily repaired. (Ahme via Schmidt)

Left: Tied up at the torpedo dock, a Type IX is having a G7a loaded into one of its four external storage tubes. Later on, after some of the internally stored torpedoes had been fired off, this 'eel' would be transferred inside, a difficult task in the best of conditions. (ECPA)

Bottom left: Standing watch meant a four-hour shift, binoculars in hand, sweeping a quadrant of the horizon. The standard practice was to alternate sweeps with and without the binoculars, so that nothing would slip past unnoticed. A watch consisted of four seamen and a watch officer. Rarely was anyone else allowed up on the tower, except, of course, the commander, who could come up whenever he wished. This view taken on U154 in 1942 shows everyone enjoying balmy weather in the Caribbean, but watches were more often endured in bitter cold with waves crashing over the tower. (BAK)

Below: The *Pairs* (ratings) slept in the forward torpedo room. Until the two torpedoes stored above the floor-plates were fired off, some men got to sleep on their 'eels'. (via Schmidt)

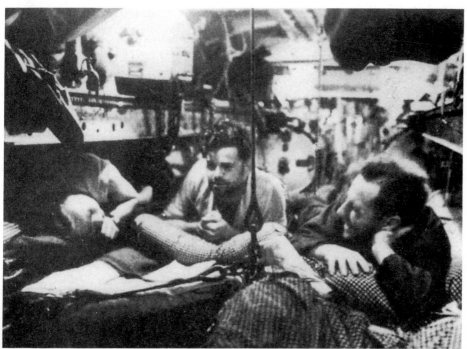

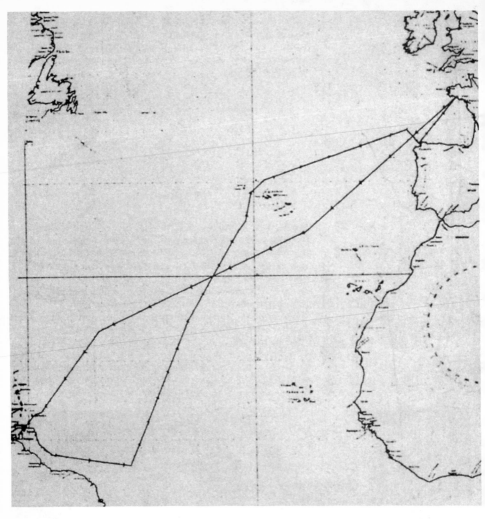

Above: US Naval Intelligence reconstructed the path of U66's sixth patrol, including its unscheduled stop at El Ferrol. (NARS)

Right: Crewmen on the broad foredeck of U460, a *Milchkuh*, go about the business of supplying oil to another U-boat. Under a warm sun, it was a difficult enough task, but later, when Allied air-power came to dominate the Central Atlantic, the life of a supply U-boat became much too dangerous.

Left: *Milchkühe* brought not only fuel but also badly needed provisions such as bread (they had an on-board bakery) and meat (they had a large freezer). These perishable supplies were hauled across between boats in large waterproof sacks.

Lower left: The *Pairs* from U66 enjoy a relaxing moment at the end of a patrol, La Pallice, June 1941. They certainly looked just like this when they came aboard the tanker *Georg Albrecht* in El Ferrol harbour the following September. (BAK)

Below: The U-boat war as seen from the air, 8 July 1943. Here U134 is being strafed by its attacker as the large water plume of an exploding depth charge erupts in the background. Even a near-miss from a depth charge could damage a U-boat, but this one exploded at a safe distance. This boat survived the attack, only to be sunk in another air attack a month and a half later, the same day U185 also lost. (NARS)

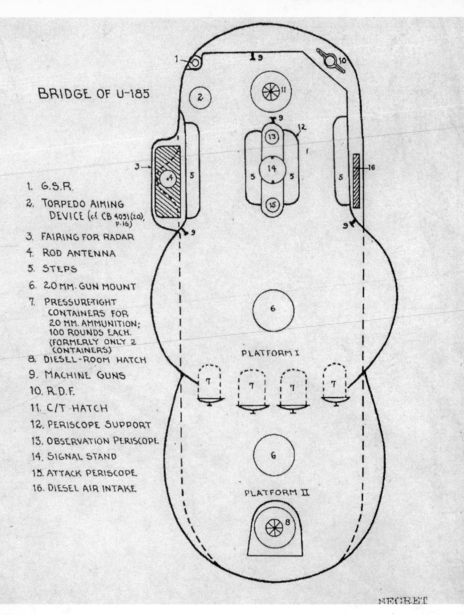

BRIDGE OF U-185

1. G.S.R.
2. TORPEDO AIMING DEVICE (cf. CB 4051(20), p.16)
3. FAIRING FOR RADAR
4. ROD ANTENNA
5. STEPS
6. 20 MM. GUN MOUNT
7. PRESSURE-TIGHT CONTAINERS FOR 20 MM. AMMUNITION; 100 ROUNDS EACH. (FORMERLY ONLY 2 CONTAINERS)
8. DIESEL-ROOM HATCH
9. MACHINE GUNS
10. R.D.F.
11. C/T HATCH
12. PERISCOPE SUPPORT
13. OBSERVATION PERISCOPE
14. SIGNAL STAND
15. ATTACK PERISCOPE
16. DIESEL AIR INTAKE

PLATFORM I

PLATFORM II

Above: The analysts at US Naval Intelligence gathered the information from U185's survivors and put together this quite accurate sketch of the layout of the U-boat's tower. (NARS)

Top right: A chart showing the track of the task group centred on USS *Block Island* (CVE-21) in mid-March 1944. As it swept the area west of the Cape Verde Islands, it found and finished off two U-boats: U801 on the 17th and U1059 on the 19th. (NARS)

Right: A schematic diagram showing the attack on U1059 on 19 March 1944. The Avenger, piloted by Lt (jg) Dowty, was hit and crashed just west of the U-boat, but not before dropping a pair of depth charges which sank the boat. Dowty and his belly gunner were killed, as were 47 men from U1059. (NARS)

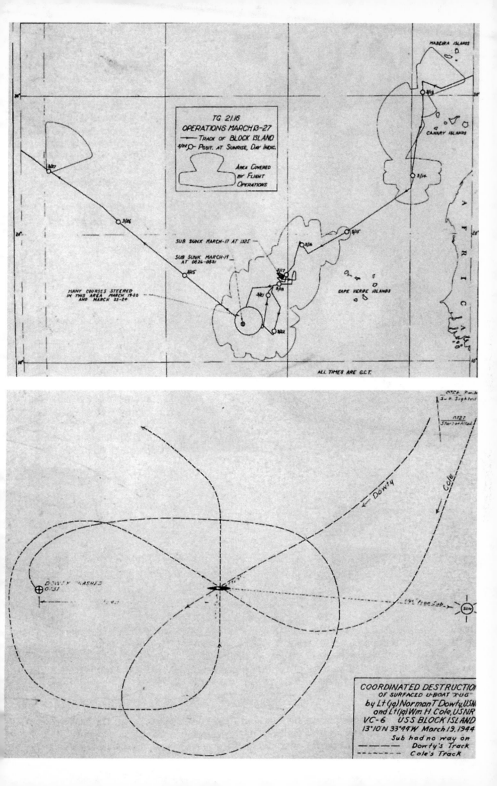

TG 21.16
OPERATIONS MARCH 13-27
— Track of BLOCK ISLAND
⊙ Posit. at Sunrise, Day Indic.

Area Covered
by Flight
Operations

MADEIRA ISLANDS

CANARY ISLANDS

A F R I C A

SUB SUNK MARCH-17 AT 1325
SUB SUNK MARCH-17
AT 0826-0831

MANY COURSES STEERED
IN THIS AREA MARCH 19-20
AND MARCH 23-24

CAPE VERDE ISLANDS

ALL TIMES ARE G.C.T.

DOWTY CRASHED
0.137

293° from Sub

COORDINATED DESTRUCTION
OF SURFACED U-BOAT "X-U16"
by Lt(jg) Norman T. Dowty, U.S.N.
and Lt(jg) Wm H. Cole, U.S.N.R.
VC-6   USS BLOCK ISLAND
13°10'N 33°49'W March 19, 1944
Sub had no way on
——— Dowty's Track
------- Cole's Track

Left: U821 in Brest, June 1944. It was one of the *Landwirt* boats intended to repel the Normandy invasion. All nine of the non-snorkel-equipped boats that sortied from Brest immediately after the invasion were either sunk or damaged in the next few days. Note the large structure built into the near side of the tower. This was a *Kohlenkasten* (coal scuttle), an armoured box into which lookouts could duck if caught on the tower by an attacking aircraft. (via Schmidt)

Below: Personal photographs of the war zone were against the rules, but the Germans loved their cameras and photographs such as this one, taken from one of the survivors of U66 who was captured on USS *Buckley* (DE-51) on 6 May 1944. It shows U66 docking at Lorient after a patrol in May 1943. (NHC)

Above and below: U977 tied up at the wharf at Mar del Plata, rather the worse for wear after its long ordeal, August 1945. The close-up of the tower shows the two twin 2cm guns on the upper platform and the single 3.7cm on the lower. The rod antenna, slightly bent, projects above the forward part of the tower. A cluster of FuMB antennas sprout from the middle mast. The mast just aft of that is not from U977; it must be a communications mast from a building on shore. (Albrecht)

Above: In US Navy hands, U977 was painted a dark colour and had its hull number displayed on its tower. (NHC)

Below: Despite the extraordinary nature of his flight to Argentina, Heinz Schäffer became just another POW in US custody, September 1945. (NARS)

DP.323M5- U-977. WORKING PAPERS

BASIC PERSONNEL RECORD
(Alien Enemy or Prisoner of War)

7G-231-NA
(Internment serial number)

F. P. C.*

SHAFFER, Heinz
(Name of internee)

Reference*

Male
(Sex)

Height	5 ft. 8 in.	INVENTORY OF PERSONAL EFFECTS TAKEN FROM INTERNEE
Weight	230	1.
Eyes	Blue	2.
Skin	Fair	3.
Hair	Dark Brown	4.
Age	24 Years	5.
Distinguishing marks or characteristics:		6.
	None	7.
		8.
		9.
		10.

The above is correct.

(Signature of internee)

DIO-7ND, Miami, Fla.   8 Sept 1945
(Date and place where processed (Army enclosure, naval station, or other place))

Right Hand

1. Thumb	2. Index finger	3. Middle finger	4. Ring finger	5. Little finger

Left Hand

6. Thumb	7. Index finger	8. Middle finger	9. Ring finger	10. Little finger

W. D., P. M. G. Form No. 2
December 9, 1941   16—25535-1   Note amputations in proper space   * Do not fill in.

the mid-Atlantic were slim. In an emergency, there was always the option of transferring fuel from the next outbound boat, but standard U-boats weren't well-equipped for fuel transfer, and taking fuel from another boat merely passed along the problem of low fuel to another captain. Fortunately for the Germans, another, illegal (and, therefore, secret) option existed: refuelling in Spain. (The significant and active German presence in Spain was an open secret, as was Franco's 'unofficial' aid to German U-boats. Spain's neutrality benefited the Allies far more than it did the Axis and, therefore, the Allies were willing to overlook a myriad small violations of that neutrality.)

The Spanish government, under Franco, was philosophically aligned closely with the fascist governments of Germany and Italy. (Actually, Franco was much closer in style and in personality to Mussolini than to Hitler; also, especially after the fall of France, Franco felt far less threatened by Mussolini.) However, Generalissimo Franco had decided early in the war that he would not be pushed into hostilities with the Allies before he was ready. By late 1942, he had clearly concluded that the benefits of neutrality to Spain and to himself personally outweighed the minimal inducements that Hitler had offered him for joining the Axis. But, in late 1942 the Axis powers were still on the ascendant, with Germany master of most of continental Europe and Japan still solidly in control of South-east Asia and much of the Pacific; so it was to Spain's advantage to be very accommodating to its German guests. A number of German merchantmen, freighters and tankers had been interned in Spanish ports in the first year of the war and these ships were resting comfortably under their German crews, well supplied with food and fuel. It certainly was not of concern to the Spanish that, in many cases, the food and fuel being supplied to these ships was significantly more than they could actually consume. The Spanish authorities didn't want to know where the rest was going.

U66 received orders to proceed to the vicinity of El Ferrol, at the north-western corner of Spain. There, on 25 September, U66 crept in towards shore, submerged, until, at 1000, it settled on the bottom at 80m to wait for dark. At 2300, U66 resurfaced and proceeded at slow speed into the harbour at El Ferrol and tied up alongside the interned German tanker *Georg Albrecht*, on its seaward side, so as to be out of sight from land, at 0100 on the 26th.[2] Spain, being a neutral country, had no worries about air attacks and, therefore, the harbour at El Ferrol was brightly lit, the lights from the city in the background reflecting off the water, making the crew of U66 feel terribly exposed and vulnerable.

The tanker's crew moved fast, with practised efficiency. There wasn't much time. U66 had to be out of sight of land by first light. No matter how open the secret was that U-boats were resupplying in Spanish ports, it still would be an embarrassment to Franco to have a U-boat sighted in a Spanish port in daylight. A single hose was hefted over the tanker's railing and connected to the U-boat's fuel valve. A few bushels of fresh apples and a couple of cases of tinned fruit were let down from the tanker's deck. These were gratefully stowed away on board the boat. Even more welcome was the invitation to come aboard the tanker for a meal. Having been at sea for three months, the crew of U66 would have traded extremities or loved ones for one meal that didn't taste like diesel fuel, garbage and sweat. The spread that greeted the crew, if it was typical of those reported by other crews that refuelled in Spain, would have included, besides fresh fruit and vegetables, precious in themselves, also roasted meats, cold beer, fresh bread and, to finish it off, sweet pastries and tortes. Sometimes, it even included the delicacy many U-boatmen reported craving more than any other: ice cream.

The stop-over in Spain, brief as it was, afforded U66 one other luxury. U66 was able to drop off a crewman, an engine room petty officer named Ehrlichmann, who was extremely sick with a stomach ailment. He was operated on in a Spanish hospital and recovered in Spain before being smuggled across the border to France and rejoining his boat before it left on its next patrol.

Before long, the abundance displayed on board the tanker was a fading memory. U66 spent less than three hours tied up alongside the supply ship. By 0400, it was outbound, on the surface, at 12kt. An hour later, having reached deep water, it submerged and began the ever more perilous crossing of the Bay of Biscay, arriving at Lorient safely four days later. U66 would have two more successful patrols under Markworth during 1943. During his third patrol in command of the boat (the boat's eighth), Markworth was seriously wounded in an attack by aircraft off USS *Card* (CVE-11). Three days later, U66 met U117 and that boat's IWO, OlzS Frerks, took over U66 from Markworth and guided the boat home. Markworth was given shore duty after that, serving as training officer for the 23rd and later the 25th Flotillas. U66's third commanding officer, OlzS Gerhard Seehausen, took the boat over for its ninth patrol (see Chapter 11).

— 9 —
U185

The Air War

April 1943 had been ominous. Suddenly, the defences around and in the air above convoys in the North Atlantic had become increasingly dense. Unknown to the Germans, a large number of escorts and aircraft, which had been reserved to protect the 'Torch' convoys, had just been released for general convoy duty, giving the impression of a sudden increase in their numbers.[1] Add to this the fact that the 'Air Gap', that part of the Atlantic not covered by long-range, land-based aircraft, had essentially disappeared in early 1943. It had been shrinking perceptibly since the beginning of the war, as the number and range of aircraft flying out of Newfoundland, Ireland and now Iceland and the Azores had steadily increased, but the commitment by the Americans of large numbers of B-24 Liberators to anti-submarine patrols had now closed the gap completely.

In April 1943, the number of U-boats lost had remained at an acceptable level. Thirteen of them had succumbed to the ever-stiffening defences, just one more than the month before. In the same month, the number of *Front-boote*, boats available for combat, increased by four, so those losses were considered sustainable. However, the efficiency of those boats actually on patrol dropped by half.[2] Even without a significant increase in losses, it was obvious that the improved defense of convoys was making it harder every day for the wolf-packs to get close enough to attack their targets.

If April was ominous, May was a disaster. Efficiency declined still further, but U-boat losses almost tripled, to 38. This represented a totally unacceptable rate of loss and Dönitz made the hard, but necessary, decision to withdraw his boats from the North Atlantic. The tactics that had worked since 1939, as conceived by Dönitz sitting in a POW camp back in 1918, were clearly no longer valid, at least in the North Atlantic, and it was necessary to re-examine all aspects of U-boat strategy.

Crossing the Bay

For a start, simply crossing the Bay of Biscay, transiting to and from operational areas in the Atlantic and beyond, had become increasingly dangerous. When the Germans had conquered France in 1940, it opened up that country's Atlantic coast for use by Dönitz's boats. Bases had been established between Brest and Bordeaux from which U-boats departed daily for the Atlantic, avoiding the bottlenecks at the Dover Straits and between Scotland and Norway which had so restricted U-boat effectiveness in the First World War. However, in the spring of 1943, air attacks in the bay by RAF Coastal Command Wellingtons and Sunderlands were daily becoming more frequent and intense. Of the 38 boats lost in May, as many as five or six were presumed to have been sunk while crossing the bay. More were attacked and forced back to base with damage to the boat or wounded crewmen. Still more were attacked and escaped damage, but had their passage across the bay slowed by the frequent dives to avoid enemy action. What made those attacks especially frightening was the fact that, with increasing frequency, the standard *Metox* radar detector failed to give warning of them. This was because the British had begun deploying, beginning in March 1943, the ASV MkIII airborne radar, which operated on a centimetre wave frequency, outside the sensitivity range of the *Metox* set.

In a few cases, U-boats were caught on the surface in such circumstances that they couldn't safely dive. For example, if the attacker was sighted too late to allow the boat to reach a safe depth before the bombs arrived, then it was better to stay on the surface and take a chance holding the attacker off with the 2cm on the tower platform. After all, U-boats were small, manoeuvrable targets and the attackers carried very few bombs. Amazingly, this defence occasionally worked and in a few cases actually resulted in the shooting down of the attacker. Unfortunately, in his desperation to find some solution to this seemingly insoluble problem, Dönitz drew the wrong conclusion, reasoning that if it was possible for a single U-boat, with a single *Flak* gun, to shoot down an occasional attacker, then a group of four boats would have four times the firepower and thus four times the likelihood of a successful defence. Such logic, in fact, was flawed, based on wishful thinking and a poor appreciation of how the RAF would react to this new tactic, but only experience would show that.

(This is somewhat like the case of four people flipping coins. The odds of any one of them getting 'heads' is 1:2. Those odds are unaffected by the fact that three others are flipping at the same time, because each act of flipping a coin is independent. Dönitz reasoned correctly that the odds that at least one 'heads' will be flipped by the group are indeed improved. When four coins are flipped, the chance that at least one will be heads is 94%. If you substitute 'damaging an attacking aircraft' for 'flipping heads', there is an equivalent, but far from identical, improvement in the odds for success. The odds of four boats getting a hit are far better than for one boat. Specifically, if the odds of one boat getting a hit are 1:20 [a totally arbitrary number used here purely for illustration], then the chances of four boats getting a hit increase from 5% to 18.5%. This didn't take into account, however, the likelihood that the RAF would react to groups of defenders by concentrating their attackers. Any benefit of supporting fire would be lost when more than one aircraft attacked at the same time.)

On 29 May 1943, Dönitz issued the following order:

> In order to make it difficult for enemy aircraft in the Biscay area to find U-boats and in order, in case of enemy air attacks, to be able to counter the enemy when surfaced, which has proved to be most practical, with heavy and successful gunfire, all boats returning in a position W of 16° should continue the return passage together, through the Biscay area in groups up to four boats.[3]

At the same time, he extended the order to cover the next batch of boats leaving port for their operational areas:

> The measure taken . . . today for boats on return passage will be introduced by way of experiment for outgoing boats, this being passage together through the Biscay area in groups of between 3 and 6 boats.[4]

The specific points enumerated by Dönitz in this order included putting this group of boats under the local tactical command of the senior commander. Boats were to proceed submerged at night, when they were most vulnerable to surprise attack, and on the surface during the day. (Obviously, Allied airborne radar was equally effective by day as by night, but at least during the day, a U-boat's lookout might sight the attacker before it got too close.) Above all, boats were to remain on the surface when attacked. This last provision would clearly be the hardest to enforce, since it went against the grain of three-and-a-half years of hard-won battle experience, which ruled that the best survival tactic, when there was time, was to dive when an aircraft was detected. And since, ultimately, each commander was responsible for the survival of his boat, the temptation to dive while the rest of the group kept the attackers at bay would be powerful. But, if this plan was to have any chance of succeeding, it required that all available guns be brought to bear, compelling all boats to stay up and fight off the attackers, no matter how great the temptation to dive.

Reality Check

Several groups of outbound boats tried out this tactic in early June and managed, for the most part, to escape detection, or, when discovered, to fight off the attacks. But this lucky streak came to an end with a group of five boats which gathered near the French coast on 10 June. Two of those boats had left Bordeaux at 1000 the previous day. One of them was U185 (see Interlude 2) still under the command of KL August Maus. After working up U185, Maus had led the boat on two successful cruises, earning the Knight's Cross along the way. Now he was leaving for his third patrol in command of the boat. Along with U185 went U564 (Fiedler), another Type IX boat. The two boats tied up for the night at the mouth of the Gironde, at the small port of le Verdon-sur-Mer, and in the morning proceeded into the bay for several hours under escort by a big minesweeper, three M-boats and three R-boats. (M-boats [*Minensuchboote* – minesweepers] and R-boats [*Raumboote* – patrol boats] were 550t and 150t minesweepers built in large numbers by the Germans and used for a variety of tasks, frequently including escort duty.) They met two more Type IXs and then waited some hours for a Type VII from Saint-Nazaire. While they were waiting, a small French fishing smack approached the group several times, at one point coming within 100m. The escort commander on the large minesweeper warned the fishermen away. Maus was furious, yelling at the commander that he should sink the intruder, since it was well known that many fishermen along the coast were smugglers or *Maquis* or both.[5] The escort commander declined, saying: 'You don't get a medal for sinking fishermen.'[6]

Shortly after that, the fifth boat joined the group and they all headed south-west in formation towards Cape Finisterre. The five U-boats were in two parallel columns, three in the starboard column and two in the port. U185 was the middle boat in the starboard column. At 1300 the escort boats turned around and headed back to Bordeaux. Approximately a half-hour later, three Ju88s showed up and provided air cover until well after dark. (Of all the remedies tried by Dönitz to counteract RAF airpower over the bay, none would have been more effective than a significant increase in *Luftwaffe* air cover. However, the very small numbers of aircraft committed to air patrol over the bay, and the limited range and capability of those few aircraft, meant that what little assistance the *Luftwaffe* could offer was inadequate at best. Like the British, but unlike the Americans or the Japanese, the Germans put all their land-based maritime patrol aircraft under the control of the air force, ensuring that decisions as to which aircraft to build and which to assign to coastal defence were being made by officers unfamiliar with the problems, or unaware of the importance, of command of the air over the water.)

The RAF did not show up until the next morning. At about 1000, the group was buzzed by a single, fast aircraft and, ten minutes later, four bombers appeared, identified as two Wellingtons, a Blenheim and a Baltimore. (The Wellington and Blenheim were British medium bombers of pre-war design. No longer big enough or fast enough for combat over Europe, they were ideal for the less demanding combat over the bay. The Baltimore was built in America for the RAF by Martin.) As Dönitz had ordered and as the boats in the group had agreed when they joined up, all five boats stayed on the surface and put up a heavy anti-aircraft barrage. The combined armament of 14 2cm guns and as many light machine guns was sufficient to hold the bombers at bay for almost two hours. During that time, they tried repeatedly to press home their attacks, but were driven back each time. At 1300, they gave up and flew back into the clouds. The defence had been everything Dönitz could have wished, but the ammunition expenditure was heavy. Between the five U-boats, 3000 rounds of 2cm were fired off.

The rest of the 12th and most of the 13th passed without further attack. Late in the day on the 13th, a single Sunderland attacked the group.[7] (The Sunderland was a large four-engined flying boat intended specifically for maritime patrol and was used in that role throughout the war. They became such a common sight that U-boatmen coined a nickname for them, calling them *müde Bienen* [tired bees], because of the distinctive buzzing sound made by their engines when first heard in the distance. This particular Sunderland was aircraft 'U' of No. 228 Sqdn, serial DV.967, flown by Flight Officer L. B. Lee.)

The group was now some 250nm west of Cape Finisterre. The tight formation of the day before had become somewhat ragged and U564, which was the second boat in the port column, had fallen several hundred yards behind the other boats. The boats started a rapid zigzag manoeuvre in an attempt to confuse the pilot. Two of the boats were sufficiently out of range that they didn't even fire at the attacker. The other three put up a heavy barrage, but the pilot of the Sunderland elected to press home the attack. The bomber had its starboard float shot off and two engines set on fire, but at a critical point in the attack, both of U564's single 2cm guns and one of U185's jammed, and U564's new quadruple 2cm mount seized up, allowing the Sunderland to carry out a straight approach and drop a stick of seven small 50kg bombs from an altitude of barely 400m. Four of those bombs hit U564 on the deck and three more splashed alongside forward, one of them carrying away the boat's starboard dive plane. U185 kept up fire with its one functional 2cm and managed to hit the bomber's cockpit right after it released its bombs. The pilot was obviously hit by that burst, because the plane immediately dipped its left wing, which caught the water. The bomber cartwheeled on contact, disintegrating as it hit, throwing the bodies of three crewmen out into the water.

(The 2cm gun used by the Germans was essentially the same gun used by the US and Royal Navies as their light AA gun for most of the Second World War. Originating from a design by Oerlikon of Switzerland, it was a simple and effective gun, albeit often too light to stop an oncoming attacker. When *kamikaze* attacks started in 1944, the 2cm – or 20mm as it was called by the Americans – fell increasingly out of favour in the US Navy, because it lacked the power to knock down an attacker. Even after being hit repeatedly with 2cm rounds, *kamikazes* would often keep on to their target. The gun became derisively known as the 'doorknocker', because its primary function seemed to be to announce the presence of an incoming *kamikaze*. It required regular and thorough cleaning to work well, something which was impossible to carry out on U-boats, and in U-boat service, the gun had the nasty habit of jamming at crucial moments. The Germans later supplemented their 2cm guns with a 3.7cm *flak* mount; the Americans and British substituted the 40mm Bofors. Both guns fired more slowly than the lighter weapon, but fired a significantly heavier shell. In general, fewer hits were obtained, but those hits were far more effective.)

Two of the bodies were brought on board U185 and were carefully examined for any useful information. (The inspection of bodies for personal effects and documents was legitimate intelligence gathering and, while a bit macabre, was carried out by all sides. Even the stripping of the bodies for useful items of clothing made sense, given the shortage of many of these items in wartime Germany.) Between the items found on the bodies and other bits of flotsam pulled out of the water, U185 was able to gather a radio code book for that day, an operator's manual for the Sunderland's radar, the plane's logbook, marked up maps of the Bay of Biscay and Norway, and Spanish-language propaganda leaflets, obviously meant to be dropped over Spanish territory sometime during the flight. The pilot's personal effects were gathered and handed over to Maus. The bodies were then stripped of all money, jewellery and useful clothing and dropped back overboard. The money, approximately £80, was distributed among U185's officers. The jewellery, a couple of gold rings, was taken by Maus and put in the drawer of his private cabinet. A waterproof wristwatch was given to the IWO. The IIWO, the recently promoted former bosun, was given a pair of leather trousers and the pilot's leather flying cap.

That grisly business out of the way, they then turned their attention to the damaged U564. Amazingly, the boat was still afloat and in no immediate danger of sinking, but, equally clearly, it was in no condition to continue with its mission. The bombs had torn up the deck-casing, particularly aft, but the pressure hull looked to be intact. The most serious problem was the number of wounded crewmen on board, some of them seriously injured. U564 had no corpsman on board, but U185 did and so Maus brought his boat close and had his *Assis* rowed over in his inflatable dinghy. For a full two hours, the remaining four boats of the group stood by while the *Assis* tended to U564's wounded. Then, an attempt was made to dive the boat, but even before it was half submerged, numerous leaks were discovered and the attempt was quickly aborted. (*Assis* was short for *Assistenzarzt*, literally 'assistant doctor', roughly equivalent to a corpsman in US Navy practice, someone who had completed at least several months of training in first aid and the treatment of wounds and common maladies. On most U-boats, the only medical care available was from a *Funker* who had received a few weeks medical training. But, by ordering his boats to fight aircraft on the surface, Dönitz knew that there would be increased casualties and ordered that every other boat leaving port carry a trained doctor; but this was wildly impractical since nowhere near the number of doctors existed to carry out this order. Therefore, the *Kriegsmarine* began training a number of *Assis*, far more skilled than the minimally trained *Funkers*, but in no way as capable as a fully qualified doctor.)

Now a hard decision had to be made. Obviously, U564 had to turn back to port. Without escort of some sort, it was highly unlikely that the boat would survive to reach the French coast. At least one boat had to accompany the cripple. Even then it had little chance of making shore, given the frequency of RAF air patrols, but at least an escorting boat could pick up survivors if, or more likely when, it was sunk. The other three commanders declined the task of escorting U564, so Maus reluctantly accepted the responsibility. (Maus's decision to escort U564 was not made purely out of sympathy for that boat's plight. He had several documents picked up from the wreck of the Sunderland and knew that the sooner these reached shore, the more valuable they would be.) BdU was radioed with the details of this predicament.

(By this time of the war, Karl Dönitz had taken over the post of *Grossadmiral* – Commander-in-Chief of the *Kriegsmarine* – from Erich Raeder, who resigned in January 1943. Dönitz, however, retained the title and authority of BdU until the end of the war. Increasingly, the daily operation of U-boat command was taken over by Dönitz's long-time assistant, Eberhard Godt, although Dönitz was involved in every major decision regarding his boats. To avoid confusion, all communication to and from U-boat command from this point on in the story will refer to BdU rather than Dönitz personally, though it is very likely that he saw the messages and dictated the responses.)

The reply confirmed Maus's decision and, as expected, ordered the other three boats to continue towards their patrol sectors. Two destroyers, Z24 and Z32, would leave Le Verdon the next morning and meet the two submarines.[8] It was already nearly dark before all this had transpired. The two boats set out at best speed towards the designated rendezvous, which was about 200nm due east of their current location. They hoped to cover most of that distance during the night, although nights in mid-June at that latitude were barely eight hours long.

Any hope they had of reaching the rendezvous unmolested faded at 1000 the next morning, the 14th, when an RAF aircraft emerged from the clouds, circled a few times and headed into cloud cover again. An hour later, two big four-engined aircraft dropped from the clouds and headed straight in towards the boats. U185 put up a heavy barrage and managed to hit one of the aircraft, which, when it veered away, revealed German markings and a familiar planform. (The aircraft were both Focke-Wulf Fw200 Condors, probably Fw200Cs of KG40 operating out of Bordeaux-Mérignac.) Only then did the aircraft drop the six red flares, which were the current recognition sign between German aircraft and U-boats. With one of their number damaged, both aircraft departed and headed back to land. At 1300, another RAF bomber appeared. Again, it circled, but didn't attack. U185 radioed a contact report to BdU, who replied that several Ju88s were being prepared and were scheduled to arrive at 1700.

The British bomber, ordered to shadow the two U-boats, circled for more than three hours, sending off homing signals, before it was finally given permission to attack the boats.[9] Even then, it took several attempts before it was able to find a favourable position to attack, because the two boats put up an effective fire. Finally, at about 1630, the bomber came in low and on a line that took it over U185 and then U564. U185's guns jammed again soon after the bomber started in, and U564 was unable to fire for fear of hitting U185. The bomber was therefore able to line up U564 precisely and drop a string of depth charges, one of which, at least, exploded directly under the U-boat and split it in two. The stern section sank instantly and the bow just moments later. The bomber turned quickly and started a strafing run on U185, which wounded a bosun's mate (*Bootsmann*) named Kamps. This was too much for Maus, who ordered a crash-dive and took U185 down to 190m. He circled the site of the sinking for more than an hour and then surfaced to find the sky clear. U185 was able to pick up 19 survivors, including U564's commander. At 1900, eight Ju88s finally appeared overhead to provide air-cover, and at 2030, one of the two destroyers sent to meet them, Z24, showed up and took over U564's survivors, the wounded Kamps and the interesting documents they had fished out of the water. The transfer of survivors was interrupted when the destroyer's radar picked up another aircraft. Z24 homed the Ju88s towards yet another RAF bomber that had been directed to the site, shooting it down.

The place of the wounded *Bootsmann* was taken by a volunteer off the destroyer, a man named Willmann who had never set foot on a U-boat before that moment. U185 turned back west again, heading towards the Azores and then on towards Pernambuco, its assigned patrol zone. (Pernambuco is now Recife, a port on the coast of Brazil.) The crew of the bomber which sank U564 had a rougher time of it. At least some of the shots U185 got off hit the bomber because soon after that U-boat submerged, the bomber's crew found that their hydraulic systems were failing. The crew fought for almost three hours to keep the plane in the air and had made it back most of the way to England when, at 1920, the starboard engine quit and ditching became the only option.

The crew survived the ditching and launched the inflatable dinghy. After floating for three days, they were picked up by a French fishing boat. They tried talking the boat's captain into taking them to England, but he said he was afraid for his family if he failed to return on time. He dropped them off near Morgat, south of Brest, where they were captured.

It took Dönitz no time at all to understand, based on these events, that attempting to cross the bay on the surface was suicidal, regardless of whether his boats could shoot down a plane or two. There would always be more aircraft than U-boats: anything like an even exchange would lose the war. On the same day that U564 was sunk, BdU recorded in his war log:

> On the basis of recent experience in Biscay, the following order has been given to the boats. With immediate effect, groups of U-boats will proceed through Biscay mainly submerged and will surface only to charge batteries. Instructions for procedure when surprised by aircraft are unaffected by this order.[10]

Just as he had a month earlier in the North Atlantic, Dönitz was admitting defeat. By ordering his boats to cross the bay submerged, he was accepting the necessary consequence that the passage to and from the open ocean would take at least a week each way rather than a few days. The extra days and the extra wear on crews would reduce the effectiveness of those U-boats which in fact reached their operational areas.

A Successful Patrol

Once past the Azores, U185 was able to proceed mainly on the surface. Approaching the Brazilian coast, U185 happened upon a small convoy running between Bahia and Trinidad, consisting of six merchantmen and seven escorts and covered in the air by a pair of Hudsons which, according to Maus, were busy performing aerobatics. Bahia, also known as Salvador, is a port city on the Brazilian coast between Recife and Rio. The convoy U185 found was BT18. Maus trailed the convoy until dark and then carried out a methodical and skilful assault. In five separate attacks, Maus lined up his targets and fired two torpedoes each at five targets. He believed he sank four of the five, a tanker and three freighters totalling 28,000GRT, and damaged the fifth.[11] The last victim was a munitions ship which exploded in a magnificent fireball and finally alerted the somnolent escorts to his presence. Even then, when U185 went deep and braced for the expected pounding, the escorts let the U-boat slip away without dropping a single depth charge. With that success under its belt, U185 reached the Brazilian coast on 10 July off Bahia, and began its patrol. On the last leg of its passage, it found calm seas and clear skies sufficient to bring all six of the torpedoes carried in the deck storage tubes into the boat, four forward and two aft. On the 8th, Maus claimed that U185 was attacked by an American patrol plane which was shot down, but post-war records indicate no such loss.

U185 patrolled for two weeks off Bahia, seeing almost no traffic and managing no attacks. In his frustration, Maus sailed north to the area of Pernambuco, where he found a similar lack of targets. This futility was momentarily interrupted on 30 July by a message from BdU to U199 (Kraus), which was operating further south, to come to the aid of U604 (Höltring), which had been damaged in an air attack. In fact, U185 was much closer to the damaged boat, but U604 had several seriously wounded crewmen, including the commander, IWO and bosun, and U199 had a real doctor on board.

(U604's IWO and bosun were both on watch when an aircraft approached undetected, firing its guns and dropping depth charges. Both men were seriously wounded and the commander, Höltring, was also hit when he came up to investigate. The attacker was a US Navy PV-1 Ventura of VB-129. U604 was reported by the pilot of the Ventura as having exploded and then sinking bow first at an angle of 60deg. It was believed to have been destroyed in the attack. In fact, however, while seriously damaged, it remained able to dive and surface, and Höltring believed it capable of surviving the ocean crossing back to France. First, however, it headed for the rendezvous set up with U199. The IWO and bosun both died during the night and were buried at sea.)[12]

U185 continued to patrol off Pernambuco and on the night of 1 August, it found and sank a lone high-speed freighter, missing it three times before getting two good hits.[13] On the 5th, Maus received another message about U604, this time specifically addressed to U185 and U172 (Emmermann). U199 had never shown up at the rendezvous and Höltring's boat had sustained two further attacks, and now was barely afloat.[14] BdU ordered the two boats to make for a new rendezvous with U604. Maus, having been through one rescue operation already on this patrol, complied with orders, but with something less than complete enthusiasm. He headed for the rendezvous at less than full speed and allowed himself, when he spotted another single target on the 6th, to be diverted from the rescue mission.

(On 3 August, U604 was attacked by a PB4Y [B-24] Liberator of VB-107, but managed to submerge and was only shaken by the six bombs dropped by the attacker. The Liberator pilot saw an oil slick where U604 submerged and claimed a probable sinking. That night, needing to recharge its batteries, U604 surfaced, only to be attacked within minutes by a surface ship firing its guns just over the boat. Höltring launched two *Aphrodite* decoy balloons and submerged. The destroyer USS *Moffett* [DD-362] kept U604 down for over 20 hours, dropping at least 17 depth charges, before tiring of the game and departing the scene. U604 surfaced late in the day on the 4th, by now so badly damaged that return to France was out of the question. Therefore, BdU ordered U185 and U172 to make for a new rendezvous with U604. U199 failed to make its appointed rendezvous with U604 because it had been sunk by air attack on 31 July.)

Maus lined up a spread of three torpedoes from the bow tubes at the single large target, but all three missed. Undismayed, he turned the boat and lined up a shot with both aft tubes. Those missed as well. There now was only one torpedo left on board. This last shot was lined up carefully and fired with fingers crossed. The torpedo hit the freighter under her foremast.[15] The ship stopped and the crew began swinging the lifeboats out on their davits, but it soon became obvious to both the attacker and the victim that the freighter wasn't sinking. With no torpedoes left, Maus had no choice but to attempt to sink the freighter by gunfire. Unfortunately, the deck gun hadn't been cleaned since they had left port two months earlier, and the ready-service rounds had been sitting in the *Spargelbetten* just as long; so, not too surprisingly, the first six rounds missed completely. One of them fell into the sea barely 20m from the gun. The crew was equally unpractised at ammunition handling and there then was a delay of several minutes as fresh rounds were manhandled out of the ammunition locker under the floor plates just forward of the control room, out of the tower hatch and down to guncrew. The crew of the freighter, meanwhile, had recovered sufficiently to man their single deck gun and an eight-barrelled pom-pom and had started firing back. Furious at this resistance and at his own crew's ineptitude, Maus ordered his 2cm flak guns manned and had a steady fire aimed at the freighter's gun mounts sufficient to discourage them from further defensive fire. Once the 10.5cm gun was again loaded and ready, a steady fire was aimed at the target's waterline, despite which it continued to creep forward slowly. After putting 30 shells into its port side, Maus ordered the boat around to the other side and hit it 39 times before it began to sink and the crew finally did take to the lifeboats.[16] Now, out of torpedoes, Maus turned his boat, still at a leisurely pace, towards the stricken U604. It had been a good patrol, with six sinkings for 38,000GRT. (Post-war analysis credited Maus with five victims grossing more than 36,000GRT.)

The Rescuer Needs Rescuing

Two days later, U185 rendezvoused with U604 approximately 450nm east of Pernambuco. Almost immediately, an American Liberator attacked and drove both boats underwater, where, using the UT (*Unterwassertelegraphie*) system, they communicated. U604 reported that the windings of both electric motors had caught fire and that the fires were put out with a foam fire extinguisher. They also reported that the boat had a 15deg angle towards the stern and depth-keeping was difficult at best. Maus suggested that they meet again two days later some 300nm to the north-east. That was nearly midway between Brazil and Senegal and was expected to be as free of aircraft as anywhere in the Central Atlantic. With that, the boats separated, each to make its own way to the new rendezvous. Not long after U185 surfaced again, it was attacked by a destroyer and then depth charged. U185 escaped by releasing six *Pillen* from its *Pillenwerfer*, which succeeded in decoying the destroyer. (*Pillen*, officially codenamed *Bold*, were small canisters of a calcium compound which broke down in sea water into a mass of hydrogen bubbles, capable of causing a sonar reflection similar to that of a U-boat.) Maus suspected that the destroyer had been in the vicinity and had picked up the UT communication between the boats on its sonar. (The UT was sender and receiver for underwater telegraphy and could be picked up on sonar as far as 20nm from the source. For this reason and because the opportunities to use the device were rare, the UT was used very rarely.)

The air attacks on U185 continued over the next day and a half. Maus had to crash-dive the boat no fewer than five times in the face of long-range Liberators which were clearly tracking its progress. On the morning of 11 August, U185 surfaced and found clear air. As hoped, they had finally shaken off the pursuit of the Brazil-based bombers. The rest of the run up to the new rendezvous point was uneventful. U604 was waiting and the two boats rested on the surface, at times less than two metres apart, and as rapidly as possible transferred all usable and portable material from U604.[17]

Despite the initial plan to scuttle U604 as soon as it had been stripped, Maus wanted to wait until they were joined by Emmermann in U172, because transferring more than 50 crewmen into his boat alone would cause severe overcrowding. At 1800, U172 arrived and the three boats were sailing together in tight formation, making final arrangements for the transfer of Höltring's crew, when a US Navy Liberator joined the party. The three boats sped up and began zigzagging and, as a result, the depth charges dropped by the Liberator near U172 failed to inflict serious damage. Emmermann, nevertheless, had clearly had enough and submerged while the bomber turned for another pass at the boats. U604 was unable to submerge at this point and Maus decided to keep U185 on the surface and do what he could to help Höltring's boat. On its next pass, the Liberator overflew U185 and, despite the fact that one of its 2cm guns had jammed, the crew of the other gun shot well and put several rounds into the bomber's belly. The plane immediately trailed smoke and flames, tried to pull up but fell off to the left and crashed into the sea.[18]

The immediate threat might have been negated, but there was no question that more bombers would appear soon. It was time to get U604's crew off the damaged boat. U185 tried repeatedly to raise Emmermann on the UT, but got no response. However, time was pressing and Maus told Höltring to begin transferring his crew. While U185's IIWO was inflating its rubber dinghy, the crew of U604 was swimming the 20m that separated the two boats. Höltring himself, wounded in the shoulder in the initial attack on 30 July, would need the lifeboat to get across. Soon, only Höltring and the LI were left on board the damaged boat. The LI set four demolition charges timed for eight minutes, opened all the ventilation ducts, removed the one remaining 2cm breech assembly and climbed into the lifeboat with Höltring and U185's IIWO. The lifeboat must have been holed during one of the many attacks aimed at U185, because it collapsed and sank under the load of three men. Höltring ended up in the water despite all the precautions and had to be hauled out by the crew of U185. Moments later, the demolition charges exploded and U604 slipped quietly stern-first under the waves.

Now filled past capacity with the addition of U604's crew, U185 started again towards the north and home. Maus kept trying to raise U172 on the radio and finally succeeded in doing so late in the day. Emmermann reported that the earlier air attack had knocked out both his magnetic and gyrocompass. A new rendezvous another 500nm further north was set for 15 August, three days hence. U185 arrived at the designated point late on the 15th, but had to wait until almost noon on the 16th for U172 to appear. Emmermann blamed his faulty compasses for being late to the rendezvous. Once the boats had met, 25 of the survivors swam across to U172, including the LI and a PK Oberleutnant.[19] Twenty-three more remained on U185. After the transfer was complete, the two boats sailed north in loose formation, about 3nm apart, heading towards the Azores. In another two days, U172 completed repairs of its compasses and parted company with U185. Both boats were low on fuel and were told to meet U847, a Type XIV *Milchkuh*, in a sector north-west of the Azores. On the 21st, Maus informed BdU that U185 didn't have enough fuel to reach the designated rendezvous with U847. BdU replied that Maus should identify a meeting point as far north as practicable and wait there for the *Milchkuh* to join him.

U185 reached the agreed-upon rendezvous before dawn on the 24th, but was informed that U847 would be delayed and wouldn't arrive for two more days. Therefore, Maus and his crew settled into waiting on the surface for the *Milchkuh* to arrive. Unfortunately, they didn't have long to wait. At 0700 a pair of aircraft, a Wildcat and an Avenger, ducked out of the low clouds from directly astern.[20] The two used a new and highly effective tactic. The Wildcat led the Avenger, strafing the tower to suppress any defensive fire. The Avenger could then drop its depth charges without worrying about flak. The tactic worked perfectly, but was in this case actually unnecessary because the two aircraft emerged from the clouds so close to the boat that there was no time for the U-boat's gun crews to reach the tower. The first pass by the Wildcat killed five of the seven men up top and wounded the other two. The Avenger, following close on the tail of the Wildcat, dropped a single depth charge which exploded under the hull just aft of the control room, damaging the aft and amidships dive tanks and starting leaks into the bilge. By the time the two planes swung back for their second pass, a new bridge crew had come up from inside the boat. Unfortunately, they suffered the same fate, being all killed or wounded by the Wildcat's .50cal (12.7mm) machine guns. The Avenger dropped its second depth charge, this one hitting forward, right by the 10.5cm gun mount.

By now it was clear that staying on the surface was suicidal, so Maus, who was in the tower, shouted down to the LI to find out if it was possible to dive. The response was that it probably was possible but not advisable, since there were leaks forward and aft and chlorine gas from the battery compartments was starting to fill the boat. Moments later, the engine room reported that both port diesels were burning and that the *Maschinisten* were fighting the fires as best they could. Thus it was clear to Maus that the fight was lost and the only recourse was abandon the boat. He ordered the crew to the deck with lifejackets and rebreathers, but another strafing pass by the Wildcat wounded more crewmen and convinced some not to come out of the boat. U185, however, was now sinking rapidly and nearly all the men who hadn't taken their chances on deck were trapped inside as the boat slipped stern-first under the waves. Höltring, too badly wounded to survive in the water, took his own life after first shooting a seriously wounded crewman.[21]

Another pair of aircraft arrived overhead and the pilots waved at the survivors in the water, reassuring them that rescue was on the way. Nevertheless, the survivors were in the water for almost six hours before help arrived in the form of USS *Barker* (DD213). Many of the men were without lifejackets and tried hanging on to the officers, who all had theirs, but Maus ordered the men to form their own group. Eventually, 36 men were pulled out of the water, including nine survivors from U604.

U1059

In the Soup Together

U1059 was conceived and designed at a time when U-boats were roaming the Atlantic and wreaking havoc among the Allies' convoy routes. Dönitz's boats were ranging across the width of the ocean and indeed were having some of their greatest successes off the coast of America. Nothing seemed to limit their potential to wage war except the unavoidable bounds set by logistics. A boat could carry only so much food and so much fuel and so many torpedoes, and when one or more of those ran low, the boat had to return to get more. That wasn't a problem in the early years of the war when the battle rarely ranged past mid-ocean, but now, in 1941, boats were finding their best hunting in increasingly distant areas and much of a boat's stock of provisions would get used up just during the passage to and from patrol. This problem had been handled originally by a network of supply ships, former merchantmen, which were sent out to meet U-boats and replenish their supplies at sea. For a while this worked fine, but the British caught wind of the scheme and 'rolled up' the surface supply network in the summer of 1941. Dönitz wasn't surprised by this and in fact had already ordered the first of the Type XIV *Milchkühe* in May 1940. These boats, good as they were, solved only part of the problem. They could give food and fuel to another U-boat, but they carried only four torpedoes and these were stored in deck containers where they were difficult to retrieve. Thus, in late 1941, Dönitz asked his designers to come up with a torpedo transport U-boat to supplement the Type XIV.

The resulting design was the Type VIIF, very much a hybrid. It was basically a Type VIIC, the main production U-boat type, with an added section 10.5m (35ft) long behind the tower to hold the cargo of torpedoes and enlarged fuel tanks to extend its range. This cargo compartment could hold 22 torpedoes.[1] Additionally, it had, like the bigger Type IXs and XIVs, external storage tubes in the deck-casing for a pair of additional torpedoes.[2] However, unlike the Type XIV, the Type VIIF was a fully armed submarine, with the same arrangement of torpedo tubes as the Type VIIC from which it was derived. Therefore, it also carried 12 torpedoes stored, as in a Type VIIC, in the five torpedo tubes and in storage locations in the fore and aft torpedo rooms.

Construction of these boats, four of which were ordered from Germaniawerft, went very slowly. They shared some sections in common with the main production Type VIICs, which were being stamped out two a month from the same yard, but many other parts had to be custom-built, so construction of U1059 took from summer 1942 until March 1943 and its commissioning didn't take place until 1 May. Because U1059 was armed like a standard U-boat, its working up in the Baltic resembled that of any other U-boat, with the full round of testing and training exercises. In fact, U1059 went through this testing and training twice, further delaying its availability. The boat was commissioned by OLzS Herbert Brüninghaus and trained under him until late September, when he came down with a serious stomach ailment and had to be hospitalised. The onset of the illness was so sudden and severe that he had to be replaced by a temporary commander in the middle of its tactical exercises. The boat returned to Kiel and on 30 September 1943, a brief ceremony was held to mark the transfer of command to OLzS Günther Leupold. Unfortunately, Leupold had never commanded a U-boat before, so the round of testing and training began again, adding four months to the boat's working up. (In fact, Leupold boasted to his captors that he was the youngest U-boat commander, just 23 years of age. His youth and, perhaps, immaturity might explain some of his subsequent behaviour.)

So it was not until late January 1944 that U1059 was ready to leave Kiel for its first operational patrol. When the boat had started loading out on 25 January, the crew was issued tropical kit, but only the officers were told their intended destination. The load-out included, besides 12 torpedoes in the torpedo rooms and two in the deck containers, 11 in the torpedo storage room (eight electrics and three air-driven). The torpedoes in the storage room were stored in pieces, the warheads and after-bodies having been removed and stored separately. The remaining space in the storage room was taken up with crates of spare parts, extra radios and spare tubes, and many boxes of provisions.

By early 1944, the war had changed dramatically since the Type VIIFs had originally been ordered. It was now obvious that at-sea replenishment of torpedoes was no longer practical or safe. It would require two boats to be stopped in mid-ocean with multiple hatches open. The density of Allied air patrols over the North and Central Atlantic was such that an operation of this type was simply too dangerous. Still, there was a high priority task awaiting U1059. As the anti-submarine defences in the Atlantic had stiffened, Dönitz found hunting grounds further afield. As early as December 1942, the Japanese had suggested the establishment of a German U-boat base at Sabang or Penang with the intent of supporting U-boat attacks in the northern Indian Ocean. Sabang is a small port on a small island at the north-western tip of Sumatra. Penang (Malay Pinang) is an island off the west coast of the Malay Peninsula. Its principal town is the port of George Town. Dönitz had shown little interest in 1942, but after the collapse of the U-boat offensive in the North Atlantic in May 1943, interest in the proposal was revived. One boat already operating in the South Atlantic was ordered to proceed to Penang and a group of nine Type IXCs was readied to leave France in June with orders to raid in the Indian Ocean and then base itself at Penang. It was estimated that the boats would arrive in the Indian Ocean in time to start operations in September at the end of the Monsoon season, hence the group was named *Monsun*.

In the meanwhile, a force of German naval personnel was gathered from various merchantmen and auxiliaries trapped in the East Indies by the war and set to work establishing a U-boat base at Penang. (Penang was chosen as the site over Sabang, despite the fact that the latter was some 300nm closer to the hunting grounds, because Penang had a much bigger, better equipped port and was closer to the Japanese supply lines.) The Japanese were eager to see German U-boats at Penang and they made supplies readily available to the German boats which arrived there starting in October 1943. Of the original nine boats in the first *Monsun* group, four actually made it to Penang.[3] However, when the base personnel attempted to provision these boats, they encountered several problems. The German torpedoes, which had been gathered from the various naval vessels in the east, were found to be in poor condition and of questionable reliability even when refurbished. Worse still, the rations supplied by the Japanese, equivalent to the diet eaten by their submarine crews, were found to be inadequate in calories and generally unpalatable to the U-boat crews. (The Japanese submariner ate a diet that would today be considered quite healthy, consisting mainly of rice garnished with pickled vegetables and tinned fish. The German U-boatman was used to sausage and other preserved meats, dark bread – fresh or tinned – and canned vegetables, mainly sauerkraut.) The Germans set up a small factory at Penang to prepare food more to their liking, but desperately needed a supply of torpedoes and spare parts for machinery and radios. Enter the newly completing Type VIIFs. The first of them to complete training, U1062 (Albrecht), left Norway on 3 January 1944 with a cargo similar to that just loaded onto Leupold's boat. U1059 was to follow as soon as possible.

U1059 left Kiel on 4 February 1944. It was a Friday. The crew was very unhappy about this. It was considered very bad luck to leave for patrol on a Friday and U-boats almost never left port on that day of the week. Leupold, however, expressed his disdain for such sailor's superstitions and ordered the boat out. Several of the survivors stated later that they knew then that this captain would be trouble.[4] The boat's orders were simple. It was to make for Penang at the most economical speed so as to arrive there without needing to resupply along the way. That meant that en route to Penang, it would be necessary to avoid all contact with the enemy. Once there it would offload the contents of its storage room and the deck containers (13 torpedoes and all the spare parts and excess provisions), undertake an offensive patrol into the Indian Ocean and then, after resupplying at Penang, return to France where it would join the 12th Flotilla at Bordeaux.

U1059 departed Kiel before daybreak, accompanied by two minesweepers, but no other U-boats. It proceeded alone up the Kattegat, past Anholt, and across the Skagerrak to Kristiansand, at the southern tip of Norway, arriving there at 0900 on the 6th. The call at Kristiansand was unscheduled. Soon after leaving Kiel, the boat had made some practice dives and, almost immediately, it was noticed that the 3.7cm gun was damaged. This was a new gun, just fitted during the boat's last yard period, and it had seemed fine the week before, but now it was clearly not working. The boat stayed at Kristiansand for three days, reluctant to continue without a fully functional flak battery. It was obvious after three days that the facilities at Kristiansand were inadequate and the boat left at 1400 on the 9th and, taking advantage of the long winter night, arrived at Bergen at 0800 the next day. There the offending gun was removed, taken ashore and completely rebuilt in the local maintenance shop. It was ready the next day, restored on the boat on the morning of the following day, and U1059 left Bergen for Penang at 1200 on 12 February 1944.

Upon leaving Bergen, U1059 followed a long looping course designed to keep it as far away as possible from air pursuit. It started towards the north-north-west until it reached the Arctic Circle. It then looped around to the south-west, through the area between Iceland and Norway, which the Germans called the *Rosengarten*, until, passing near the Faroes, it entered the dangerous North Atlantic. (That stretch of ocean between Iceland and Norway was known as the *Rosengarten* [Rose Garden] by the Germans because by this time of the war it was so densely strewn with drifting mines that it might 'bloom' into life at any moment.) During this part of the voyage, Leupold was rather conservative. He surfaced the boat at night and proceeded at the most economical speed, approximately six knots, carefully monitoring the radar and the search receiver. During the day, he submerged and the boat crept along at barely two knots. Still, few aircraft were detected and U1059 made good progress, averaging about 120nm a day.

U1059 made it through most of February without distraction and managed to reach mid-ocean safely. However, in late February, due west of Ireland, U1059 encountered three fast freighters, steaming together but without escort. Contrary to orders, Leupold ordered the boat to give chase. Only after more than an hour of high-speed pursuit did it become obvious that the U-boat wouldn't catch the freighters in the near future. Reluctantly, Leupold gave up the chase and the boat resumed its southward course, but now it did so without sufficient fuel to reach Penang. Leupold radioed BdU requesting resupply and was told to meet U488 south-west of the Cape Verde Islands on 23 March.

Passing the Azores in early March, U1059 found itself in a dangerous predicament not of its own making. The two main air compressors, the diesel-powered *Junkers* and the battery-driven electric compressor, both failed at the same time. Even the small emergency compressor, carried for just this eventuality, failed as well. (These kinds of material failures would have been unheard of earlier in the war, but now, in 1944, they were all too common. It has to be remembered that by this time, dockyard work was done almost entirely by conscripted French or Polish workers, and sabotage or plain shoddy work caused many a system to fail on U-boats at sea.) For four days they were without a working compressor of any kind and, during that period, they were unable to dive. Their luck held and the *Maschinisten* were able to repair the compressors under clear skies. Unfortunately, Leupold came to trust his luck just a bit too much, as his subsequent behaviour would show.

Incredible Laxness

Maybe it was the sheer pleasure of encountering a tropical sea and warm sunshine after a long, cold and depressing wartime winter. Maybe Leupold had become a little unbalanced, as some of his crew later intimated. For whatever reason, he began to let caution slip as the boat neared its designated rendezvous point. Due in part to the four days during which the boat had been unable to dive, it was now nearing the meeting point days ahead of schedule. Leupold's laxness certainly couldn't have stemmed from any illusion that they were out of danger. They knew from monitoring the radios that another U-boat, located less than 100nm from their current position, was being pursued by naval aircraft.[5] Despite this known threat, Leupold began allowing off-duty men to come up on deck to enjoy the pleasant weather. While there was no specific rule against this, Leupold's decision falling under the discretion of the commander, it has to be seen as unusual, to say the least. It was well understood that a U-boat's safety, especially in the face of threat from the air, often rested on its ability to dive quickly. And it was equally well understood that the speed with which a U-boat could dive was a function, in part, of the number of men who had to get below and the number of hatches which needed closing before the boat could submerge. Put simply, the more men on deck, the longer it takes to dive, the greater the danger to the boat. Thus permitting men on deck for reasons other than standing a watch or manning a weapon in a region of known air threat has to be seen as high-risk behaviour.

Nor was this something Leupold did only once. Encouraged by the boat's doctor, who argued that time on deck was good for the men's health and morale, Leupold allowed this dangerous luxury more and more frequently as the boat passed the Tropic of Cancer and approached the rendezvous point. Organised social activities began to be allowed on deck, including a concert and games of chess. But the most dangerous luxury of all was swimming. Three times in those quiet days of March 1944, Leupold stopped the boat and allowed up to 20 of the men to swim in the water around the boat. That he was aware that his boat was indeed in danger is shown by the fact that during the second of those 'swimming parties', on the 18th, Leupold arranged for an air alert to be sounded, which sent the off-duty men in the water scrambling back on board to their battle stations at the guns or passing ammunition up from the magazines. (Several of the survivors stated that, well intended as that practice alert undoubtedly was, it probably did more harm than good. When the real attack came the next day, and the real alert was sounded, some men hesitated briefly, thinking that it was another drill.)

Dawn on 19 March 1944 was particularly beautiful in the Central Atlantic. The Obersteuermann, Hartmann, who had the watch, called down to the commander to come up and see the brilliant colours painting the eastern horizon. Leupold climbed up to the tower and, as dazzled by the beauty as Hartmann, passed down word that all off-duty men would be allowed a ten-minute swim. At the same time, he ordered all engines stopped and the boat gradually lost way. As the boat slowed, Leupold stripped off his clothing. Just before he jumped in the water, he shouted back up to Hartmann: 'Watch out for aircraft in this fine weather!'[6]

Besides Leupold, others in the water included the IIWO, the LI and the boat's doctor. In all, about 18 men were soon swimming. Many of those who opted to remain on board were still following Sunday routine. This meant that few of the crew had duty: most of them were playing cards or sleeping. A number of others were playing a variant of 'Name that Tune', a musical quiz show that the crew staged regularly, the winner of which got a bottle of wine or some fruit. (The *Kriegsmarine* had a policy of no drinking on board ships, just like the US Navy, and similarly, the enforcement of that prohibition was the responsibility of the ship's officers: thus, in most cases, an occasional off-duty drink was tolerated, but drunkenness on duty was severely punished. Type VIIFs, due to their increased size and range, were fitted with a large refrigerator, so that fresh fruit might indeed have been available more than a month into a patrol.)

Meanwhile, the very danger that Leupold had warned of, but, apparently, feared insufficiently, was indeed approaching out of the sky. The hunter-killer group based on the aircraft carrier USS *Block Island* (CVE-21) was approaching from the north-east. Alerted by signals intelligence about the planned replenishment, *Block Island's* aircraft were sweeping the sky, looking for surfaced U-boats. This group was experienced and successful. Just two days previously, they had dispatched another U-boat in the vicinity and now they wanted more. As was standard practice, search sweeps were launched well before dawn so that they would be in their patrol areas at first light. At 0826Z, 0726 local time, a search team made up of a Wildcat and an Avenger spotted, much to their surprise, a U-boat dead in the water, surrounded by swimming men.[7] The aircraft attacked immediately, the Wildcat leading and spraying the boat with .50cal machine-gun fire, the Avenger following, dropping two depth charges.

Amazingly, the boat managed to put up a defence. Leupold saw the aircraft as they started their run and gave the alarm. By the time the Wildcat passed overhead, two of the boat's flak guns were manned and had started to put up defensive fire. All but one of the swimmers had already climbed back onto the U-boat's deck, which, unfortunately, made them the target of the Wildcat's strafing run. A number were killed or wounded, including Hartmann. The Avenger's depth charges were devastatingly accurate. One hit the deck aft and exploded on contact, blowing a number of the swimmers, including Leupold, back into the water. The second depth charge exploded under the boat's starboard side just aft of the tower, in the way of the torpedo storage room. A number of the survivors stated later that they'd always thought the big open space in the boat to be a source of structural weakness and events proved them right. U1059 broke neatly in two right aft of the tower and the halves disappeared beneath the waves in barely more than a minute.

Approximately 15 men were in the water in the oil slick left by the sinking. Most owed their survival so far to having been on deck and being blown overboard by the first depth charge. Some, like Leupold, had been picked up and thrown a second time by the explosion of the second depth charge and were now wounded and dazed. A series of explosions was heard from the sinking U-boat. Whatever the cause of the explosions, they were fortuitous for the survivors because considerable flotsam rose to the surface from the sinking boat, including two intact torpedo bodies. A number of the survivors clung to these until they were rescued.

In the Soup

They were about to be joined by one more survivor. Both aircraft immediately began to circle to the left in order to make a second pass at the U-boat. The Wildcat lined up the boat and made a second strafing run on the sinking boat. The Avenger, piloted by Lt (jg) Norman T. Dowty, started to turn but was clearly in trouble. It continued turning to the left, then straightened briefly and started to turn again. It stalled in mid-turn and slid on its left wing into the water, approximately a half-mile from the site of the sinking. Dowty and the belly gunner/bombardier were killed in the crash. The rear gunner, a pilot who was sitting in to observe Dowty's technique, ended up in the water unharmed.[8] Ens M. E. Fitzgerald found a seat-pack life raft floating nearby, inflated it and pulled himself out of the water. The Wildcat passing overhead reported these events back to *Block Island*, which immediately instructed all available aircraft to the scene and ordered the destroyer USS *Corry* (DD-463) dispatched as well. The Wildcat also reported that a shark was in the water near the survivors.

Fitzgerald, confident that rescue was on the way, settled back to enjoy a quiet float. He could hear faint shouting from the direction of the sinking, but that was a half-mile away and into the sun, still low in the sky, so he couldn't see any survivors. After a short while, the Wildcat, running low on fuel, waggled its wings and headed back to *Block Island*. Perhaps an hour later, Fitzgerald heard the sound of a swimmer and looked up to see a German survivor dog-paddling slowly towards him. Fitzgerald recounted later that he was 'scared to death', afraid that he'd have to fight a Nazi fanatic for possession of his life raft. When, after some time, the man had pulled within 50m of his raft, he called out to the man, asking if he spoke English. The man answered in the negative. As the German closed the last few metres to the raft, another Avenger from *Block Island* arrived at the scene and counted eight men in the water. Assuming that the man swimming near Fitzgerald was another American survivor, the pilot of the Avenger unhooked his own seat-pack life raft and dropped it near Fitzgerald and the swimmer. Fitzgerald directed the German to retrieve the life raft and showed him how to inflate it. He then lashed the two rafts together and, looking over his new companion in the other raft, noticed that he was wounded. Fitzgerald opened his first aid kit and began treating the astonished German's wounds.

Presently two more swimmers approached. Both appeared to be badly wounded. One identified himself, in passable English, as the U-boat's commander. Günther Leupold pulled himself up onto the rafts; the other man hung on in the water. Fitzgerald, afraid that he was now outnumbered and in the presence of an ardent Nazi in Leupold, hitched his sheath knife around where he could easily reach it and asked Leupold: 'Did you fire on my plane?'[9]

Leupold, afraid that this American, the man with the power to save his life, might be angry, answered him cautiously: 'You're mad?' Fitzgerald responded: 'No, I'm not mad, just want to know.'

Leupold relaxed and said: 'Sure, my gun crews shot at it. We shot it down.'

Fitzgerald then told Leupold to lie back and he examined his wounds. One of Leupold's knees was shattered and his scalp nearly laid bare.[10] Fitzgerald later expressed amazement that any man could swim for an hour-and-a-half in Leupold's condition. Leupold, for his part, was astounded at the compassionate treatment he was receiving from the American. Finally, Leupold extended his hand to Fitzgerald and said: 'You good fellow. Damn war!'

Now completely relaxed, Leupold began to expound to Fitzgerald about his theories on the war. He explained at length that he thought it was sad that the Germans and the Americans were fighting, saying that they should join forces against the Russians, who he claimed was the common enemy of both countries. (This was a fairly common Nazi propaganda line and was used by a great many German prisoners on their American captors. Few among the Americans agreed with this idea, with the notable and well-publicised exception of General George S. Patton. The Americans were in the odd position of being instinctively anti-communist but strongly allied with the Russians in the war.) Leupold seemed relieved that Fitzgerald was a Navy flier. He claimed to be unaware whether the aircraft which attacked his boat were carried-based or land-based. He said that since Fitzgerald was a Navy pilot, it meant that they'd be rescued soon. He stated several times that he was very glad that his captor was American and not British or Canadian. He said that he knew that he'd be treated well by the Americans, while the British, in particular, were believed to treat captured U-boatmen rather harshly. Leupold showed himself to be fully in sympathy with Nazi racial prejudices when he asked Fitzgerald if there were any 'Negroes' on the aircraft that crashed. He expressed considerable fear that he might be turned over to 'Negroes' once he was taken on board a US Navy ship.[11]

The other German, who was hanging on to the rafts, began to lose his battle with the water shortly after this. He clearly was exhausted and complained of cramps. Fitzgerald thought that he would soon just let go and drift away, so he asked Leupold to convey to him that a rescue ship was coming. This seemed to cheer the man up and allowed him to hang on a while longer. Only minutes later, *Corry* appeared on the scene and rescued Fitzgerald and eight survivors from U1059. One of the torpedoes floating amidst U1059's wreckage was taken on board *Corry*; the other was sunk. *Corry* herself didn't have long to live. While supporting the Normandy landings on 6 June 1944, she struck a mine and sank off the coast of France.

— 11 —
U66

'Central Atlantic Worse than Biscay'

U66's eighth patrol had been a marathon, lasting five months, taking it to the American coast and Bermuda. On the way home, it was attacked by aircraft and its commander, 'Fritz' Markworth, was seriously wounded. Under temporary command, U66 limped home, arriving at Lorient on 1 September 1943. The boat then entered the yard for a period of repair and overhaul that lasted more than three months. By the time it emerged in January 1944, it had lost its deck gun, gained an enlarged *Wintergarten* with a single 3.7cm gun on the lower platform and two twin 2cm on the upper. It was also fitted with the new, sophisticated underwater sound gear, the *Balkon-Gerät*, which consisted of 48 sound-receiving diaphragms arrayed round a circular platform set into the bow of the boat. This arrangement allowed far better target location while submerged than the older version, which simply had a semi-circular pattern of sound diaphragms set into each side of the bow. However, the most significant change was the replacement of Markworth with a very young commanding officer, OLzS Gerhard Seehausen. (Seehausen's youth wasn't exceptional. By this time of the war, all the old guard of U-boat commanders, trained before the war, were either dead or had been promoted to shore jobs. The new commanders commissioning the 20 or more new boats joining the fleet every month were generally very young men who'd had a few patrols as watch officer before taking over a new boat.)

Seehausen took his rebuilt boat out on 16 January 1944. It was escorted as far as Ile de Groix and then headed at its best speed due west across the Bay of Biscay, proceeding mainly submerged, surfacing only to recharge batteries. It actually sighted only one aircraft crossing the bay and, in that instance, the U-boat was able to dive before it could be attacked. After two weeks, U66 had reached a point almost due north of the Azores. Gradually its course was altered to south-west until it passed west of the islands and then it came around to the south-east until it passed east of the Cape Verde Islands and approached the African coast near Freetown in mid-February. The effect of travelling primarily submerged was obvious. A passage that would have taken a couple of weeks on the surface had taken more than five weeks mainly underwater.

Near Freetown, Seehausen sighted a convoy and attempted an attack, but aircraft and a pursuing destroyer drove the U-boat away. A T5 was fired at the destroyer and a detonation was heard after 12 minutes, but no one on board the U-boat really thought they'd hit the destroyer, especially since no sinking sounds were heard.[1] U66 continued to the south-east until it passed Cape Palmas and then turned east. Its assigned patrol area was the Bight of Benin between Cape Palmas and Lagos, but Seehausen stretched his patrols to the east as far as Douala and Libreville. Near Abidjan, on the 26th, another convoy was located and attacked, this time with more success. This convoy had ten or more merchantmen with a thick screen of escorts, but Seehausen got favourable position ahead of the convoy and waited until it steamed into range. He launched four torpedoes at two targets and believed he hit them both. As he took the boat down to 120m to await the inevitable depth charges, the crew heard the distinctive sounds of a target's bulkheads collapsing as water broke into closed compartments. They knew they'd got one and hoped they'd got two.[2] The depth charges came, as expected, and continued for hours. In all, they counted 53 of them. Lights were broken and fuses popped and one T5 was disabled, but, all in all, U66 got away without serious damage.

Just off Accra, on 1 March, U66 caught a single steamer and put two torpedoes into her.[3] Four nights later, they caught another solitary steamer as it approached the harbour at Douala. This steamer, SS *John Holt*, was a new, fast cargo ship headed from Lagos to Douala on a high-speed run carrying mail and 2600t of general cargo, mainly cement.[4] She was zigzagging at 13kt when she came into U66's sights. (Away from the main convoy routes, ships faster than 12kt were generally allowed to proceed alone, on the theory that their speed offered them as much protection as a convoy would.) Again, two torpedoes were fired and both hit forward. The steamer rapidly settled by the head and the captain immediately saw that she was sinking and ordered the crew overboard. Three of the four lifeboats, including the captain's motor launch, were lowered successfully and a number of rafts were also pushed over the side before the ship sank no more than five minutes after being hit.

Most of the men who jumped from *John Holt* were pulled onto the rafts. Once the ship had sunk, the men in the three lifeboats rowed over to the rafts and the remaining survivors were transferred into the lifeboats. A quick count showed that there had been no casualties in the sinking. All 97 passengers and crew were in the three lifeboats. (That number broke down into 91 crewmembers and six passengers. The crew was further divided into the following categories: 36 'Europeans', 5 Navy gunners, 4 Army gunners, 6 native firemen and 40 Kroo 'boys'. The Kroo are a tribe that inhabits the coastal regions of Liberia.)

Approximately a half-hour after the sinking, U66 surfaced not far from the lifeboats and closed to within hailing distance. A machine gun was fired over the survivors' heads, presumably to get their undivided attention and then a voice was heard, in heavily accented English, ordering the boats to pull up to the U-boat's side. The captain's boat tied up alongside the U-boat and all the 'Europeans' on board were ordered onto the U-boat's deck and lined up facing a guard with a sub-machine gun. The steamer's captain was interrogated by the English-speaking officer who remained on the *Wintergarten*, being asked the ship's name and other particulars. The captain answered all the questions as best he could, and, when the questioning was complete, the survivors were ordered back into the lifeboat with the exception of the captain, the senior radio officer and one passenger, a Mr Eliot, who was a shipping agent of the steamship line. During the confusion of men scrambling down the side of the U-boat and back into the lifeboat, the radio officer slipped in with the crowd and climbed into the lifeboat without being noticed. (As far as the survivors could tell, his absence on board was never noticed by the Germans.) As the lifeboat cast off, the officer on the *Wintergarten* called out to the survivors:

Your captain will be in Germany in three weeks time. I am sorry I had to sink your ship, but war is war. Good luck and a safe passage.[5]

With that, the U-boat pulled away from the lifeboats and headed off into the night. The motor launch took the other two boats in tow and started towards land. The sinking occurred barely 20nm off the coast of Nigeria. Soon after first light on the 6th, they were spotted by a steamer and taken into Port Harcourt.

Creeping Homeward

Unfortunately, Seehausen was far too optimistic about his prospects for returning home. He had indeed made up his mind to head towards France, but he still had torpedoes and provisions and he continued hunting along the coast of Nigeria for several more weeks. On 21 March, U66 attacked a large tanker near Lagos with three torpedoes and left it in sinking condition.[6] After this, U66 moved more steadily towards the west, sighting a convoy in early April off Cape Palmas that it was unable to close. Running low on fuel and provisions, although he still had five torpedoes left, Seehausen radioed BdU that he was heading home and needed replenishment; he was assigned a rendezvous with U466 (Studt) north-west of the Cape Verde Islands for late April.

Like so much else about U-boat warfare, the process of replenishing from *Milchkühe* had been changed dramatically for the worse by the increasing dominance of Allied air-power. Beginning in mid-1943, the Allies had made a concerted effort to break the back of the resupply system and by April 1944, U466 was the only *Milchkuh* left afloat. Seemingly every time it surfaced to meet another U-boat, Allied aircraft appeared to break up the planned replenishment. As U66 crept steadily towards the north-west, U466 was repeatedly attacked and only carried out its assigned mission through persistence and a good deal of luck. U66's progress was slower even than expected and on 21 April, Seehausen contacted Dönitz to inform him that he was still far south of the planned rendezvous point and that the boat had provisions for no more than a week. Obviously, U66 would be unable to reach the rendezvous point; U446 would have to come south to meet Seehausen. A new rendezvous was set for the 26th due west of the Cape Verde Islands.

During the evening of 25 April, U66 surfaced at the designated rendezvous point only to find numerous aircraft overhead. The boat submerged and, opting to be safe rather than sorry, remained underwater for the rest of the night. Unknown to Seehausen, Allied signals intelligence and HF/DF had determined that a rendezvous was to take place in the area and an anti-submarine group based on the escort carrier USS *Croatan* (CVE-25) was in the vicinity intent on crashing the party. An Avenger flying off *Croatan* had pinpointed U66's location, but lost it again when the boat submerged. The commander of the 'hunter-killer' group ordered that *Croatan's* destroyer escorts conduct a concentric search, starting at U66's last known location. That search paid off early in the morning on the 26th, when USS *Frost* (DE-144) obtained a sonar contact and USS *Inch* (DE-146) attacked with Hedgehogs. (A Hedgehog was a fixed, forward-firing multi-barrelled mortar which fired small depth bombs. The weapon was often installed on small ASW vessels during the later stages of the Second World War. The depth bombs exploded only on impact, so they didn't disrupt sonar contact when they missed like a standard depth charge did. The system was given the name Hedgehog because the bank of mortar tubes vaguely resembled the quills of a hedgehog.) Hits were obtained with the Hedgehogs, but sonar interference of unknown origin prevented the search from continuing until first light.

Meantime, U66, which was not the U-boat being pursued by *Frost* and *Inch*, had surfaced nearby and watched impotently as the destroyer escorts continued their pursuit, completely unaware of U66's presence. The dilemma facing Seehausen was difficult at best, impossible at worst. To slink away without doing anything to assist another U-boat in danger bore more than a trace of cowardice, but to intervene would only put his boat in mortal danger. After a while, the escorts disappeared into the gloom and U66 lost track of their presence until near dawn, when a flare was seen being fired into the air just three miles away, too close for Seehausen's taste, and U66 submerged again. Once underwater, the crew listened in horror as an attack developed soon after, with several separate patterns of depth charges being heard, then the unmistakable sounds of a sinking boat and finally silence. In fact, first light had revealed a distinct oil slick to the waiting escorts. Searching at that spot, they obtained a stationary sonar contact at 190m. Three escorts dropped patterns of depth charges, after which the contact had disappeared. Despite the fact that no debris ever rose to the surface, they were credited with the kill. U66 reported these events to BdU later in the day, stating that it had just eight days provisions remaining and asking again for guidance from home.

(The inconsistency of the radio reports made by Seehausen to headquarters deserves an explanation. When the survivors of the crew of U66 were taken on board USS *Buckley*, they were found to be in very poor health. This was partly because U66's crew, with rare exceptions, hadn't seen daylight for three months. However, the crew was also found to be in a state of reduced mental capacity, due to the fact that they were suffering from relatively advanced vitamin deficiency. U66 left port with an inexperienced corpsman [*Sanitätsmaat* Wolf Loch] who was on his first patrol. Before departure, he had been sent to the medical supply depot to pick up vitamin tablets for the crew. He was given a large container, presumably with sufficient tablets for the patrol, and left the depot without checking the invoice. The boat was already a day out to sea when he opened the container and discovered to his horror that it was mostly packing material surrounding a small bottle of tablets, only enough to last the crew a week. They waited eight weeks before distributing the pills and after that, for the last month of the cruise, the crew's physical and mental state deteriorated. Many of the crew were found to be suffering all the classic symptoms of scurvy.)

Orders came back to wait a while longer for U488 and then, if that boat failed to appear, to set up a rendezvous with U515 (Henke), which was supposed to be approaching that area outbound from France and had been scheduled to resupply from U488 five days earlier. Neither BdU nor Seehausen were aware that U515 had itself fallen victim to another US Navy hunter-killer group over two weeks earlier.[7] After another 24 hours, the Germans accepted the loss of U488 and a specific rendezvous was set between U66 and U515 for the 29th, two days hence. Three more days passed as U66 crept slowly northward. The rendezvous with U515, obviously, failed to occur and, on 30 April, an urgent message was sent to U68 (Lauzemis) and U188 (Lüdden) to meet with and replenish U66, which reported that it was down to 3m³ of fuel. U68 was supposed to reach Seehausen later on the 30th and U188 sometime after that.

The next day, 1 May 1944, BdU was scrambling to cope with another missed rendezvous. U68 had failed to appear at the appointed time and place. Once again, BdU was moving chess pieces blindly on his situation maps, unaware that, as often as not, the boat in question had gone to a watery grave days or weeks previously.[8] The Germans knew that their boats were losing the war against Allied air-power; they were still ignorant of the totality of the devastation. Now aware that U68 had disappeared in the waters off Africa, BdU turned to his last available candidate to resupply Seehausen. U188 was itself nearing the end of a long return voyage from Penang and barely had enough provisions to reach France, but there was no choice but to order it to share what little it had. An elaborate scheme was worked out whereby

U188 is to give half its fuel and provisions to U66. The boats can exist for three weeks on this. U198 and U543 are to proceed full speed to DR 60.[9] The boats should meet in about nine days. The boat to arrive first in this area is to supply U188 and U66 with fuel and provisions.[10]

There was little that Seehausen could do now but wait for U188 to show up. This meeting was scheduled for 5 May. If this boat failed to materialise, U66 might end up adrift. U188 was in fact still afloat, but it was running late. From the 1st onward, U66 was again almost continually under surveillance from the air by single-engine naval aircraft passing overhead, indicating the presence of an aircraft carrier nearby. There was indeed a carrier-based hunter-killer group in the vicinity. The group, based on USS *Block Island* (CVE-21) had been sent to that spot because, once again, a combination of direction finding and signals intelligence had deduced that two U-boats were to meet in the near future at that location.

In the early morning of 6 May, U66 surfaced, under a clear moonlit sky, only to find itself less than 5000m away from the carrier. Seehausen took the boat down again immediately.[11] In a subsequent radio message to BdU, Seehausen reported attempting an attack on *Block Island*, but none of the survivors recall such an attempt being made. U66 had, however, been detected by *Block Island*'s radar and the carrier turned away at high speed and dispatched an escort, USS *Buckley* (DE-51), to investigate. *Buckley* had no luck finding the target until, at 0530 on the 6th, a night-adapted TBM-1C Avenger spotted U66 moving at high speed on the surface, now some 18nm away from *Block Island*.[12] Seehausen apparently had decided that his only hope was to put as much distance between himself and the carrier as quickly as possible, despite the obvious risk of detection and the drain on his dwindling fuel reserves. The Avenger had been specially adapted by maintenance crew on *Block Island* for all-night reconnaissance flights. The modification of the Avenger involved the removal of all armament and the fitting of extra fuel cells. Thus, the only weapon carried by that aircraft was the pilot's side-arm, but U66 had no way of knowing that. The U-boat's lookouts didn't spot the Avenger until it was quite close, and at that point Seehausen decided that it was too late to dive. But, instead of attacking, the Avenger pulled up and began circling, so Seehausen decided to press his luck and stay on the surface as long as possible. Every minute increased the charge on his batteries and would add to the boat's submerged endurance when he did have to dive. While the Avenger circled, U66 got off two messages to BdU. One simply reported the presence of the shadower. The other was even shorter and more disturbing to BdU:

Central Atlantic worse than Biscay.[13]

For almost an hour, the Avenger circled and U66 made full speed away from the carrier group. The Avenger would periodically manoeuvre as if commencing a bomb run and U66 would respond with evasive manoeuvres and a few rounds from its 2cm guns. While this was going on, *Buckley* was making its top speed of 23kt towards the location of the Avenger. At 0545, *Buckley*'s radar picked up the U-boat at 14,000m. At 0608, *Buckley* saw what it believed were three red flares being fired by the U-boat, but in fact they were tracer rounds from the 2cm guns, which were being fired at the Avenger. Manoeuvring to keep the U-boat in line with the moon, the escort's crew was rewarded when U66 was sighted, silhouetted against the moonlit ocean, at 0617, at a range of 4000m. *Buckley* held fire as long as it could, but when the range had dropped to a little over 2000m, U66 sighted the escort and opened fire with its 2cm guns. Moments later *Buckley* opened up with its forward 3in guns and the battle was joined.

An Old-Fashioned Brawl

It was a terribly uneven fight and the outcome could hardly have been in doubt for an instant, but there were nevertheless a few exciting moments before it was over. *Buckley*'s first round sealed the U-boat's fate. One of the two 3in shells hit U66 just forward of the conning tower, holing the pressure hull and rendering the boat unable to dive. The range closed rapidly and soon reached the point that *Buckley* could no longer bring its 3in guns to bear because they couldn't depress far enough. Even without its main battery, the escort kept up a withering fire with its 40mm and 20mm secondary armament, effectively suppressing any return fire from the U-boat. Sometime in these first few minutes, Seehausen realised the impossibility of his situation and ordered the boat to be abandoned. Few men were able to comply at this point because of the continual fire from *Buckley*'s secondary battery sweeping the U-boat's deck.

By 0627, *Buckley* had drawn even with the U-boat and they both continued for a brief moment side-by-side, barely 10m apart. The escort continued to pump 40mm and 20mm shells into the U-boat, but it showed no sign of sinking or even slowing down. *Buckley*'s captain, concerned that the U-boat might still, at this point, dive and thus escape, had to act decisively. He ordered hard right rudder and the escort responded quickly. Its bow swung quickly to starboard and rode up over U66's foredeck, locking the two antagonists together. What happened next was like a scene from the days of wooden ships:

> Men began swarming out of the submarine and up on *Buckley*'s forecastle with their hands up. Machine gun, tommy gun, and rifle fire knocks off several before ship's company realise U-boat's crew is surrendering. (There were several hand-to-hand engagements at this moment. One boarder fell over the side as the climax of a fist fight with a pharmacist's mate. Another was brained by a gunner with an empty shell case.) *Buckley* suffers only one casualty of engagement when man bruises fist knocking one of enemy over the side.[14]

Concerned that his ship was indeed being boarded, as in the days of wooden ships, *Buckley*'s captain ordered his engines stopped and U66 slipped out from under the escort and, engines still running at full speed, pulled away towards *Buckley*'s port side. Again, *Buckley* was ordered to full speed and within minutes the two antagonists were once more side-by-side, with fire from the escort's 20mm and 40mm guns raking the U-boat over the escort's starboard side. Twenty-five metres separated the two. Anyone foolish enough to attempt to come out of the U-boat's tower hatch was instantly the target of a devastating hail of fire.

Chaos must have reigned inside U66. The original tower watch, including Seehausen, were all long since dead or had jumped overboard at the commander's first order to abandon the boat. Below, in the tower and control room, crewmen were waiting for a break in the fusillade to try to make their escape through the tower. At this point, deliberately or, more probably, by accident, the boat swerved suddenly to port and hit *Buckley* amidships.[15] The U-boat's bow slid under *Buckley* in the way of her forward engine room. Fearful that the U-boat might damage his rudder and propellers, *Buckley*'s captain ordered his starboard engine stopped and his rudder hard right in order to swing his ship away from the U-boat as quickly as possible.

U66 slowly scraped along *Buckley*'s starboard side, rolled over by the drag of hull scraping against hull so that, at one point, the U-boat was leaning at a 60deg angle. Meanwhile, some resourceful torpedomen on *Buckley* broke out the ship's supply of hand grenades and several were lobbed at U66's tower, including one that was seen to drop through the tower hatch before it exploded in the conning tower. A number of crewmen waiting to escape were killed in the blast, as were, in all likelihood, the two British prisoners off *John Holt*.[16]

Incredibly, U66 survived its two collisions with *Buckley* and as the escort swung free, the boat righted itself and started forward again at high speed. By now it was a macabre sight. Its upperworks were battered and holed and flames were shooting out of its forward and tower hatches. By now, anyone who was still alive and capable of escaping had done so. As *Buckley*'s crew watched in fascination, the U-boat slipped under the surface at full speed and with hatches open. Three minutes later a loud explosion was heard from far below the surface, followed by several smaller explosions and then silence.

In total, 36 survivors of U66 went into American captivity. Twenty-four, including Seehausen and the two British prisoners didn't survive. Eleven of the survivors were wounded, none seriously. *Buckley* was damaged, though not critically. Specifically, her bow was bent and the shell plating on her starboard side was buckled in a number of places. She maintained her place in *Block Island*'s screen for two more days, transferring her prisoners to the carrier, before she was detached at midnight on the 7th and made her way independently to Bermuda and then to New York.

Before U66's prisoners were transferred, there proved to be some difficulty retrieving the personal effects of the men who boarded *Buckley*'s forecastle and surrendered there. (It was normal practice for the Intelligence Officer to gather all the contents of prisoners' pockets and keep possession of them until the prisoners were landed, both as an aid to their immediate interrogation and as a possible source of information.)

In the natural confusion attendant upon them being boarded before dawn by fifteen or more Nazis, having to get them under control while finishing off a still active submarine, and picking up the remainder of the survivors, it appears that *Buckley*'s crew had a chance to make a start towards getting souvenirs. However, order was soon restored. The prisoners were segregated by rank: officers, petty officers, and enlisted men. All personal effects were confiscated; *Buckley*'s crew were required to yield up the articles that had been taken from the prisoners.[17]

For the Germans, even before the loss of U66, and before Seehausen's comment on the ever-present danger from the air in the Central Atlantic,

Dönitz had reached the only possible conclusion. At sea replenishment of U-boats had simply become far too dangerous.

> All boats have received instructions to commence return passage in good time so that they can reach port without refuelling.[18]

Interlude
U821

The Death Ride
The continuing dominance of Allied air-power over the Atlantic forced Dönitz to seek innovative solutions. Something had to protect his boats against the constant danger from the sky. By early 1944, it had reached the point where the issue wasn't even whether his boats could wage an effective campaign against Allied shipping; it was whether his boats could even survive the passage to and from the battle zone. BdU had ordered that all boats passing through regularly patrolled areas, like the Bay of Biscay, should proceed submerged, surfacing only long enough to charge batteries. But even this proved unworkable, since the recharge took several hours and the density of the air patrol over the bay was such that a boat was often located by aircraft within minutes of surfacing. Boats would eventually be forced to the surface because their batteries were depleted and they'd been unable to recharge them sufficiently. Once up, unable to submerge again, they had no choice but take their chances with the aircraft and, all too often, they lost.

The best solution would be to discover a way of running the diesels while the boat remained submerged. They could be run off the air within the boat for only a few minutes. Clearly, a much bigger air supply was required. The German Navy had been experimenting with a number of advanced designs, such as the Walter and closed-cycle boats, but none of these were close to being ready for deployment and that still left the problem of how to carry on the war while a radically new boat was designed and put into mass-production. (The Walter process used hydrogen peroxide (H_2O_2) as a source of oxygen, broken down by a catalyst into oxygen (O_2) and water (H_20) and used to create high-pressure steam which drove a turbine. The closed-cycle designs used large quantities of compressed oxygen, stored in banks of high-pressure cylinders, as the air supply for specially modified diesels. Both designs showed promise, but had many complex and difficult engineering and production problems.)

In the event, these totally new concepts were too ambitious to be practical and new boats of a somewhat less radical design were indeed designed and mass-produced, based not on a new idea but rather several concepts which had been around for some time. The new boats were the Type XXI and XXIII designs which entered production in 1944 and were just reaching operational status at war's end. These new types relied heavily on one particular idea that showed promise not only for the new boats, but, even better, could be retrofitted to the existing fleet of Type VIIs and IXs while the new boats were being built.

This was the snorkel (officially *Schnorchel* in German or *Snort* for short).[1] It wasn't even a German idea. A Dutch naval officer had been experimenting with the idea of an air-mast, capable of supplying air to a submarine's diesels and carrying away exhaust gases, since 1933. By the time his country was overrun by the Germans in 1940, he had refined the concept to include hinging the mast, so that it could be lowered when not needed, and a ball-float valve at the top of the mast to prevent the entry of water if it dipped below the surface. Snorkel-equipped Dutch boats fell into both German and British hands in 1940 after the collapse of the Netherlands. Both countries put the interned boats into service after removing the snorkels, for which they saw little use. The Germans went so far as to test one of the snorkel-equipped boats they captured, the former Dutch O26, before removing the mast. They concluded it was technically interesting but of no immediate utility.

However, the emergence of Allied air-power during 1943 as a decisive weapon forced a re-evaluation of the snorkel's utility. But snorkels, once it was decided that they represented the best response to the aerial threat, took some time to be designed, manufactured, delivered and fitted to front-line boats. U821 (Knackfuß), like other late-production Type VIIs, had no snorkel when it arrived at Bergen, Norway, from training in the Baltic and it still had none when it left Bergen on its first war patrol on 19 March 1944.

Nothing could indicate how dramatically the situation had changed for the German wolf-packs in less than a year than to observe the reduced expectations that accompanied U821 on its first patrol. The boat's orders were to establish a patrol area approximately 400nm west of Ireland. There were now so few boats in the North Atlantic, barely more than a dozen, and the defences now so intense, that it was impractical and even dangerous to form those boats into groups. Just as they had in the first days of the war, boats hunted alone. Only now, their chances of success were small indeed.

U821 departed Bergen and headed into the hostile sea. Until it was well west of Scotland, it proceeded primarily submerged, surfacing only long enough to recharge batteries. Most of the time, it progressed at only three or four knots, the maximum cruising speed allowed by its electric motors. As long as it proceeded in this manner, its daily progress would average only 60nm per day. Thus U821 crept slowly across the north of the British Isles, passing the Shetlands to the north and intending to pass the Faroes to the south.

Along the way, however, they discovered one of the inherent problems of oper-ating primarily submerged. In the days before inertial navigation, the only way to determine a boat's position accurately was to take a fix on the stars or the sun. Between such fixes, boats used dead reckoning to estimate their position based on the course and speed of the boat. It was understood that the inherent inaccuracy of dead reckoning was a direct function of time. The longer it had been since the last fix, the less accurately the boat's position was known. Normally, a boat would take a navigational fix every four hours, though, obviously, many things could interrupt that routine. Now that boats were required to remain submerged much of the time, it became more critical than ever for a boat periodically to fix its position.

One of the many things that could get in the way of taking a navigational fix was overcast skies, unfortunately quite common in the North Atlantic in March. When fixes were obtained on a four-hour cycle, missing one or even a whole day's worth of sightings wasn't critical. But the standard operating procedure now required boats to surface only once a day, for several hours to recharge batteries and, at the same time, take a fix. If, as happened to U821, several days passed with each chance for a navigational fix obscured by overcast, a boat could easily end up 50 or 100nm from its estimated position. Thus, as U821 approached the Faroes on its passage to the open ocean, they thought they were well to the south of the islands, but, in fact, they were headed directly towards the group. (The ocean currents in that part of the Atlantic flow mainly north or north-east, which would account for the mistake.)

The first they knew of the navigational error was when they heard one of the most dreaded sounds a submariner can hear, the slow scrape of a wire along the side of the hull. Everyone knew instantly what that meant. U821 had stumbled into a minefield. For a veteran crew that would be frightening enough. For a new boat composed mainly of kids with very little experience in a U-boat, the effect could be paralysing. There simply was no way of knowing how far into the field you were or what course and depth would point to safety. You just had to wait and mutter supplications to whatever force you believed rules the world and wait for the scraping to stop or for the sea to crash in on you. (Stabsobermaschinist Warnecke, a veteran with long years of experience, was so terrified that, according to a witness, Ernst Schmidt, his hair turned from coal black to pure white in a matter of 15 minutes. It later grew in black again.)

Ernst Schmidt, U821's IWO, sensed that the crew was near breaking point and needed something to calm them down. Schmidt returned to his bunk and extracted an old felt hat which he wore on patrol as a good luck charm. He announced in a loud voice, so that everyone around him would hear, that he was tired and was going to lie down and nap. He then stretched out on his bunk in the wardroom, drew the hat over his eyes and was snoring a minute later. The effect was exactly as he had hoped. His nonchalance and ability to fall asleep even as mine cables scraped against the boat's hull was precisely the model of calm and steadiness the crew needed to keep their nerve. Hours later, when the danger had passed, Schmidt got up, carefully stashed his lucky hat back in his wardrobe and took his watch in the control room.

U821 passed safely the rest of the way around the British Isles and arrived at its operational area south of Iceland at the end of March. However, it was immediately recalled because the Germans had determined that a major invasion of France was in the offing and they were gathering U-boats at Brest to be ready to attack the invasion fleet. The passage to France was supposed to have followed the same routine of cruising primarily submerged and surfacing only to charge batteries. However, Knackfuß had other ideas. He was aware of the problems other boats had faced crossing the Bay of Biscay and opted to take his chances on the surface. Above all, he wanted to avoid the dilemma of those boats that surfaced with depleted batteries and never had a chance to recharge them. His plan was to spend the night submerged and to surface at first light, making best speed towards the coast. He wouldn't submerge at the first sign of radar detection. The accumulating experience of those boats equipped with the improved FuMO 30 GEMA radar was that many aircraft whose radars could be detected by a U-boat's radar detectors had in fact not detected the U-boat, so that diving at each detection was unnecessary.[2] Rather, he would rely on the trained eyes of his lookouts and wait until an aircraft was actually sighted before diving. (The reason for this is a function of the physics of radar. Radar signals are simply short bursts of radio waves, which fall off in power as a function of distance until they become undistinguishable from background noise. A radar, when it detects a target, is picking up a reflected signal, i.e. a signal that has travelled twice the distance from the sending antenna to the target and is much attenuated by the process of reflection off the target. Reflection off a curved surface, such as a U-boat's hull, scatters and further weakens the signal. Thus the theoretical maximum target detection range for a radar is half the range at which an unreflected signal would become too weak to be distinguished by a receiver, such as a German radar detector. In practical terms, the effective range at which a radar could detect a U-boat may be a quarter or less than the range at which a radar detector would pick up a signal. Obviously, a radar detector, when it first picked up a signal, was almost certainly detecting a radar far beyond the range at which the radar could detect the U-boat.)

For the most part, Knackfuß's plan worked. It wasn't until the last day, as the boat approached Brest, that his luck ran out. The day had become increasingly cloudy and the overcast dropped lower, but the boat pressed on despite the danger this involved. Finally, a Sunderland dropped out of the clouds behind the boat, too close to give it time to dive. Schmidt, who had the watch, was able to get the guns manned and to put up enough defensive fire to cause the attacker to swerve before any bombs could be dropped. The pilot put his plane into a long slow curve and then started a bomb run from in front of the boat, hoping to avoid U821's flak. Schmidt waited until the last moment and then turned the boat, giving his gun-crews a shot at the approaching bomber. They were able to put a few rounds into the Sunderland and must have caused some damage, because the aircraft pulled away and then coasted to a landing on the water. By this time Knackfuß had come up on the bridge, had sized up the situation and had ordered the boat to dive. Once underwater, he took a look through the periscope, observed the Sunderland floating quietly on the water for a few minutes and then ordered that the boat's small arms, consisting of four rifles and three or four pistols, be broken out and the boat be resurfaced. The sky appeared to be clear, and he started to bring the boat over to the floating aircraft when another Sunderland was seen to drop out of the clouds. Deciding that discretion in this case was very much the better part of valour, he dived the boat and departed the scene. Later that day, he surfaced the boat again and completed the run in towards Brest. Arriving at Point A, where escorts generally met incoming U-boats, he found no waiting escort. He radioed the port commander for assistance and was informed that there must have been a mistake, that U821 wasn't expected for two more weeks.

U821 arrived at Brest on 12 April, having seen no enemies and fired no torpedoes. It remained in Brest, awaiting the invasion, for almost two months. During this long period, Ernst Schmidt renewed an old acquaintance with KK Winter, commanding officer of the 1st Flotilla, who ordered Schmidt detached and sent to *Komandantschule*, the training school for prospective commanders.[3] Because of that fortuitous assignment, he lived to tell his story. His former mates on U821, with only one exception, were not so lucky.

Finally, on 6 June 1944, the massive Allied invasion of Normandy began and U821 was sent out, along with 34 other U-boats, with orders to disrupt the invasion by any means. Most of the boats were from Brest, but others left Lorient and St-Nazaire at the same time. One was delayed and didn't depart Brest until the next day. Of those 36 boats, eight were snorkel-equipped and were given orders to penetrate as far as they could into the bay of the Seine and sink as many transports from the invasion fleet as possible. These boats at least had a chance. The rest, Dönitz knew full well, would be up against the most concentrated defensive screen the Allies could muster and their chances of even getting close to fleet were nil. He was sending them on a death ride.

(There was a noble precedent for just such a death ride. In the battle of Jutland in May 1916, Admiral Scheer, the German fleet commander, guided his fleet into a deadly trap, where the head of his battle-line was steaming right into the centre of the massed Grand Fleet. His only option was to turn his line and his only chance of performing that manoeuvre without disastrous losses was to find a way to distract the British fire. To cover his retreat, he ordered his four remaining operational battlecruisers on what became known popularly in German as their 'death ride'. These four warships swung across the line of vision of the British, drawing the fire of the entire fleet on themselves until, battered but still intact, they were able to disappear into the smoke of their own fires. The difference between May 1916 and June 1944 was that the battlecruisers' death ride achieved a very worth-while purpose – the extrication against all odds of the vast bulk of the German fleet. It remained to be seen whether the sacrifice of the U-boats at Brest and in the other French ports would achieve anything approaching the legendary success of the battlecruisers at Jutland.)

Dönitz's feelings were expressed in so many words in his order to the Group *Landwirt*, the boats assigned to attack the invasion fleet:[4]

> This morning Commander-in-Chief of the Navy ordered whole of Group *Landwirt* to sea and all-out operations. As issues of invasion will have decisive effect on the war, all boats lying in Brest, both with and <u>without</u> *Schnorchel* put into the Channel. For those boats without Schnorchel this means the last operation.[5]

The non-snorkel boats were given theoretically safer patrol quadrants, near the south coast of England, away from the immediate invasion area, but they were attacked repeatedly and remorselessly by RAF squadrons assigned the specific task of keeping U-boats away from the fleet. In the first day alone, six of the *Landwirt* boats reported nine separate air attacks. Fortunately, none of these attacks were successful, but more were to come. However, four non-snorkel boats from Brest were damaged to the point that they had to put back into port. Two more boats (one with snorkel) returned the next day, leaving 30 boats to continue this dubious operation.

> The risky operation of boats in the Channel, above all those without *Schnorchel*, had to be undertaken in this decisive situation. . .
>
> The operation is especially difficult for boats without *Schnorchel*. The return of six of these boats already is no evidence to the contrary, since they put to sea on the surface in order to reach operations area quickly and were bombed in so doing.[6]

The attacks continued unabated on the 8th and, on this day, the RAF had spectac-ular success, sinking no fewer than three U-boats from the *Landwirt* group, all of them non-snorkel boats. Two more boats (one with snorkel) put back into Brest the next day and another was sunk by aircraft. Now, only U821, of the nine non-snorkel boats which had departed Brest, was still in the Channel. At 1300 on the 10th, the staff of the German observation post on Ushant watched in horror as a swarm of RAF Mosquitoes repeatedly attacked a U-boat which had surfaced just eight miles north of the island.[7] The boat under attack was U821 and the attack was efficient and successful. Repeated strafing runs caused the tower crew to jump overboard and prevented any attempt to man the boat's guns. A Liberator then appeared on the scene and made two bombing runs, the second of which straddled the U-boat and, when the waterspouts fell back to the surface, U821 was gone. U-boat command hadn't heard from U821 for several days and it can only be assumed that the boat was returning to port in damaged condition. An R-boot rescued some of the crew but was in turn sunk by aircraft from the same RAF squadron. Eventually, one wounded chief was rescued early the following morning.

Of the 17 boats that had left Brest on the 6th and 7th, eight with snorkels and nine without, four of them had now been lost (all non-snorkel boats) and seven more had put back into port in damaged condition (two of which were snorkel-equipped). With remarkable efficiency, the RAF had demonstrated to Dönitz beyond any doubt that the day of the U-boat operating on the surface was over.

On account of the great number of air attacks, above all on boats without *Schnorchel*, and the extensive damage caused thereby, for the present, further sailings of these boats has been stopped.[8]

U371

The Technical War

Earlier in the war, when U371 had first entered service, the technology of U-boat warfare was relatively simple. U371 was a Type VIIC which had been launched in January 1941 and left on its first patrol, under OLzS (later KL) Heinrich Driver, in early June 1941. Back then, the war was still being fought much as it had been in 1939. U-boats, when there were enough at sea, formed groups to scout and, if a convoy was found, to swarm and attack. Of course, finding convoys seemed to be getting harder. Somehow, even though there were more U-boats and more convoys, the enemy appeared to have an uncanny ability to route convoys away from the U-boat groups. (Between the rapidly improving HF/DF [High Frequency/Direction Finding] system set up by the British and the increasingly timely stream of 'Ultra' decrypts coming from Bletchley Park, the British could by mid-1941 pinpoint the location and movements of the German wolf-packs with considerable accuracy.)

But when the U-boat groups found a target, the tactics were the same as they had been from the beginning. The boat that first sighted a convoy would act as a beacon, sending out homing signals on a high-frequency band to help the rest of the pack find the target. As the second and subsequent boats came on the scene, they were free to attack as soon as the opportunity arose. In general, attacks were made at night and on the surface, counting on the U-boats' small size to render them undetectable by the convoy's lookouts. The human eye was the sole resource available to the convoy and its defenders to locate approaching U-boats. One of the reasons for attacking on the surface was because sonar is ineffective at locating surfaced U-boats. The more U-boats that could attack at the same time, the better. This was because multiple attacks spread confusion and reduced the chances of evasive manoeuvring by the convoy, and also because multiple attacks spread the defences, increasing the odds that attacks could be made without interference. Each U-boat acted entirely independently of any other that might be on scene. Targets were lined up and torpedoes fired without regard for any other boat that might be attacking at the same time. The odds of one U-boat's torpedoes hitting another U-boat were infinitesimally small. (There are no verified cases of a U-boat being lost to torpedoes fired by another U-boat. There were a few instances of U-boats colliding with each other while attacking a convoy. A small number of U-boat losses remain unexplained and may be the result of fratricide. There is one case in which it is believed that a U-boat torpedoed itself. This will be described later in this chapter.)

The torpedoes that a U-boat fired in 1941 were still relatively simple machines. There were two basic torpedo types: the air-driven G7a and the electric G7e. U-boatmen preferred the electrics because they left no tell-tale trail of exhaust bubbles, but G7as were produced in small quantities throughout the war because they had greater range and because they could be stored in a U-boat's external storage tubes. G7es required daily maintenance to remain functional. In particular they had to be recharged daily or their batteries deteriorated. This kind of care couldn't be lavished on torpedoes stored externally. The torpedoes carried at the beginning of the war caused a myriad of problems, leading Dönitz at one point to state that 'the failure of the torpedoes is the cause of our lack of success'.[1] These problems suffered by early torpedoes included premature detonation and multiple failures of the magnetic exploder. They proved to be difficult to cure because they were caused by a number of seemingly unrelated problems whose effects often masked other deficits.[2] Gradually, the problems were isolated and fixed. Eventually, by late 1942 a thoroughly reliable electric torpedo, the T3, was in the hands of U-boatmen.

Setting up and firing one of these torpedoes was also a fairly straightforward, albeit time-consuming, affair. U-boats operated with relative impunity on the surface at night and, thus, had the time to go through the lengthy set-up process. This included: identifying targets, estimating the bearing, course, speed, tonnage and draft of the selected targets, entering that information in the attack computer, waiting a minute or two for the computer to generate a solution, designating which tubes would be fired and then waiting a while longer for the settings to be entered into the torpedoes and the torpedoes' gyros to sync. After all that, if the target hadn't changed course in the interim, the torpedoes were fired and the crew waited for explosions and sinking sounds. Once a torpedo was fired, it would run straight for a pre-set distance and then turn to a new course that would take it towards the target. The whole process required time and skill and constant practice. If you missed the target, the torpedoes would run in a straight line until they ran out of fuel or electricity, and then they would sink.

The Mediterranean Misadventure

It was this world into which U371 emerged, but it was a world that was already changing. The boat's first two patrols under Driver were standard North Atlantic convoy battles. They were moderately successful, with one sinking on the first patrol from Kiel to Brest and two more on its second patrol from the

French port.[3] Before departing on its third patrol, however, other strategic issues got in the way. The Germans had become involved in North Africa after Italian attempts to expand its holdings from its colony in Libya ran afoul of stiff British resistance. Having driven British forces from Greece and then Crete, the Germans found themselves facing the same troops in North Africa. Rommel's first great offensive towards Egypt bogged down during the summer of 1941, due primarily to effective British naval and air attacks on his supply convoys from Europe which cut his supply line. Hitler reacted by ordering Dönitz to send U-boats into the Mediterranean. Much against his will, Dönitz complied, ordering the first group of six boats, *Gruppe Goeben*, to slip through the Straits of Gibraltar, starting in late September, do what damage they could to Royal Navy units they encountered and then continue operations based at Salamis, near Athens. One of that first group was U371.

The Mediterranean had been the site of great successes for German U-boats in the First World War, and it was where Dönitz himself had fought, but he was extremely reluctant to send any boats into that sea. The primary reason was his knowledge that any diversion of effort from the North Atlantic would be of infinitely greater aid to the enemy than could be recouped by any level of success in the Mediterranean. Also, he knew that these boats wouldn't find the rich traffic on which they had feasted in the first war. In that war, both France and Italy had been Germany's enemies and a large percentage of the victims of such aces as Lothar von Arnauld de la Perière or Walther Forstmann had been traffic carrying goods northward from the North African colonies of those countries. A lot more had been British shipping carrying goods from the east, through the Suez Canal, heading for southern France and the Western Front. None of that traffic would be there this time. But orders were orders, particularly when they came from Hitler himself, and Dönitz did as he was told. The effect on the convoy battles was devastating. As of 1 January 1942, 23 U-boats, including many of the newest, had been transferred into the Mediterranean. That was fully one-quarter of his operational boats.[4]

When those first boats in the *Goeben* group broke through the Straits, the defences were still fairly loose and perhaps a bit too relaxed, since no boats had attempted to pass through in the first two years of the war. The following was typical of these first passages through Gibraltar:

| 1200 | Sector CG9575[5] | Location: 35° 58,5' N; 6° 20 W' A look around at periscope depth; a fishing trawler in view, probably a picket, at a bearing of 70°, 5000m off; creep slowly until it is at bearing 170°, changing course occasionally.[6] |
| 1600 | Sector CG 9582 | The mountains on the Spanish side, as well as |

on the African, come into plain view. Near
shore, some mist.

2000   Sector CG 9591   As of 2000, running at periscope depth. The
full moon shining, virtually daylight; the
current is giving us a good push forward,
despite it being low tide. The Cape Spartel light
at least is visible on the right side.[7] Our course
now wanders somewhat towards the European
shore. Tangiers to the starboard, 9nm across.
After dusk, surfaced to ventilate the boat and
proceeded on the surface. Cloudless, starry
night. The night is lit up so brightly by the light
of the full moon that we can easily make out
almost every detail on shore on both sides of
the Strait. As long as we stay on the surface,
there is unfortunately nothing to be done
about it.

Because it is so bright, we submerged in order
to continue the passage underwater. At first,
proceeded at periscope depth; Tarifa to port
3.9nm across.[8] Starting 2140, continued at 20m,
looking around every half-hour.

Destroyers to starboard bearing 210°, lying 90
and 900-1000m off, crept away quickly. It would
have been impossible to come to a complete
stop at high tide. The listening device picked
up no sound. Heading of the destroyers 50°,
high speed.

Out of sight.

0000   Sector CG 9593   At bearing 357° about 5000m off, a steamer
without At bearing 357° about 5000m off, a
steamer without neutrality-markings in Morse-
communication with picket. The steamer is
heading for Ceuta.[9]

Distant explosions heard.

Directly across from the lights of Ceuta.
Distance 2.1nm. At bearing 220° with heading
320°, a steamer about 600t, 4000m off. Heavy
smoke. Surfaced under the cover of this cloud
of smoke; Ceuta lighthouse is at bearing 225°,
2.4nm off; ran above water at full speed.

		Gibraltar is very easy to identify. Newspaper reading is possible on the bridge without difficulty.
0400	Sector CG 9675	Thicker fog.

U371 was the first of the boats through, passing the Straits on the night of 21 September 1941. The remaining boats all passed through in the next two weeks without any serious problems. The British learned quickly, however, and barely two months later, U96, commanded by Lehmann-Willenbrock, was badly damaged and forced to turn back by the now much stiffer defences.[10]

Once in the Mediterranean, U371 headed for Salamis. Along the way, it was diverted to the site of the sinking of *Albatros*, an old Italian torpedo boat. *Albatros* had been completed in 1934 as a submarine chaser, but was later reclassified as a torpedo boat. Ironically, she was used during the war in her original role. Even more ironically, she was sunk by the British submarine *Upright* on 27 September off Sicily. U371 rescued 42 survivors and then resumed its course for Salamis.

Patrols in the Mediterranean tended to be shorter, because the distances to and from operational zones were much less than in the Atlantic. U371 conducted patrols off the coast of Lebanon and Palestine and also off Algeria, operating out of Salamis. In March 1942, Driver was replaced by OLzS Karl-Otto Weber, and Weber, in turn, was succeeded on 21 April 1942 by KL Heinz-Joachim Neumann. (Weber and Neumann appear to have been interim commanders only.[11]) On 24 May, U371 was taken over by KL Waldemar Mehl, who commanded the boat until April 1944, almost exactly two years. During that time, U371 changed home ports, to Pola temporarily and then to La Spezia and later still, after the invasion of Italy, to Toulon. Under Mehl, the boat was very successful, sinking nine ships, including three warships, and damaging four more.[12] His biggest prize was the American destroyer USS *Bristol*, sunk on 13 October 1943 off the coast of Algeria. On 25 March 1944, U371, by now a veteran of 17 operational patrols, returned to Toulon. Mehl and his crew left the boat at this point. Mehl took a position on the staff of *FdU Mittelmeer* (Commander U-boats Mediterranean) and the crew returned to Germany to be distributed among the crews of the new, advanced boats that would soon be joining the fleet.

On 6 May 1943, U410, a boat whose fate would be intimately linked with U371, broke through the Straits of Gibraltar and entered the Mediterranean. This boat had been originally commanded by KL Kurt Sturm, who later took over U167 (see Chapter 8). By the time it entered the Mediterranean, it was under the command of OLzS Horst-Arno Fenski, who led U410 for the last five of its seven patrols. Fenski had more success than Sturm in command of U410.

All told, he accounted for eight ships, including the Royal Navy light cruiser HMS *Penelope*, and damaged one other steamer.[13] Like Mehl, he was awarded the Knight's Cross for his successes.

While in the Mediterranean, U410 operated from the U-boat base at Toulon. It was there that, on 11 March 1944, it was seriously damaged while docked in port. Eleven days later, it was officially written off and decommissioned. Fenski and his crew, temporarily without a boat, simply moved over to U371 when Mehl brought it in on the 25th. Thus it was Fenski who took U371 out on its next and last patrol.

Smart New Weapons for a Much More Dangerous World

While Mehl and Fenski had been achieving success in the Mediterranean, the world in which U-boats operated had changed dramatically. The vast technical resources available to the Allies were threatening to overwhelm Dönitz's U-boat forces. Nothing, it seemed, was as simple and easy as it had been in 1941. The seemingly omnipresent air cover over convoys, described in so many of the preceding chapters, was a constant threat to any U-boat operating on the surface. But that was by no means the only threat to U-boats. The amazing ability of the British and the Americans to build anti-submarine vessels meant that all convoys were closely protected and enough escorts existed to form attack groups which could be detached from a convoy's escort screen to stay with a contact until it was destroyed.

But the many aircraft and the many escorts would have been far less effective were it not for the many advances in sensor technology which stole the night from the wolf-packs. By early 1943, every escort ship and every patrol aircraft was equipped with radar of sufficiently high resolution and range that a U-boat could be detected at a range of 1.5nm or greater, depending on the height of the antenna. The introduction of higher frequency radars on both aircraft and ships in 1943 doubled the effective range of the radar and increased resolution to the point that a periscope could be detected in a calm sea. Against sensors of that quality, U-boats lost the ability to remain on the surface near convoys. And with that loss came a dramatic reduction in the offensive capability of the U-boats.

Once a U-boat was forced to dive, the Allies had new sensors and weapons to use against a submerged boat. Sonars continued to improve in their resolution and capability. Sonar could find a target's range and bearing and a good operator could make a reliable estimate of its depth. By late in the war, depth finding sonar and doppler sonar were being deployed which also gave a target's depth and speed. However, the greatest advance was in weaponry. Besides the depth charge, anti-submarine ships were being fitted with forward-firing, contact-detonated weapons, such as the 24-barrel Hedgehog and three-barrel Squid. These fired a salvo of multiple small charges ahead of the escort. The main advantage of this new weapon was that it allowed sonar contact to be maintained with a target during an attack. Depth charges so disturbed the water that sonar was ineffective for some time after depth charges were dropped. Since they exploded only on contact, and not at a predetermined depth like a depth charge, a detonation with these new weapons indicated that the target had been found. A miss wouldn't explode and thus enabled sonar contact to be maintained. Airborne weapons improved with the introduction of the air-dropped homing torpedo called Fido in 1943.

In response to these technological advances, the Germans responded with defensive measures. Some of them were quite effective but all, ultimately, were intended to keep a U-boat safe. They didn't in any way make up for the dramatic lessening of the offensive potential of the U-boats. Against Allied radars, the Germans developed radar detectors. These were simply radio receivers tuned to the frequencies used by Allied radars. They would tell if a nearby radar was transmitting at a detectable level. This, however, wasn't the same as telling if a radar had indeed detected the U-boat. Experience using radar detectors showed that many times it detected radars on aircraft or ships which in fact hadn't detected the U-boat. So U-boat commanders learned to play a game with their radar detectors, not responding to the first indication of a radar's presence, but waiting for the signal to reach a certain strength or go into target mode. (By mid-war, airborne radars had separate search and targeting modes. These differed in that in search mode the radar beam was swept back and forth across the forward quadrant of the aircraft. To a radar detector with audio feedback, this mode had a characteristic warbling sound. When a target was found, the radar operator could fix the antenna in the direction of the echo. In this mode, the radar detector would give off a steady tone.) Anti-aircraft armament was steadily increased on U-boats, but except for a brief period in 1942, no one seriously thought that fighting back against aircraft was anything but a desperate last resort. Ultimately, the only meaningful protection against radar-directed attack was to dive.

The Germans developed some counter-measures against both radar and sonar detection that were quite technologically advanced. They deployed a radar-reflecting float called *Thetis* and a radar-reflecting balloon called *Aphrodite*. These were reasonably effective when first introduced, but Allied radar operators quickly found that *Thetis* reflections were steady and didn't move, and learned to ignore them. *Aphrodite* was more effective because it would drift with the wind and show some variability in the radar return, but it also acted differently than a U-boat would, and experienced operators learned to discriminate between the decoys and the real thing. Against sonar, they had a decoy called *Bold*, which generated a mass of bubbles that would reflect sonar just like a real U-boat. This was the most effective of the decoys. It was only defeated by doppler sonar, which could distinguish between a stationary bubble mass and a moving U-boat. The Germans also developed radar and sonar absorbent coatings for U-boats. Problems with manufacturing and adhesion prevented them from being widely used. (A number of these approaches have led directly to current technologies. For example, the stealth materials used on modern aircraft are the direct descendants of the anti-radar coatings developed by the Germans during the Second World War.)

Regardless of the technical sophistication of these engineering achievements, the upshot was that U-boats were getting less and less effective at doing what they were designed to do: sinking Allied merchant shipping. Increasingly, U-boats were being forced underwater, where their effectiveness was a mere fraction of what it had been when they still could operate on the surface. Snorkels allowed U-boats to operate submerged all the time, but experience quickly showed that while snorkel-equipped boats had a far better survival rate, they were no more effective at sinking enemy shipping. Besides, in 1944 most boats still didn't have snorkels. Better boats were coming. The Type XXI and Type XXIII boats were entering production, designed from the outset to operate continually submerged with snorkel and much enhanced battery equipment, but those boats were a year away from combat. In the meanwhile, U-boatmen still left port in Type VIIs and Type IXs designed for a very different technical environment.

To fight in those old boats in this new, far more dangerous battlefield required new tactics and new weapons. The old days of the leisurely set-up for firing torpedoes were long gone. U-boatmen learned to attack as best they could, approaching on the surface until forced to dive, firing their torpedoes quickly with minimal set-up and then retiring as quickly as possible. This new tactic required new torpedoes designed to operate as much as possible without the precise set-up needed by the old T3 and its predecessors. These torpedoes had to do a lot of the work themselves. In a very real sense, they were the precursors of the smart weapons increasingly found in today's arsenal.

The first of the new torpedoes was the FaT (*Flächenabsuchender Torpedo* – shallow-searching torpedo).[14] The idea behind the FaT was simple. The guidance of a standard G7a was altered so that, after a set distance of running straight like a standard torpedo, it would make a wide turn of 180deg and start back in the direction it came. After a leg of 800m or 1600m, it would turn again and head back parallel to the original course, but now two-turn widths from the original track. (The course run by a FaT was called a 'ladder course' because the back and forth legs ran a track that resembled the rungs of a ladder. Optionally, FaTs could be set to run a loop course rather than a ladder course by always turning in one direction rather than alternating the direction of the turns.) This turning back and forth, each leg offset by the diameter of the turn, would continue until the torpedo ran out of fuel or hit a target. Of course, it was to increase the chances of the latter that the FaT was invented. It was an elegant solution to a fundamental problem. U-boats no longer had enough time to properly aim a torpedo, and a poorly aimed torpedo, one which missed its intended target, was most likely wasted unless it happened to strike another target in another row of the convoy. The chances of that happening were small, but what if, instead of just running a straight course, the torpedo might loop back and have another try at the original target or at another ship in the convoy? That would have the effect of multiplying many-fold that slim chance of a hastily aimed torpedo hitting something.

The first FaT prototypes were demonstrated in September 1942 and by November, the first operational models, based on the long-running G7a, were being delivered to front-line boats. Of course, it wasn't just a matter of delivering the torpedoes. The attack computers and torpedo tubes had to be modified so that additional parameters (the length of the straight run, the length of the 'rungs' and the turn direction) could be input and passed to the torpedo in the tube. Also, commanders had to be trained how to use the new torpedo. New doctrines for attack were required as well. Because of the danger that FaTs might hit other attacking U-boats, an attacking U-boat was required, before firing a FaT, to radio a standard warning message on the medium-wave band. If another boat was attacking at the same time, it was supposed to dive to at least 50m or exit the area at high speed. No new attack was to be made for 30min after a FaT warning was issued. (These rules were overly cautious and were often ignored in combat. For example, the required 30min gap between attacks was about twice what was really needed, since a G7a, even on its most economical speed setting, could run for only slightly more than 15min before running out of fuel.)

FaTs were an immediate success, at least from the subjective point of view of U-boat commanders. The only problem with them was that there weren't enough to go around. The maximum monthly production of G7as was 350, and when the requirements of other uses were taken into account, only 100 were available to be made into FaTs each month. Dönitz needed more. So, despite the much shorter range of the G7e, that torpedo was used as the basis for the FaT II, identical in all other aspects to its air-powered predecessor. Initially, because of their shorter range, FaT IIs were intended as an interim anti-escort torpedo and were initially loaded only in the stern tube of a Type VII. The introduction of a longer-range variant of the basic G7e, the T3a, in early 1944, gave the FaT II sufficient range to serve as the standard anti-convoy torpedo, for a while at least. In mid-1944, all models of the FaT were superseded by the LuT (*Lagenunabhängiger Torpedo* – course independent torpedo), which added a second course-correction turn into the FaT's pattern, so that axis of the 'ladder' could be different from the course of the straight run. This added one more needed factor in setting up a shot and required further modification of the attack computer and torpedo tubes, but otherwise, it was sufficiently similar to the FaT to have not much impact on U-boat commanders or the success rate of their boats.

The anti-escort torpedo for which the original FaT II was considered a stand-in was the T5 *Zaunkönig*. (There was a T4, codenamed *Falke*, which was a design predecessor to the T5. It was produced in very limited quantities and was quickly replaced by the more capable T5.)[15] This was a standard electric torpedo fitted with an acoustic seeker head. The seeker was a simple affair, composed of two acoustic sensors placed side-by-side. The seeker's circuitry would compare the strength of the sound received by each sensor and steer the torpedo towards the stronger signal. This would cause the torpedo to turn until the other sensor picked up the louder noise, at which point it would turn back towards the other side. The net effect was that T5s would steer a snake-like course towards a target, swinging back and forth across the line leading towards the noise source.

The T5 was designed specifically for use in the situation, becoming more and more common in the Atlantic, in which a U-boat found itself on the surface and being pursued by a faster escort ship. In that situation, the U-boat was frequently doomed, because it had very little ability to fight back and no time to dive to safety. Some commanders tried firing a conventional torpedo out from the stern tube as a last desperate measure. The fortunate few who succeeded in hitting or at least diverting the pursuit freely acknowledged that it was luck rather than skill that had won them a chance to do it all over again. The T5, because it would home in on the loudest noise it could hear, would naturally be attracted to the sound of the onrushing escort.

When the T5 was introduced, it was immediately popular with commanders. Unlike the FaT or LuT, it required no modification to the attack computer or the torpedo tubes, since it had no settings. The only 'rule' that had to be followed when firing a T5 was that the boat had to dive immediately and to at least 60m. Because the T5 had been designed as a last-ditch defensive weapon, it was given a very short arming distance, only 400m. At that distance, if the U-boat continued at high speed on the surface, the loudest noise the T5 would sense might well be the U-boat itself. The only defence against a T5 looping back against the boat that fired it was to dive to sufficient depth. This was an annoyance to many commanders, especially since later analysis showed that most fired their T5s at a range of 3000m. Unlike the case with the FaT or LuT, whose firing regimes many commanders politely ignored, the danger of a T5 looping back was very real and the requirement to dive after firing one was ignored only at grave risk to the boat. (There is one instance in which it is considered likely that a U-boat sank itself with a T5. The loss of U377 on about 15 January 1944 while attacking a naval task group has never been and probably never will be explained, but there are indications that it was sunk by torpedo and the task group it was attacking fired none during that time period.)[16]

T5s had some success when they were introduced. In September 1943, T5s were used to try to defeat the escort of convoy ON.202 and did manage to sink one destroyer and sank or damaged three other escorts. Not nearly the success that the Germans had hoped for, but still impressive and a cause for considerable concern on the part of the Allies. By the end of the year, the Allies were deploying an effective counter-measure, the so-called Foxer, which was a pair of towed noise-makers intended to draw a T5 away from the ship. It was far from perfect and was difficult and time-consuming to deploy and take in, so the T5 continued to have some success throughout the rest of the war.

A High-Tech Arsenal

Thus it was with a full load of these new and clever torpedoes that U371, now under Fenski, left Toulon on 23 April 1944 on its way to a familiar hunting ground off the coast of Algeria. It carried a full internal load of 12 torpedoes: 10 in the forward torpedo tubes and torpedo compartment and two aft. Three of these torpedoes were T5s: one loaded in the aft torpedo tube (Tube V); one stored as a reload under the floor plates of the aft torpedo room, and one in Tube II forward. The other three forward torpedo tubes were filled with FaT IIs. The four reloads stored under the floor plates of the forward compartment were standard T3s. The two other reloads, stored in cradles above the floor plates of the forward compartment, were one FaT II and one T3. (These two final reloads were thoroughly hated by the ratings, the *Pairs*, who bunked in the forward torpedo compartment. This compartment had 12 bunks, two rows of three on each side, which were shared by at least 20 men. It was unpleasant enough sharing a bunk with others, but as long as those two extra reloads were there, the bottom row of bunks had to be folded out of the way, so it was 20 or more men sharing six bunks. The numbers obviously didn't add up. Inevitably, men who came off duty late would have to grab their blanket and pillow and make themselves as comfortable as they could on top of a torpedo. Needless to say, the men were eager for the first contact with the enemy, so that at least two forward torpedoes would be fired off and those damned reloads would get moved into a tube and out of the way.)

U371 was escorted as far as Cap Cépet, just outside the entrance to the port, by two small harbour craft. It was 1900 when the boat departed and

Fenski kept U371 on the surface all that night, steering due south at high speed, and submerging at dawn to pass the day underwater. It arrived at its patrol area after two days and started a slow sweep along the Algerian coast. On the 26th or 27th, a small high-speed convoy was detected by hydrophone as U371 patrolled submerged. Coming up to periscope depth, Fenski found two troop transports escorted by three destroyers. He shot the FaTs from Tubes I and III at the larger transport, the FaT from Tube IV at the smaller transport and the T5 from Tube II at one of the destroyers. It was a wasted effort. None of the torpedoes hit anything. The targets were unaware that they'd even been attacked.[17] U371 left the scene at slow speed at a depth of 50m.

On the 29th, U371 was directed to intercept a huge convoy, GUS.9, consisting of 97 vessels, including eight tankers and 15 escorts. Fenski sighted the convoy as it was passing close offshore by the town of Djidjelli, east of Algiers, late in the evening of 2 May.[18] Actually, the term 'sighted' doesn't do justice to the closeness of his encounter with the convoy. Aware from sound contact that the convoy was nearby, Fenski decided to surface the boat in order to recharge batteries. U371 had been down most of the day on the 2nd and, while the batteries weren't critically low, they certainly could use a fresh charge. When U371 reached the surface, he found himself virtually in the middle of the convoy. He immediately crash-dived the boat to 100m and settled down to let the convoy pass ahead of him. After an hour, he brought U371 to the surface and began to chase the convoy down from astern. His hope was that he'd be able to complete recharging his batteries while he approached an attack position. Once again, he had over-estimated the distance to the convoy; before very long his radar detector picked up the unmistakable signs of search radar and screw noises were heard increasing in pitch as an escort turned towards the boat. Fenski quickly ordered a course away from the convoy at high speed, hoping he could keep the pursuer at bay long enough to achieve a usable level of charge on his batteries.

Fenski's hope was once again in vain. The pursuer quickly closed the distance separating them and, when the range had dropped to 3000m, he knew he couldn't wait any longer. Any moment the escort would open fire and his chances of escape would get slimmer. In quick succession he ordered the stern tube fired, launching the T5 there at the pursuit, and took the boat deep, down to 100m. This was exactly the situation T5s had been designed for and if ever one needed to work as designed, this was the moment. The crew waited an agonising five minutes while the pursuer came on at high speed and then were rewarded by an explosion and the distinctive sounds of a ship sinking. This time, the T5 had operated exactly according to plan. (The victim was the destroyer escort USS *Menges* [DE-320]. It was struck aft by a torpedo at 0142 on 3 May and seriously damaged. *Menges* didn't sink and eventually limped into port. T5s, in reality, weren't very good at sinking escorts, but they had a creditable record of damaging them. Because they were attracted to the sounds of an escort's screws, they would home in on the aft end of a target. A torpedo hit right aft was rarely fatal, but it would effectively disable a pursuer.)

Satisfying as that hit and presumed destruction of his pursuer were, Fenski was too smart to believe that he was out of trouble. Sinking an escort would only serve to make the remaining defenders angry. The escort commander reacted swiftly and with more than sufficient force. Immediately detached were the destroyer escort USS *Pride* (DE-323) and the Coast Guard cutter USS *Campbell* (WPG-32). During the course of the pursuit, these two were joined by four other escorts: the minesweeper USS *Sustain* (AM-119), the escort destroyer HMS *Blankney* and the French destroyer *L'Alcyon* and destroyer escort *Sénégalais* (American-built, laid down as DE-106). On top of that, elements of at least three land-based bomber squadrons maintained air patrol over the scene. The idea simply was to hold U371 down underwater until it ran out of battery power, air or luck.[19] That meant that six escorts and tens of aircraft were committed for the duration of the chase to the destruction of a single U-boat. The idea would have been absolutely unthinkable back in 1941. With such a plenitude of resources, it's hardly surprising that the odds had tipped so steeply against the U-boats.

Fenski held U371 at 100m for a short while and, hearing nothing from the surface, began slowly to bring the boat up. At around 60m, the *Horchgerät* began to pick up screw sounds from the surface and then a series of depth charge explosions off in the distance. As they remained at 60m for a few minutes, they heard the screw sounds grow louder. Convinced that the pursuit was very much still alive, Fenski took the boat deeper again, this time to 160m. He set a course due south, towards the Algerian shore, because he thought that would be the most unexpected move he could make. Within minutes, a distressingly accurate series of depth charges exploded around the boat, knocking out the main lighting system, damaging the depth planes and starting leaks in the trim tanks. These leaks caused the boat gradually to sink lower until, at 210m, Fenski ordered No. 3 dive tank blown to stop the downward drift. Thereafter, the attacks came at half-hour intervals, just like clockwork, each attack seemingly more accurate than the one before, each one adding to the growing list of damaged or failed systems on board.

At 0600 on 3 May, after the most damaging series yet, Fenski decided he needed to bottom the boat, both to make it harder to find on the enemy's sonar and to save precious battery power, which was now starting to get critically low. The boat first grounded at 170m, but the ocean floor was steeply sloped, so Fenski drew the boat back and tried again further from shore, finally finding a level soft bottom at 240m. Leakage through the valve packings and other discontinuities in the pressure hull were much worse at that depth, but it was quiet and the boat lay there unmolested for the rest of the day. By dark, however, the air in the boat was getting bad, the emergency lighting system had failed and there were about 15t of water in the bilges from the various leaks. Even though screw noises were again being heard from the surface, Fenski knew he couldn't delay surfacing the boat. U371 would just have to take its chances on the surface.

Fenski ordered all tanks blown. The results couldn't have been worse. Despite using all the remaining high-pressure air in the cylinders, the boat didn't budge. It simply was too heavy with all the water that had leaked in during the day. A sticky mixture of oil and water was knee-deep in the control room. Worse, if anything could be worse, the noise of the blowing tanks had alerted the escorts, patiently waiting for U371 to move, and soon more depth charges were exploding near the boat. The only hope now was that there really was enough buoyancy in the boat, but that it was failing to rise because of adhesion to the muddy bottom. Their only recourse was to try rocking the boat, attempting to break the seal. Of course, if the boat was just too heavy to rise, then none of this mattered and they faced an inevitable, slow, but relatively peaceful, death by asphyxiation.

Rocking the boat was a simple proposition. A Type VII U-boat was small enough that the weight of the crew could seriously affect the trim of the boat. That was why, during a crash-dive, all off-duty crewmen would run at top speed to the bow compartment and pile in as close to the torpedo tubes as they could get. The same idea applied here, except that the running wasn't necessary. The crew was ordered aft, tilting the boat up by the bow, and the electric motors were set to full speed ahead. The boat still was stuck tight to the bottom and so the crew was sent forward and the motors were reversed. It took several repetitions of this cycle, but finally the boat broke free and began to rise. Fenski ordered all tubes readied and, as soon as the boat broke the surface, all guns manned.

Amazingly, U371 found itself in an empty sea, the horizon free of enemy ships. It was 0315 on 4 May 1944. The boat had been resting on the bottom for 21 hours. Fenski ordered a course of due north and full speed on the diesels. The only hope was to get as far away from that spot as fast as possible. For a brief few minutes it looked as if it might work, but perhaps 15 minutes after surfacing, escorts were sighted coming up fast from astern and everyone on U371 knew they'd run out of chances. With no more compressed air or battery power, the boat couldn't dive, and there simply was no way that it could fight multiple escorts on the surface. Word passed through the boat: 'Prepare to scuttle the boat'. The leading pursuer was *Sénégalais*, which opened fire at about 0400. Almost immediately, the French escort scored a couple of hits with its two forward 3in guns. After firing back a few rounds with its four 2cm and single 3.7cm, Fenski gave the gun crews permission to abandon the boat and ordered the rest of the crew to do the same. Just before the *Mechanikers* abandoned the after torpedo compartment, they fired off the T5 remaining in Tube V.

Once again, the torpedo performed exactly as designed. It weaved its way up to and alongside *Sénégalais* and looped back, hitting the escort right aft. It was a final, futile act of defiance. By this time, the other escorts had caught up as well and, when only the LI and a control room mate remained on board, Fenski ordered the dive tanks flooded and then he too jumped into the water. The boat sank so fast that the two men still inside never made it out.

Sénégalais also survived being hit by the T5. Only four men of U371's crew died that night. Fenski and 48 others were picked up and spent the rest of the war in the relative comfort of an American POW camp.

Interlude
U534

The Last Dash

It was May 1945. Everyone, even the most fanatical of diehards, knew that the war was lost. How could there be any other result? The Allies were pushing deeper and deeper into Germany from both the east and west, and, while the waters of the western Baltic and the straits around Denmark had yet to be breached by the Allies' vast surface fleets, the air above was now as hostile as the Bay of Biscay had ever been and the passages were strewn with floating mines.

It was known that new and better boats were coming, boats that might bring back the happy days of three or four years before. The first Type XXIIIs had already gone on patrol and had had some success, but those were small boats, a mere promise of bigger vessels to come. They carried only two torpedoes and had just enough endurance to reach the coastal waters around Britain, patrol briefly and scoot back home. They could annoy the British and force them to divert resources, but they would never win the war on their own. The bigger Type XXIs were another story. Here was a boat that could change the rules. Sleek, with a streamlined hull and tower, complete with automatic, unmanned flak turrets fore and aft, it was designed to live underwater rather than on the surface. Fitted with a snorkel and many times the battery cells of earlier boats, a Type XXI could cruise submerged on its diesels at 12kt and hit 17kt at full speed on its electric motors. That was fast enough to catch almost any target while remaining submerged. But that would drain the batteries very quickly. At its normal submerged speed, a Type XXI could maintain 6kt for two full days, and at silent creeping speed, it could remain submerged for a phenomenal 11 days. That was surely long enough to wait out the most patient pursuit. But the real revolution was its ability to fight completely submerged. With an advanced listening system, the bearing to targets could be pinpointed and attacked with advanced versions of the LuT and T5, all from 50m below the surface. Clearly, these boats had the potential to nullify, in one stroke, the Allies' tremendous advantage in air-power, and their relatively fast silent speed would make the job of surface escorts much more difficult.

Great boats indeed, but they were arriving too late and in too small numbers to be of use. The first, hand-built examples had been in the water for almost a year, but the hundreds more which were supposed to be coming off assembly lines at the three designated construction yards at a rate of 25 per month were simply not arriving. Between the teething problems that had to be expected with the introduction of a totally new boat and an equally new production network, and the effects of constant Allied bombing, supplies of prefabricated sections to the U-boat 'factories' were intermittent and those boats that did get built were often attacked from the air before they could leave the builder's yard.

Meanwhile, the war had continued. From mid-1943 on, it was increasingly obvious that the older boats still at the front, the workhorse Type VIIs and Type IXs, would have to soldier on as best they could until the new designs reached combat readiness. It was unthinkable that the U-boat offensive would simply be abandoned just because the available boats were dangerously overmatched by the Allied defence. Every day, a few boats left ports in France and Norway, crept across the Bay of Biscay or the Norwegian Sea mostly submerged, and took up patrol areas in the North Atlantic, where they tried, with little hope of success, to get close enough to a convoy to attack. Every day, fewer boats returned. U534, however, hadn't known this war at all.

U534 had indeed had a very unusual career. A big Type IXC/40 launched in February 1942 and commissioned under OLzS Herbert Nollau in December 1942, it was still under Nollau's command two-and-a-half years later, having achieved not a single sinking. That sad distinction wasn't Nollau's fault in any sense: the boat had never been assigned to combat. For the first year and a half of its life, U534 never appears in the records of the combat flotillas. The presumption must be made that it spent this period as a school boat, kept in the Baltic to train new crews and test new systems.[1] Nollau wasn't a particularly popular commander and U534 wasn't a particularly happy boat. He was described by crew-members as being a very stiff and formal man, dapper and a bit pompous. His was one of the few boats in the fleet never to carry an insignia (*Bootswappen*) of any kind. It was quite common for boats to carry one or even several insignias. They could be the crest of the sponsoring city, the naval academy class badge of the commander, the insignia of the flotilla or any of a myriad cartoons or caricatures referring to literature, folk tales, politics or some quirk in the personality of the commander or the boat. They could be very serious or entirely whimsical. The crew was often involved in thinking up the insignia but the commander had the ultimate say. The crew of U534 suggested various designs to Nollau but he always turned them down. He thought that painting an insignia on his boat would be frivolous.[2]

In May 1944, U534 was released for operational duty, but even then, it wasn't sent on offensive patrols. It was assigned the unglamorous, but crucial, duty of weather reporting. With the outbreak of war, Germany had lost contact with the international meteorological community which had previously provided data to its weather forecasters. Central Europe's weather comes from the North Atlantic. The prevailing winds flow from the north-west. With no other means of obtaining data on weather conditions in the North Atlantic, Dönitz was tasked by his government with providing at all times at least one boat on dedicated weather duty in the waters near Greenland. This boat was required to avoid all contact with enemy forces in order to maintain a regular flow of weather data. U534 was selected for this duty and spent one long patrol (8 May 1944 – 13 August 1944) monotonously following a looping course that took it close to Greenland's eastern coast and then many hundred miles south into the open ocean.

At the end of its gruelling four-month-long stint as a weather boat, U534 headed back to the coast of France. Only, by this time, the bases there were no longer well supplied with the materiel necessary to restock or refit a U-boat. In mid-August 1944, the Allied armies were breaking out of Normandy, spreading rapidly eastward towards the German border. Bordeaux, where U534 put in on 13 August, was still well behind the lines, but the supply routes from Germany had been cut and stocks of food and all other supplies were dwindling. Not surprisingly, under the circumstances, BdU ordered all boats at the French ports capable of making the trip to Norway to depart as soon as possible. U534 was replenished and refuelled and hastily fitted with a snorkel. Unfortunately, the parts necessary to hinge the snorkel weren't available, so it was fixed in the upright position. Nor was there the time to train the crew in its use. So, U534 left Bordeaux on 25 August and almost immediately came within a hair's-breadth of disaster due to inexperience with its new *Snort*.[3] More by luck than skill, the boat survived this first experience and went on to complete a slow, two-month-long circuit of the British Isles, passing well west of Ireland, north of the Orkneys and finally down the North Sea to the Skagerrak. While still in the Bay of Biscay, U534 had encountered and shot down an RAF Wellington. (The aircraft, Wellington S/N MB.798, was aircraft 'B' of No. 172 Sqdn, shot down just after midnight on 27 August 1944. Three survivors, two of them wounded, made their way out of the aircraft before it sank and were later found and picked up by a Sunderland.)

U534 put into Kristiansand on 24 October 1944 and the next day departed for Flensburg. There it joined the 33rd Flotilla. The Norwegian ports lacked the repair and refit facilities necessary to handle all the U-boats now concentrating at those ports, big and small, along the western and southern coasts. A good many longer-range U-boats were sent back to German ports in order to relieve the pressure on the over-burdened facilities in Norway. After U534 arrived at Flensburg, it once again drops from the records of the U-boat flotillas. For the remainder of the war, it performed anonymous duties without again heading out into the Atlantic. In all likelihood, it operated once more as a training boat and an experimental platform. It might also have made some supply runs to Kristiansand. During late 1944 the regular coastal traffic which had run steadily between Norway and Germany, carrying iron ore south and supplies for the German forces north, had fallen prey to increasingly frequent aerial sweeps by RAF bombers. Keeping the U-boats now operating out of a half-dozen Norwegian ports in repair required a regular supply of spare parts and other supplies. U534 was most likely engaged in this activity as well. All that is known for certain is that it remained based at Flensburg until it was forced, along with many other U-boats, to make a desperate dash for Norway at the beginning of May 1945.[4]

The Final Collapse

At the beginning of May 1945, the end was rapidly approaching. Rumours were flying that Hitler was dead. Other rumours talked about 'national redoubts', mountain strongholds where Nazi fanatics had gathered gold and food and secret weapons of great power and were prepared to hold out indefinitely. One was supposedly in the Bavarian Alps, appropriately enough since that was where Hitler had his holiday retreat. The other was rumoured to be in Norway, the one German conquest which, so far, was uninvaded and largely undamaged. Since 30 April, Dönitz had succeeded Hitler as head of what was left of Nazi Germany. There wasn't much that he could do to stem the Allied tidal wave, even if he had wanted to. As it was, he was smart enough to realise that the best he could do was to make the collapse as painless as possible. Nevertheless, he did intend to prolong the war as long as he could because he felt that the ongoing evacuation of German troops and refugees from the eastern Baltic was the most important task left to him and that would come to a stop as soon as the surrender took place.[5] There was also one additional small step he could take to save some of his boats from capture at German ports.

Hitler, in a demented dream of a final *Götterdämmerung*-style funeral pyre for a nation, ordered on 30 April that all German warships be scuttled. Dönitz, as the new head of state, passed the order along, but modified it to exempt those U-boats in German waters which were still capable of combat operations. Those boats were to head for Norway and remain prepared to continue offensive operations. The remaining boats, those incapable of diving, were to be scuttled in port. Many commanders of these latter boats, refusing to see their boats ignominiously scuttled, opted to take their chances making the run for Norway. One of the boats to attempt that trip was U534.[6]

Boats left Kiel and Flensburg individually and in groups over the next few days. Most were loaded with supplies to take to the forces in Norway. U534 was loaded up and then, in company with two other boats, headed north at high speed on the surface, hoping against hope that some of the boats would get through. Very few did. The RAF had a field day. Sweeps of Liberators, Mosquitoes, Beaufighters and Typhoons roamed without opposition over the Kattegat, the Great and Little Belts and the various bays and fjords off the Kieler Bucht, attacking everything afloat. In five days, between 2 and 6 May 1945, RAF squadrons sank no fewer than 21 U-boats in these narrow waters. U534 was just another one of these.

Only a few elements make the story of U534 stand out from any of the 20 other U-boats that were destroyed trying to reach Norway. One was the fact that U534 put up a better fight before succumbing. An even more interesting part of the story has to do with what happened after it went down. Having departed Germany in the dark, late in the evening of 4 May, U534 and its two companions made their best speed up the Great Belt, reaching the wider waters of the Kattegat at dawn on the 5th. Not surprisingly, given the intensity of RAF activity over these waters, the trio of boats were soon discovered as they made their way up the Kattegat, approaching the Anholt lightship, off the north-eastern tip of Anholt Island, almost exactly in the middle of the Kattegat. The first aircraft to attack was Liberator 'E' of No. 547 Sqdn, which got caught in a burst of flak from U534 and crashed flaming into the water. It was a satisfying victory, but there was no time to enjoy the feeling. No sooner had one attacker crashed than a second Liberator, this one aircraft 'G' of No. 86 Sqdn, appeared on the scene. U534 put up a steady defensive fire and at 'zweimal AK' circled the Anholt lightship in hopes of damaging the attacker or causing it to miss. This time it wasn't as lucky. It took two bombing runs, but the Liberator managed to put a depth charge under the U-boat's aft end and the boat rapidly started to sink. Within minutes, 50 of the 52 crewmen were in the water and the boat settled in shallow water, less than 40m deep, close by the lightship.[7] Lifeboats from the lightship picked up the survivors.

An Unquiet Grave

That should have been the end of the story: an uninteresting career ending in an unexceptional death. For 30 years the wreck of U534 rested in peace close by the Anholt lightship. On land, considerable speculation surrounded the boat. Because it was known to have had an exceptionally undocumented career, it was rumoured to have been involved in secret missions. Because it was known to have been carrying supplies to Norway on that last sortie, the rumours were embellished to include the replacement of U534's lead ballast bars with gold bullion. The interior was supposedly crammed full of stolen artwork of untold value. It was even rumoured that part of the crew had been replaced by high-ranking Nazis seeking refuge in Norway. Survivors of the boat, contacted after the war, steadfastly maintained that there was no gold on board and that the full regular crew was present when the boat sank.[8] The only unusual crew-member was an Argentinian radio operator who was one of those who died in the water.

In the mid-1970s, the remains of U534 were located by Danish divers, who applied for permission to salvage the wreck. Due to the persistent rumours of gold and other valuables on board, the Danish government would only grant a salvage permit on condition that the government would retain any valuables found. That dampened the interest of the divers and led to a long delay in the raising of the wreck. It was only in 1993 that U534 was finally salvaged and the boat's contents revealed. It turned out that U534 contained, besides the ordinary equipment of a combat U-boat, only some extra quantities of spare parts and tinned food and numerous cartons of condoms.

When the U-boat was found to contain nothing particularly valuable, interest in the remains waned to the extent that the consortium which had raised the boat offered it up for scrap. At that point, the Warship Preservation Trust from the United Kingdom stepped in and made arrangements to move the boat to England and put it on display. The boat was moved to England in May 1996 and is now an exhibit at the Nautilus Maritime Museum in Birkenhead.

— 13 —
U977

The Last to Surrender

U-boat commanders were an independent lot. They were selected for and trained to enhance their intelligence and initiative. The last person you wanted in charge of a U-boat was a man who couldn't think through problems quickly and creatively and then act decisively to remedy the situation. Once a boat left port, the 'old man' decided everything. Orders would arrive from home, changing patrol assignments, arranging rendezvous or assigning targets, but it was always understood that the commander was responsible for the success and the safety of his boat and crew and no one would second-guess his decisions. Out in the middle of the Atlantic, those messages from home were recommendations, to be followed if possible, ignored if necessary. This was understood and accepted. However, nothing in the cumulative experience of the U-boat commanders who preceded Heinz Schäffer and his contemporaries could prepare them for the decision they were now facing.

Stated simply, the question was how to bring the long, disastrous war to an end. More specifically, how to end the war for yourself, your boat and your crew. In those last days, every commander knew that the war was lost and that the slaughter of U-boats had become pointless. Schäffer certainly knew, before he left port, that Hitler was dead, that Dönitz was head of state and that behind the continuing propaganda broadcasts that preached ultimate victory or a glorious death, the reality was that Germany was out of time and chances. The order was bound to come soon. The only question was whether and how to comply. Fighting on wasn't really a choice: it would be pointless and suicidal. Yet a lot of other options existed. You could comply with the orders, surface your boat, fly the designated black flag and head for an Allied port. You could try to make it home and, once there, hope you and your crew could avoid capture and melt into the civilian population. You could bring your boat up to the nearest shore and scuttle it there, denying the victors the pleasure of gloating over this prize that had been your home and companion for as long as you could remember. Or you could defy the order and try to find a neutral port somewhere, where you could intern your boat and maybe even start a new life, away from Germany and its enemies. There were 43 boats at sea on 8 May 1945. Forty-three commanders had to make that choice.[1] Heinz Schäffer was one of them. (Of those 43 boats, 23 surrendered at UK ports, three in

Canada and four in the US. Seven returned to German-held ports in Norway or to Kiel. One other boat struck a mine and sank while attempting to enter the Elbe near Brunsbüttel. One was beached and abandoned on the shore of Amrum, one of the North Frisian Islands. Two were scuttled off the Portuguese coast. The remaining two boats opted to try a more dramatic attempt to find a neutral haven.)

Young Commander, Old Boat

Heinz Schäffer was a very young man, just 24 years old, when he took command of U977. He had entered the Navy as a cadet after the war broke out in 1939, had graduated from the naval academy in May 1941 and had progressed through assignments as IIWO and IWO before being posted to commander's school in late 1943. His first command was a school boat, an old Type IID, U148. For a year, he dutifully turned raw recruits into competent U-boatmen and passed them on to combat boats while he fretted away in the Baltic. Finally, in December 1944, he was given command of a combat-ready boat, though it wasn't the new boat he'd been hoping for.

U977 was far from new. It had been launched in March 1943 and commissioned in May of that same year. It should have completed training before the end of the year and gone on to join a combat flotilla. However, the boat was rammed no fewer than three times during its working up and, in October 1943, it was assigned as a school boat to the training flotilla at Pillau.[2] (Pillau is on the eastern shore of the Gulf of Danzig, at the tip of a long barrier island. It is now the town of Baltiysk in that small isolated slice of Russia carved out of the northern part of East Prussia at the end of the Second World War, surrounded by Poland and Lithuania.) In late 1944, it was refitted and repaired and prepared for combat assignment. This included the assignment of a new commander, Heinz Schäffer. For two more months the crew trained under their new commander and then the boat entered the yard to have a snorkel fitted and in general be prepared for its first combat patrol. From the Howaldtswerke in Hamburg, it returned to Kiel to be loaded with supplies and fuel, departing on 16 April 1945. Unfortunately, the supply situation was so critical in Germany that Schäffer chose to make a stop at a Frederikshavn, Denmark, before setting out across the Skagerrak to Norway. At the Danish port, they were able to find and requisition plentiful fresh meat and produce, enough for an extended patrol. U977 arrived at Horten, near Oslo, on 20 April and underwent ten days of training in the art of using the snorkel, leaving for Kristiansand on the 30th. While the stop in Denmark had remedied their food shortage, nothing could help the scarcity of fuel in Norway. U977, which was assigned a patrol zone in the English Channel, was given a scant load of fuel oil, only 85t, about two-thirds of the boat's capacity. It was also given a light load of torpedoes. Instead of the 12 it could carry, it left port with only ten (six LuTs and four T-5s). On 1 May, the crew was given a day off, in part to celebrate the traditional May Day holiday and in part to observe the death of Hitler, which was announced by Dönitz that day. Amid exhortations to fight to the death and never surrender, the boat put to sea the next day.

From Kristiansand, the boat made its way slowly around the southern tip of Norway and up its western coast. Starting on the 4th, when German forces in the north of Germany surrendered, Dönitz broadcast orders to all his boats to cease all combat operations immediately. Most commanders complied without hesitation. After all, the war had been long and the losses appalling. Most U-boatmen were grateful that the agony was over. (Four sinkings by U-boats are known to have taken place after Dönitz issued his cease hostilities order on the 4th. In each case, it was clear that the U-boat in question had simply failed to receive the message.)[3]

For some, it took a while for the news to sink in. Most, like U977, were running submerged most of the time, approaching the surface for only a few hours a day. Despite the fact that the signals announcing Germany's surrender were being continually rebroadcast on the standard U-boat frequencies, nevertheless it took several days for it to become clear that the signals were authentic and that, therefore, Germany had indeed surrendered. Some, like Schäffer, initially suspected the signals were a trick by the Allies. Once it was clear that the war was indeed over, it was equally clear that Germany's political and military leadership was in captivity. The oaths which bound Schäffer to obey his superiors, oaths which he took very seriously, were now dissolved. So, now the question was, what to do?

There can be no doubt that Schäffer's youth and his relatively limited combat experience influenced his decision. He was young and unmarried and had few ties to Germany other than family. Rumours abounded that the Allies, having fought Germany twice, intended to turn the country into an agricultural zone, sterilise all the men and use the women to 'breed' a more docile strain, content to remain on the farm. Schäffer appears to have given these dark fantasies at least minimal credence because he recalled that as one of the reasons he gave to his crew for deciding on his chosen course of action.

One of my main reasons in deciding to proceed to the Argentine was based on German propaganda, which claimed that the American and British newspapers advocated that at the end of the war, all German men be enslaved and sterilised. Another consideration was the bad treatment and long delay in return home suffered by German prisoners-of-war held in France at the end of World War I. Then again, of course, the hope of better living conditions in the Argentine.[4]

He had decided to head for a country with a large expatriate German population. Undeterred by the fact that it lay across the ocean and in a different hemisphere, he had decided to head for Argentina.

The Long Way

With the war over, not only was Schäffer no longer bound by his oaths to his superiors, but neither was his crew bound to theirs. If they were going to seek refuge half-way around the world, it had to be done on a voluntary basis. Schäffer assembled the crew during the day of 9 May, explained his decision and asked each man to decide whether he wanted to chance the run to Argentina. Any who opted not to, for whatever reason, would be let off near the Norwegian coast that night. As expected, the older, married hands chose to leave the boat. They had families to worry about. In all, three ratings and 13 petty officers made that choice. The loss of so many of the technical division was a problem to be solved, but Schäffer really had no choice but to permit them to leave. Accordingly, starting at 0230 on the 10th, 16 men strapped on their individual life-rafts, took three of the boat's inflatable dinghies and paddled ashore on the island of Holsenøy, near Bergen. They were picked up within hours and made prisoners, but in the process they described themselves as the 'survivors' of U977, which immeasurably aided the boat's escape.

With 32 officers and men remaining on board, the boat was now less cramped and the food was certainly going to stretch longer, but the issue of whether the boat was up to the voyage to Argentina, since it was an older vessel and hadn't had a complete overhaul prior to this mission, remained to be answered. This was particularly of concern since so many petty officers had opted to disembark on the 10th. They were the men who, if a breakdown occurred, would normally be relied upon to make the repairs. Nevertheless, Schäffer and the remaining crew were determined to take a shot at Argentina. One thing was certain, it would be a slow trip. Despite the fact that the war was over, they had to assume that they were still being hunted with wartime intensity. If they were sighted by any Allied ship or aircraft before they reached Argentina, they'd be expected to surrender and, if they didn't, they'd certainly be attacked. It was even a real possibility that, having chosen not to surrender right away, they'd be considered a 'rogue' warship and attacked without hesitation. It was critical that they remain undetected, and that meant remaining submerged until they were at least as far south as Gibraltar. That meant snorkelling or running deep on their electric motors 24 hours a day for the foreseeable future. A grim prospect indeed.

To understand how grim that prospect was, it is necessary to remember how primitive these boats really were. They weren't designed for continual submerged operation. Forget any images of modern nuclear submarines with clean, dry interiors and filtered air, showers and a laundry. U977 almost immediately began to rust and everything inside started to mould. Food, clothing, woodwork, even the painted metal surfaces of the interior, began to sprout a soft, green covering. Even the men, it seemed, were moulding. As the long days underwater passed, they grew paler and more listless. Skin rashes and fungal infections multiplied. Unfortunately, the corpsman had been one of the crewmen who had left the boat in Norway, so what little medical knowledge the boat had possessed was now gone.[5]

The normal miseries of an extended patrol in a U-boat were magnified by this enforced submergence. Garbage, the natural detritus of a human population, even a reduced population such as now inhabited U977, gathered in ever-mounting piles. Empty food tins, the mouldy rinds of bread and sausage, the spoiled remains of the last few meals, it all added up. Normally, the rubbish would be thrown overboard whenever the boat surfaced, but now it hadn't surfaced in days and might not surface again for weeks. In the dank, foetid atmosphere inside U977, the accumulating refuse became a serious threat to the health of the crew. The solution was actually relatively easy, much easier than if the war was still on and the boat was hunting enemy targets. There were only two ways of getting garbage out of a submerged U-boat: through a torpedo tube or through the *Bold* ejector, known as the *Pillenwerfer*. (*Bold* was an anti-sonar decoy, a large effervescent tablet in a small tin can. It had a special ejection tube just big enough to handle the small can. It was possible to pack the crew's waste into small cans, the same size or smaller than a *Bold* round, but that required a supply of small cans and filling them was an extremely unpleasant and unpopular activity.)

Using the *Bold* ejector was far more difficult than using a torpedo tube, but it was often chosen despite the difficulties involved because using a torpedo tube brought with it the risk that the tube would be full of refuse when targets were encountered and the boat would be missing 20 per cent of its offensive power. It wasn't sufficient just to empty the tube by firing the garbage out into the water, a *Müllschoss*, because the tube still had to be cleaned before it was ready to reload with a torpedo. That concern was no longer germane, since they no longer were hunting targets. In fact, a number of the crew suggested that they fire off one or more of torpedoes and use the empty tubes to hold garbage. Schäffer would have none of this, claiming that it was important that they be able to prove that they arrived at Argentina without firing any of their torpedoes. He insisted that a torpedo be brought into the boat from one of the forward tubes and reloaded later after they had resurfaced. Needless to say, this decision was wildly unpopular with the crew, who not only had to manhandle the torpedo into a storage position, but would then have to live with one row of bunks in the forward compartment folded up until the torpedo could be replaced.

There was no question that the RAF was maintaining its patrols of the waters around England with wartime intensity. Time and again, as they crept slowly around the north of the Shetlands and through the *Rosengarten* between the Faroes and Iceland, their radar detector, its antenna mounted on top of the snorkel, would scream a warning. The tension at this point was exacerbated by the fact that the attack periscope had been damaged back on 7 May, even before they'd decided to head to Argentina, and had been inoperable ever since. (The damage had occurred when the IWO had left the periscope extended when the boat had crash-dived. The prisms at the periscope head had been knocked loose and broken, rendering the periscope unusable and irreparable. A Type VII U-boat had another periscope, the sky periscope designed to give a panoramic view around and above the boat. Unfortunately, the sky periscope was shorter than the attack periscope and couldn't be used while snorkelling.) So, with the exception of the radar detector and hydrophones, the crew of U977 had no information on the state of the world around them. On one occasion they heard what sounded like depth charges in the distance. They would dive deep when they got a radar contact. Otherwise they kept plodding slowly southward, averaging barely 25nm a day.

Finally, after 66 days continually submerged, Schäffer concluded that they were far enough south, approximately due west of Cape St Vincent, and that they'd reached the limit of their endurance. The crew needed to breathe fresh air and see the sun. Equally important, the boat had to use its remaining fuel oil more efficiently or they'd never reach Argentina. Snorkelling, it turns out, isn't very fuel efficient. They had covered only 1800nm in those 66 days; they still had nearly 6000nm to go. Yet they'd already consumed 40t out of their original 85t of fuel oil. Clearly, a much more economical regime was required, even if it meant risking detection. Fortunately, it was well known that Type VIIs could cruise most economically on one engine at a speed of 6kt. This had allowed these boats, designed for mid-Atlantic patrols, to operate successfully off the American coast. The same scheme would be used by U977. It would run submerged on its batteries 14 hours a day, throughout the daylight hours, surface after dark and run on the surface for ten hours, recharging the batteries in the process.

That was the plan anyway, but the crew's need for sunlight gradually overcame caution and the boat spent more and more hours surfaced. The FuMB antenna was erected and full lookout watches were stood, but within a few weeks the life of the crew had gravitated to the deck as everyone enjoyed the warm sun and tropical water. After clearing Madeira to the west, the boat cruised steadily towards the south-west, staying well clear of the African coast. On 14 July, U977 sighted the Cape Verde Islands. Since first surfacing, they had encountered not a single ship or aircraft. This far south, the war was over. They felt sufficiently safe to allow themselves a rare, delicious luxury. They stopped the boat under the lee of the tiny uninhabited island of Branco in the Cape Verdes and celebrated their success so far. They swam and sang songs on deck. Then, four hours later, they started their engine and resumed the slow, relentless south-westward progress.

Over the next few days they began encountering ships and aircraft again. One ship, a passenger liner brightly lit from stem to stern, passed close enough that they could hear the band on board playing dance tunes. If nothing else had yet proved to them that the war was over, those lights and that music did the job. They didn't dive for ships they encountered at night, relying on the U-boat's small size and low silhouette to enable them to remain undetected. The qualities that had made the Type VII such an effective weapon in the first three years of the war stood them in good stead now. They did dive upon detecting aircraft, even at night, and as they approached the Brazilian coast, the frequency of those sightings increased. It was impossible to tell whether the aircraft were civilian or military. There was no point in trying to find out.

Progress came faster now that they were surfaced most of the time. On 22 July, they passed 25nm east of St Paul Rocks, and the next day, with full cere-mony, they crossed the Equator. (The German version of the Equator crossing ceremony includes Neptune and his court passing judgment on the 'polli-wogs' – men who hadn't yet crossed the Equator – and the infliction of appro-priate punishment, generally paddling with the Chief of Police's wooden sword, before the neophytes are accepted as 'shellbacks'.) Twenty-eight of the 32 men on board had never crossed the line and were subject to Neptune's arbitrary punishment. The ceremony was interrupted by the sounds of an aeroplane passing nearby, but it, like the other alarms, turned out to be a high-altitude flight with no interest in or curiosity about the small boat miles below. On the 30th, a news report revealed that another German U-boat, U530, had also made the decision to attempt internment in Argentina, but that boat and its crew had been turned over by the Argentinians to the United States. The U-boat's crew was already headed for a POW camp in the US and the boat itself was resting in an Argentinian port, awaiting a US Navy crew to sail it north. Schäffer had no reason to believe he and his boat would be treated any differ-ently, but by now U977 was committed to reaching Argentina. They were long past the point where they had other options.

The only question remaining was what to do when they reached their desti-nation. One option which had a lot of support among the crew was to scuttle the boat offshore, row to land and attempt to disperse among the local population. If there really were as many Germans in Argentina as they'd been told, maybe they could blend in. Most of the crew were experienced technicians and shouldn't have a problem finding work. Schäffer, however, pointed out the weaknesses of this plan. Even if there was a sizeable German population in Argentina, it was almost certainly concentrated in the cities. The odds were very much against them finding a sympathetic greeting as they paddled up to the beach. To make things worse, none of the crew spoke Spanish. But the greatest reason for rejecting that plan was the difficulty they would have, when inevitably caught, explaining who they were and why they shouldn't be treated as die-hard Nazi fanatics attempting to infiltrate the country. The only way they had any chance at all of being treated as they wanted to be, as refugees seeking asylum, would be to sail their boat intact into Argentinian waters and surrender as German sailors rather than as fleeing Nazis.

That decision made, the only other question was where to surrender. Schäffer had friends and relatives in Buenos Aires and would have loved to have sailed his U-boat up to the Argentinian capital, but they had no charts of the Rio de la Platà, so a submerged passage up the inlet was out of the question, and, on the surface, they would be stopped and captured by coastguard vessels in a matter of hours. Therefore, it was decided to head for Mar del Plata, a major port and naval base just south of the Rio de la Plata. U977 arrived at the limit of international waters, three miles offshore, soon after dawn on 17 August 1945, having spent 107 days at sea. Schäffer had his *Funker* broadcast in English that there was a German submarine waiting to be interned. It didn't take long for the Argentinians to react. First some fishing trawlers circled the boat and then a small minesweeper and two submarines came alongside and informed Schäffer, in English, that the local commander was on his way and that nothing should be damaged. Schäffer assured the Argentinians that he intended to surrender the boat intact. Finally, at 1105, he formally turned the boat over to the commander of the Mar del Plata base and thereafter took his orders from a Lieutenant Rodolfo Saenz Valiente. Schäffer recalled later how impressed he was with the crisp white uniforms of the Argentinian sailors.

As expected, the crew of U977 were taken into custody. They were well treated and especially well fed, but they were nevertheless in custody, awaiting transfer to the US. Schäffer was formally recorded as an internee at Miami, Florida, on 8 September. The boat was transferred to Buenos Aires, without Schäffer, and was put on public display for a few days. Then, on 11 September, U977, along with U530, left Buenos Aires for Trinidad, accompanied by the tug *Cherokee*. U977 was sunk as a target by the torpedoes of an American submarine on 2 February 1946.

Notes

Note

Sources, when mentioned in the notes, are identified by short tag-names. The key to the tag-names is provided in the Bibliography which follows the text.

Chapter 1: U9

1 Many of the details of U9's early war career come from Spiess. Johannes Spiess was IWO on U9 at the beginning of the First World War.

2 Diesel engines were still too bulky, too heavy and too unreliable, at this point in their evolution, for practical use on submarines. In November 1908, the German Navy ordered test engines from four firms, with the sole stipulation that they be able to demonstrate six days of continual operation without a failure. It was 1911 before engines from MAN and GW (Germaniawerft) were able to pass the test (cf. Rössler, pp. 25–8) The first German diesel-powered boats were U19-22 with MAN engines and U23-26 with GW engines, both groups ordered in 1911.

3 The Russian boats were finally launched in 1906, but their completion was slow and the third was not turned over to the Russian Navy until the following year. Named *Karp, Karas* and *Kambala*, two of the three were still in service in the Black Sea Fleet in 1914. The diminutive *Forelle* was known to have been transported to Vladivostok, but no record exists of its fate.

4 See Preston, p.10.

5 Gray, pp. 19, 21–2.

6 Gray, pp. 31–7; Preston, pp. 17–18.

7 In U-boat slang, torpedoes were *Aale* (eels).

8 Gray, p. 35.

9 This was the official figure given at the time. Preston, p. 18, says 1135. Tarrant, p. 10, says 1459. No matter which figure is correct, the losses were appalling.

10 Stevens, p. 314.

11 Tarrant, p. 10.

12 Gray, p. 73.

Chapter 2: UC74

1 Kemp, p. 17. Stevens, pp. 393–400.

2 Tarrant, p. 148. In the last month prior to the start of the first campaign, January 1915, seven merchant ships were sunk, totalling 17,577 GRT.

3 Kemp, p. 23.

4 GRT – Gross Rated Ton: a unit of cargo capacity for merchant ships. It measures the weight of the vessel and the weight of standard cargo it was designed to carry.

5 Kemp, pp. 36–7.

6 Guy letter. That was the theory, but in fact, Q-ships often sailed without the aid of a suitable cargo. As Captain Guy stated concerning HMS *Wonganella*, 'Could anything be more foolish than to give a decoy ship sand ballast?'

7 All of the details of *Wonganella*'s actions on 11 March 1917 come from Basil Guy's letter to Marschall dated 15 September 1929 and the attached copy of his official report on the action.

8 Ibid. Cape Bougaroni is better known as Cap Bougaroun. It is a prominent cape on the Algerian coast near the border with Tunisia. Algeria was then a French colony.

9 Rössler, p. 40.

10 Yet the UCIIs still were only a bit more than half the size of the ten UEI ocean-going minelayers, U71-80,

and were only one-third the size of the ten massive UEII boats, U117-126. The UE boats carried a different type of mine in internal dry storage, so that settings could be adjusted before the mines were laid.

11 UC74 log.

12 *Wong*. The time difference is due to the fact that the U-boat was keeping Central European Time while the Q-ship was maintaining Greenwich Mean Time, an hour earlier.

13 UC74 log.

14 Op. cit. UC74's log makes no mention of the timing of these events.

15 Ibid.

16 Ibid.

17 UC74 log. The fact that Marschall identified three guns firing at him, when in fact *Wonganella* only had two on each broadside, can be ascribed to the confusion of the moment. In the rush to get his boat below, he may be forgiven for believing that the rapid-fire 12pdr next to the funnel was two guns.

18 In the First World War, German torpedoes could only run a straight course from the U-boat, so it was necessary to line the boat up with the target in order to sink it.

19 Op. cit.

20 Op. cit.

21 Ibid. Basil Guy, in his letter to Marschall dated 15 Sept 1929, claimed bafflement as to what could have been the obstruction UC74 encountered. Q-ships were not equipped with nets or any other items intended to be dropped in the path of pursuing U-boats, since this wasn't a situation they were intended to handle.

22 Tarrant, p. 159. This author was able to find no further trace of HMS *Wonganella*.

Chapter 3: UB81

1 *Killing*, p. 224. Post-war analysis reduced that claimed total considerably, as happened to a great many U-boat aces. It is very easy to over-estimate the tonnage of ships actually sunk and to claim as sunk ships that were only damaged. The reduced total for which Saltzwedel is credited is 150,000t.

2 TL, pp. 51–5, gives a detailed account of the encounter between UC71 and *Dunraven*. This was not only a battle between two capable warships, but it was also a match between two talented and audacious warriors, Saltzwedel and Captain Gordon Campbell, VC. UC71 won, but just barely. Saltzwedel left *Dunraven* still afloat, but in obviously sinking conditions. Its aft magazine had exploded and fires raged aft. Its hull was holed in numerous places by one torpedo and countless shells. Campbell had tried the Q-ship trick of dispatching panic parties into lifeboats no fewer than three times, but Saltzwedel had been wary and avoided every trap. Finally, with no more torpedoes to fire, UC71 crept away. *Dunraven* took two days to sink.

3 *UB81*, p. 11. All further quotes in this chapter are from this document.

4 The 'he' referred to in the quote was KK Bartenbach, commander of the Flanders Flotilla.

5 This problem seemed to plague the UBIIIs. See the story of UB68 in Chapter 5.

6 Convoy, p. 32.

7 Tarrant, pp. 61–2.

8 This statement needs clarification. The Germans knew of no minefields there. This author has been unable to find evidence proving (or disproving) the existence of a British-laid minefield there, but the location where UB81 hit the mine would have been an unusual place indeed to lay mines, offensive or defensive, and the author is assuming that there was no minefield there.

9 The calculated survival time of an average-sized person submerged in water at the temperature of the Channel in December was approximately two hours, but a host of factors reduced that theoretical

maximum. For example, if the person was treading water rather than being supported by a functional life jacket, the survival time was much reduced. If the person treading water was fully clothed, the weight of clothing would increase the energy required to stay afloat and thus dramatically shorten survival time. Also, the effects of shock, caused by sudden immersion in cold water, could further reduce survival time.

10 UB81, p. 5. The reference is to a very curious sentence in the record of the interrogation of the boat's survivors. 'The Engineer Officer said that he had difficulty in keeping them away from the oxygen flasks, as this was a recognised method of providing an easy death when there is no further hope of rescue.' The author is uncertain as to what exactly the mechanism of death might be, such that it would gain the reputation among U-boatmen of being an easy death. The author would appreciate any assistance on this point from readers.

Chapter 4: U152

1 Rössler, pp. 54–6. Twelve enlarged *Mittel-Uboote* of a design called Project 42 were ordered in May 1916 as U127-138 after a lengthy review of war needs. They were to have been almost a third larger than the largest of the mainstream boats. However, construction of these boats was constantly delayed by the demands of the UB and UC programmes and by the desire of the German Navy for even larger U-cruisers. In the event, only two of the 12 were ever completed. U135 and U136 were launched in 1917 and completed in 1918. Only U135 actually became operational and that only in October 1918. Its captain was Johannes Spiess (see Chapter 1) and the only action it saw was its attempt to quell the mutiny in Wilhelmshaven. A second series of 16 slightly improved Project 42a boats (U213-228) was planned but never even started.

2 Rössler, p. 67.

3 Ibid. The boats proposed by Vulcan were U79 and U80, the last two of the six-boat UE minelayer series, then under construction and scheduled for launch in April 1916. The UE boats, unlike the UC series minelayers, were big vessels designed for internal stowage and launching of their mines. Vulcan's plan was to replace the mine handling and launching facilities, which took up much of the aft third of the 755 ton boat, with cargo space.

4 All sources, with one exception, report that *Bremen* was lost without a trace and without explanation. That one source, Gray, p 121, reports that *Bremen* was damaged, but not sunk, and returned to Germany. According to this account, *Bremen* served out the war as a surface vessel. No mention is made of its ultimate fate.

5 This and all other quotes from KK (a.D.) Adolf Franz are from an essay he wrote in 1928 to commemorate the tenth anniversary of his gun battle with *Ticonderoga*. This document was included by the archivist of the *Reichsmarine* in the same folder as U152's war diaries and fell into the hands of the Allies at the end of the Second World War.

6 The Germans knew the battle of Jutland as the *Skagerrakschlacht*, after the Skagerrak, the strait between Norway and Denmark near which it was fought.

7 *Spargelbetten* – cylindrical watertight ready-use ammunition containers set vertically into the deck-casing. Given that name because, seen from above, the shells packed nose-up in the container looked like a bunch of asparagus.

8 It is strange indeed that U152 sighted the cruiser as it was departing the convoy, which caused Franz to order his boat to submerge, but apparently neither the cruiser nor *Ticonderoga* sighted each other, because the cruiser never deviated from her course and *Ticonderoga* never called

NOTES

for assistance (or if she did, her calls were never heard).

9 The survivors estimated that 190 out the 231 on board were killed, blown overboard or injured by U152's shelling.

10 *UB72.*

11 U-boat veterans with whom the author spoke were all reluctant to talk about the experience of being depth charged, though they did all agree that the scenes of depth charging in the book and film *Das Boot*, by Lothar-Günther Buchheim, were quite accurate, except for the scene of the machinist going mad. The survivors all agreed that men might indeed be driven temporarily over the edge by extended depth charging, but would have been restrained by crewmates long before it became a problem for the commander to handle.

12 *UB72.*

13 *Type VII*, pp. 14–16. The later models of the Type VII, from the VIIB on, stored some fuel oil externally because there simply wasn't enough room inside the boat for fuel sufficient to provide the greater range demanded of the type.

14 The course was slightly westward because Franz intended to pass north of the British Isles and head south through the North Sea, the narrows north of Denmark and then south to Kiel.

Chapter 5: UB68

1 Pola is now the Croatian port of Pula.

2 Cattaro is now Kotor in Montenegro. It, too, is on the Adriatic.

3 Steinbauer commanded UB47 and UB48 before taking over U48.

4 Credit for the origination of these ideas is reported differently by the two sources consulted for this part of the story. Page 1 of *Ten Years*, written by Dönitz, one of the participants in the conversation, but not put on paper until nearly 40 years after the event in question, refers to 'our plan' and 'our idea', giving neither man

exclusive credit for the ideas. On the other hand, Wolf, pp. 14–15, clearly credits Steinbauer with originating the ideas. Be that as it may, Dönitz adopted the ideas as his own and implemented them 20 years later.

5 *UB68*, p. 2.

6 *Invest.*

7 *Ten Years*, p. 2. The account in this section of the convoy attack and loss of *UB68* is an amalgam of several different accounts of this incident, accounts which disagree in a lot of the details. My primary references were *UB68* and *Ten Years*, accounts both written by Dönitz, though *UB68* was written within days of the incident, while *Ten Years* was written more than 30 years later. For that reason, despite the fact that it's rather incomplete and sometimes confusing, I've tended to give the most credence to *UB68*.

8 *UB68*, p. 1. Dönitz was informed after his capture that the steamer he had torpedoed was SS *Oopack* of 3883GRT, which sank several hours after the attack.

9 *UB68*, p. 3. Dönitz wrote: 'According to the later report by Masch. Meinke, the packing of the gasket of the stern-tube was blown completely into the boat. The depth gauge in the aft compartment at that time read 86m, which would put the bow at a much greater depth (about 120m).'

10 The author has found four sources that give a figure for the number of *UB68*'s crew who died in its sinking. No two of those sources agree. TL says that six died, while *Destroy*, *UB68* and *Ten Years* say one, four and seven respectively.

11 TL, pp. 69–71.

Chapter 6: U47

1 *Destroy*, pp. 9, 58–9; *Killing*, pp. 49–50, 211–13. U18 attempted to break into Scapa Flow on 23 November 1914, following an inbound ship as far as the Hoxa Boom. A quick sweep of the harbour through the periscope revealed that

it was empty of major warships. Due to fears of exactly this kind of intrusion, the Admiralty had moved the fleet to several subordinate anchorages, primarily Loch Ewe on the western coast of Scotland. Turning away from the entrance, U18's periscope was sighted and a chase began which included two rammings of the U-boat by defenders before it finally ran aground on the Skerries in the Pentland Firth and had to be abandoned.
UB116 was the last U-boat sunk in the First World War. It also tried to enter Scapa Flow through Hoxa Sound on 28 October 1918. The boat's commander had been erroneously informed that there were no defences at that entrance. In fact, the defences there included hydrophones, remotely detonated minefields linked to magnetometers, as well as nets patrolled by anti-submarine vessels. UB116 had been sighted in the North Sea en route to Scapa Flow, so the defences were already on alert, but even if they hadn't been warned, the U-boat's fate would probably not have differed. The boat was picked up on hydrophones while still navigating the outer sound. When magnetometers indicated it was over a minefield, the mines were detonated and UB116's noises ceased. The irony was that, as had been the case with U18, Scapa Flow was empty. The Grand Fleet had moved south to Rosyth seven months earlier.

2 Today, causeways that link South Ronaldsay and Burray with Mainland (largest of the islands) block all the eastern entrances.

3 *KTB*, U47, 13 October 1939; TL, pp. 79–101; *Black*. The account that follows is an amalgam of these sources. Note that all times in this account are taken from Prien's log, which remained on German rather than local time, and thus were an hour later than the local time used in British accounts. The German habit

of keeping German time while on patrol in the Atlantic will come up again in this book.

4 *BdU*, short for *Befehlshaber der Uboote*, Commander-in-Chief, U-boats, the position to which Dönitz was promoted soon after the outbreak of war. *Der Alte*, literally 'the old man', was a slang term often used by U-boatmen to refer to their captain. It was more than a bit ironic, given that most U-boat commanders were men in their early 30s commanding a crew of men in their 20s and teens.

5 *Black*, p. 16.

6 *KTB*, U47, 13 October 1939.

7 Type VII, p. 128. The GHG sound receiver wasn't terribly good at determining the bearing of a sound source, but it was quite sensitive and would have picked up the sounds of a ship as close as that which Prien saw.

8 Accounts of survivors from *Royal Oak* differ as to whether there were two or three hits from this second salvo. Prien's log just mentions 'explosions' without giving a number.

9 The entire 13th chapter of *Black* is an attempt to cast doubt on whether Prien and U47 ever were in Scapa Flow.

Interlude: U556

1 *BdU*, 24–30 May 1941; *Pict*, pp. 221–7. Most of this section comes from Schmidt. The Chief Motorman (*Elektro-Maschinist*) on U821, Schmidt's boat, had previously served on U556, transferring just before its last patrol, and told Schmidt this story.

2 In the German Navy of the time, as in most other navies (and the US Navy to this day), there existed a cavernous cultural divide separating the submarine force from the surface fleet. The main difference is in mindset. Submariners succeed by breaking the rules and traditions that sustain surface sailors. In the US Navy, there's even a difference in uniform.

Submariners (and aviators) wear brown shoes; surface sailors wear black. Submariners in both navies refer to their vessels as 'boats'; surface sailors call their vessels 'ships'.

3 *Success*, p. 51. Wohlfarth thought this was an anti-submarine vessel, but in fact it was the fishing trawler *Emanuel*, out of the Faroe Islands, of 166t.

4 *Success*, p. 52. The steamer damaged in the first attack was *Aelybryn* (4986GRT). The victim of the dawn attack was *Empire Caribou* (4861GRT). The last victim was the Belgian steamer *Gand* (5086GRT).

5 *Success*, p. 52. The damaged tanker was *San Felix* (13037GRT). The confirmed victims were the tanker *British Security* (8470GRT) and the freighter *Darlington Court* (4974GRT). Wohlfarth claimed eight victims totalling 48,000GRT. The actual count was five ships sunk totalling 23,557GRT with two more ships of 18,023GRT damaged. Over-claiming was a chronic habit of submarine commanders (and fighter pilots as well) on all sides.

6 *BdU*, 27 May 1941.

Chapter 7: U156

1 *Ten Years*, p. 255; MoD, p. 41.

2 *Success*, p. 118. This was the British steamer *Clan Macwirter*, 5941GRT.

3 *KTB*, U156, 12 Sept 1942. The evening fix taken at 2100 put the boat at 4° 58' south, just within the letter of the law.

4 Ibid. The message was in standard Admiralty submarine report form. The repeated 'SSS' at the beginning indicated that a submarine was involved.

5 *KTB*, U156, 13 September 1942. The number of prisoners reported by Hartenstein, 1500, was based on reports he received from the Italian survivors. The actual figure, 1800, is derived from British records.

6 The two Freetown boats were U506 (Würdemann) and U507 (Schacht).

7 Op. cit. U156's radio continued to pick up what appeared to be a steamer quite close broadcasting on the 25m band, but this ship, if it ever existed, never was sighted.

8 Ibid.

9 *KTB*, U156, 14 September 1942.

10 The French warships were the cruiser *Gloire*, the sloop *Durmont D'Urville* and the minesweeper *Annamite*.

11 MoD, §234. The Germans referred regularly, from mid-war on, to the Allied bombing of German cities as justification for many of their actions in the Second World War. On the one hand, this really was unnecessary, since the logic of 'total war', as practised by all sides, had long since removed any distinction between civilians and combatants. At the same time, this was a rather self-serving attitude on the part of the Germans, given the fact that they had practised the indiscriminate bombing of civilian targets from the beginning of the war, and they certainly would have retaliated against British cities in 1942 had they had the means.

12 Conway, pp. 305–6.

13 *Wahoo*, p.5.

14 *Destroy*, pp. 186–7.

15 *Wahoo*, Attachment.

Interlude: U185

1 *U185*. The notes used for this interlude are from an early and a later draft of 'Chapter III – *Early History of U185*'. Deschimag was the successor to the firm known as AG Weser. Deschimag is a contraction of *Deutsche Schiff und Maschinenbau AG*.

Chapter 8: U167

1 MoD, §314.

2 KTB , U167, 15–16 March 1943. This KTB was reconstructed by Sturm after his return to France. The original KTB had gone down with the boat. Understandably, there are some discrepancies between the dates Sturm recalled and other sources,

since Sturm was working without notes. In general, I've favoured other sources over Sturm's memory when it comes to dates. The fact that this KTB was written after the fact and at some leisure makes it a far more interesting read than most boat's logs. It is dated 'Lorient, 23 April 1943

3 Type VII, pp. 85–6

4 BRT – Bruttoregistertonne, the equivalent of GRT (Gross Registered Tons), the capacity of a cargo ship expressed in registered tons. A registered ton equals 100 cubic feet.

5 *Success*, p. 159. According to postwar records, Sturm's four torpedoes obtained one hit. That ship was indeed only damaged and the American steamer *Molly Pitcher* was indeed found and finished off by U512 (Bargsten). The same system that denied Sturm credit for the damaged ship he sank back in Oct 1942 awarded this sinking to him.

6 *KTB*, U167, 17 March 1943.

7 *Success*, p. 160. U167 sank the Belgian motorship *Moanda* (4621GRT).

8 *KTB*, U167, 3 April 1943. The steady tone from the *Metox* meant that the aircraft had already acquired the submarine. Even in 1943, airborne radars had separate search and attack modes. In the former mode, the antenna swept an arc in front of the aircraft and would produce a warbling note on the *Metox*. In attack mode, the radar was aimed at a single location and thus produced a steady tone on the *Metox*. Loudness indicated range. The higher the number on the *Metox* scale, the closer the aircraft.

9 *KTB*, U167, 4 April 1943. The reference to 'zT' obviously refers to a warning signal of some sort, but the author has not seen this abbreviation in any other German documents and has been unable to find even what German words it represents. Any help on this from readers would be appreciated.

10 *KTB*, U167, 5 April 1943.

11 Ibid.

12 Ibid.

13 *Schlüssel M* (short for *Schlüssel Marine*) was the name for the naval version of the Enigma coding machine used by the Germans during the Second World War and broken by the British at Bletchley Park and distributed under the codename 'Ultra'.

14 The T3 was a standard G7e torpedo equipped with a new and fully functional magnetic detonator (Pi2).

15 The rudder and planes controls on a U-boat were power-assisted by compressed air. With no more air pressure, the boat could be manoeuvred only by manual controls. (Some U-boat commanders believed that the power-assist system was a source of noise and would steer their boat manually when under attack.)

16 *KTB*, U167, 6 April 1943. In fact, none of the scuttling charges detonated. The boat sank in intact condition.

17 *Destroy*, p. 109. This source says that Sturm was badly wounded during this action; however, the KTB, written by Sturm immediately after his return to Lorient, makes no mention of being wounded and the fact that he commissioned U547 only two months later would also argue against that possibility.

Interlude: U66

1 *U66*, p. 14; Rössler, pp. 166–7. The survivors of U66 couldn't recall whether the refuelling was from U460 (Schnoor) or U117 (Neumann). Rössler's notes on *Milchkuh* activities, however, indicate that U66 in fact replenished from U462 (Vowe) on its first patrol.

2 *Boot*, pp. 329–40. The description of the fictional boat's victualling at Vigo is quite accurate.

Chapter 9: U185

1 This really was an illusion. The number of available escorts had been steadily increasing as American

production came on line, but many of the new ships had been reserved for the 'Torch' convoys (carrying troops and supplies for Operation Torch, the Allied invasion of North Africa in November 1942). Because they passed south of the normal convoy routes, almost none of these convoys were even spotted by U-boats, much less attacked. The successful conclusion of that campaign in late spring 1943 led to a reduction in the number of convoys needed to support that theatre and the subsequent release of those ships to the North Atlantic.

2 MoD, §333. The actual loss in efficiency, measured in tons sunk per U-boat per day, fell from 147 in March to 76 in April.

3 *BdU*, 29 May 1943.

4 Ibid.

5 *Maquis* – members of the French resistance.

6 *U185*. This account, as was the case for Interlude 2, is derived from rough drafts of the final survivors' report. In this case the drafts are of Chapter VII. One of these drafts is dated 11 September 1943.

7 *Destroy*, p. 125.

8 *BdU*, 13 June 1943.

9 *Destroy*, p. 125. This was aircraft 'G' of No. 10 OUT, a Whitley, serial BD.220, piloted by Sgt A. J. Benson.

10 *BdU*, 14 June 1943. Dönitz may have remained BdU, but after mid-January 1943, the BdU KTB was signed by Eberhard Godt.

11 *Success*, p. 169. According to post-war records, Maus actually sank three ships and damaged a fourth on 7 July 1943. The victims were all American ships; the tanker *W.B. Thompson* (7061GRT) and freighters *James Robertson* (7176GRT) and *Thomas Sinnickson* (7176GRT). The damaged ship was also a tanker. Note the identical tonnages of the last two victims. These were American Liberty ships, mass-produced freighters of identical characteristics, produced far faster than Germany was building U-boats.

This was one of the reasons why, despite his best efforts, Dönitz was bound to lose the war of attrition in the Atlantic.

12 *U604*.

13 *Success*, p. 170. The victim was the Brazilian steamer *Bagé* (8235GRT).

14 *U604*; *Destroy*, p. 142; BdU, 5 August 1943.

15 *U185*. These notes include the comment that one of the crew revealed that this shot hit even though, or perhaps because, the torpedoman responsible for firing the torpedo was distracted and actually fired the torpedo four seconds after the order came down, an inexcusable slip-up. No one in the crew told this to any of the officers.

16 *Success*, p. 170. This victim was the British steamer *Fort Halkett* (7133GRT).

17 *U185*. The transferred material included 33m³ of oil, three sheets and one pillow case packed with food, 12 pairs of lookout's binoculars, 30 practice and 2000 regular rounds for the 2cm guns, a breech assembly for a 2cm gun, rotors for the Enigma and all of U604's secret papers, assorted medicines, radar detector, short- and long-wave radios, a typewriter, two sextants and 150 potash canisters (used to absorb CO_2 while submerged). Maus bemoaned the fact that the seas were too rough to transfer torpedoes.

18 The aircraft in question was another PB4Y of VB-107.

19 PK (*Propagandakompanie*), war correspondent.

20 *Destroy*, p. 143. The aircraft were from VC-13 off the escort carrier USS *Core* (CVE-13). The Wildcat was piloted by Lt(JG) M. G. O'Neill and the Avenger by Lt R. P. Williams.

21 *Destroy*, p. 143.

Chapter 10: U1059

1 Sources differ on how many torpedoes could be stored in a Type VIIF's torpedo storage room. Rössler (p. 162) says 21; MoD (§407) says 39,

total inventory, which, given the 14 carried elsewhere, leaves 25 for the storage room; Bagnasco (p. 66) also says 25; the survivors said 22 and I have gone with that figure.

2 Type IXs and XIVs each had four such external storage tubes. The Type VIIFs had two. Early models of the Type VII also had these external storage tubes, but they were rarely used by combat boats and were deleted from the main production sequence of Type VIICs.

3 MoD, §363. U168, U183, U188 and U532 reached Penang. U506, U509, U514 and U533 were sunk en route. One boat, U516, was used to refuel the others when the designated tanker failed to show up.

4 *U1059*. One survivor described the commander as being 'very pleasant but very irresponsible'.

5 *U1059*; *Destroy*, p. 178. This was U801 which reported the attacks to BdU on 16 March. It was sunk the next day by aircraft from USS *Block Island* (CVE-21) and two destroyers from the carrier's screen.

6 Ibid.

7 Ibid. As elsewhere in this book, there is a discrepancy between the time kept on the U-boat which, in the Atlantic, was always German time, and the time reported by the attackers, who used local time or ZULU (GMT). In this case, Leupold reported that the attack came at 0930.

8 Ibid. Dowty was worth observing. He was credited with sighting and damaging U801 just two days earlier. He was awarded the Navy Cross posthumously.

9 Ibid. This conversation is taken verbatim from 'German Prisoners of War Taken 19 March 1944 from U-boat X-U-G, Report on'. X-U-G was U1059's radio call sign.

10 Ibid. Leupold's scalp wound required fifty stitches to close and his kneecap, damaged beyond repair, was removed.

11 Ibid. Leupold is reported to have

reacted in terror when, on board USS *Corry*, he saw a black mess steward serving in the officer's mess. Of course, he had little to fear from the Americans on this score, because prevailing racial prejudice was such that blacks were permitted on board only in the most menial of capacities.

Chapter 11: U66

1 *Success*, p. 178. The attack occurred on 19 February 1944. No escort was damaged or sunk that day in that area. The T5 *Zaunkönig* (Wren) was an acoustic torpedo designed to be fired at escorts.

2 Ibid. One of the two was sunk, the British motorship *Silvermaple* (5313GRT). Since no other ship was damaged, both hits Seehausen heard must have been on *Silvermaple*.

3 *Success*, p. 179. This victim was the French steamer *Saint Louis* (5202GRT).

4 Ibid; *U66*. *John Holt* was a British steamer launched in 1943 and was rated 4964GRT. Most of the information in the following paragraph comes from a report of an interview with *John Holt*'s Chief Officer which is included in the ONI file on U66 at NARA.

5 Ibid.

6 *Success*, p. 179. This ship indeed sank. She was the British tanker *Matadian* (4275GRT).

7 *Destroy*, p. 182. Henke's boat fell victim to USS *Guadalcanal*'s (CVE-60) group on 9 April 1944.

8 Ibid. U68 fell victim to the same hunter-killer group as had U515 just one day later.

9 DR 60 was a map quadrant about 250nm north-north-west of U66's current location.

10 *BdU*, 1 May 1944.

11 It is hard to imagine, given U66's excellent sound equipment, that it was unaware of *Block Island*'s presence just 5km away. This and other odd behaviour that morning can only be explained by a combination of exhaustion and the above-mentioned

vitamin deficiency.

12 *Destroy*, pp. 188–9; *U66*; BdU, 5 May 1944. The times given here all correspond to the German time maintained by U-boats operating in the Atlantic. The time kept by the attackers was true local time and was two hours earlier.

13 *U66*; *BdU*, 5 May 1944. At the same time, Seehausen reported a much greater supply of fuel and food than previously reported, leading BdU to conclude that he'd resupplied from U188, when, in fact, he hadn't.

14 *U66*. This quote is from *Buckley*'s log, which is quoted in a document entitled 'Surviving Prisoners from U-66, Report on', which is included in U66's file in the ONI records at NARA.

15 Ibid. With the exception of Seehausen, all of U66's officers survived and none recalled ordering or hearing anyone else order the turn towards *Buckley*, so it almost certainly happened unintentionally.

16 Ibid. The fate of the two prisoners is unknown, but this is the most logical conclusion, since they were reported to have been seen in lifejackets in the conning tower just before the hand grenade explosion.

17 Ibid.

18 *BdU*, 28 April 1944.

Interlude: U821

1 *Type VII*, pp. 58–62.

2 MoD, §419.

3 Schmidt graduated that school and was offered command of a new Type XXI boat. He declined the honour.

4 *Landwirt* – farmer.

5 *BdU*, 6 June 1944. Underlining was in the original.

6 *BdU*, 7 June 1944. In fact the log is in error here, since one of the returned boats, U212, is listed in the previous day's log entry as being one of the eight snorkel-equipped boats leaving Brest.

7 *BdU*, 10 June 1944; *Destroy*, p. 195. Ushant (Ouessant in French) is a large island about 10nm off the northern headland of the Breton

peninsula and a major navigational landmark for the harbour at Brest.

8 *BdU*, 10 June 1944.

Chapter 12: U371

1 *BdU*, 17 April 1940.

2 *Type VII*, pp. 78–84. This section covers the whole twisted story of the problems suffered by German torpedoes and their eventual resolution.

3 *Success*, pp. 57, 61. On 24 June 1941, U371 sank the Norwegian motorship *Vigrid* (4765GRT) from convoy HX.133. On 30 July, it sank the British steamer *Shahristan* (6935GRT) and the Dutch steamer *Sitoebondo* (7049GRT), both from convoy OS.1.

4 *Ten Years*, p. 197.

5 The Germans used a sector grid notation system to designate any spot on the oceans. It was a flexible system that used two letters and up to four numbers to define a position. The crudest locator, the two-letter grid sector, defined an area 486nm square. This grid sector was divided into nine subsectors, which were in turn divided into nine sub-subsectors and so on, two more times. At its finest level, described by two letters and four numbers, a grid sector six miles square was defined. The Straits of Gibraltar were in sectors CG95 and CG96.

6 *KTB*, U79, 4–5 October 1941. This account is from the log of U79, another of the *Goeben* boats, that passed the Straits two weeks after U371.

7 Cape Spartel is on the African side and marks the western entrance to the Straits.

8 Tarifa is at the southernmost tip of Spain and is at western end of the narrowest stretch of the Straits, a stretch approximately 5nm long and 6-7nm across.

9 Ceuta is a Spanish-held city on the African shore at the eastern end of the Straits. It is due south of Gibraltar.

10 *Boot*. Despite this being a novel, the account of the attempted passage of

the Straits in this source is quite accurate. The author was on U96 when it attempted to pass the Straits and the fictional account accurately retells what happened to that boat.

11 Weber subsequently commissioned U709 in August 1942 and commanded that boat until December 1943. Neumann commanded U372 from its commissioning in April 1941 through its loss in the Mediterranean in August 1942. His stint in command of U371 was obviously a temporary assignment.

12 *Success*. Mehl's victories in command of U371 were:

7 Jan 43	British A/S trawler HMS *Jura* (545t)
7 Jan 43	British steamer *Ville de Strassbourg* (7159GRT) damaged
23 Feb 43	British steamer *Fintra* (2089GRT)
28 Feb 43	American steamer *Daniel Carrol* (7176GRT) damaged
27 Apr 43	Dutch steamer *Merope* (1162GRT)
10 Jun 43	Americam steamer *Matthew Maury* (7176GRT) damaged
10 Jun 43	American tanker *Gulf Prince* (6561GRT) damaged
7 Aug 43	British steamer *Contractor* (6004GRT)
11 Oct 43	British minesweeper HMS *Hythe* (656t)
13 Oct 43	American destroyer USS *Bristol* (DD453) (1630t)
15 Oct 43	American steamer *James Russell Lowell* (7176GRT)
17 Mar 44	American steamer *Maiden Creek* (5031GRT)
17 Mar 44	Dutch motorship *Dempo* (17024GRT)

13 *Success*. Fenski's victories in command of U410 were:

6 Mar 43	British steamer *Fort Battle River* (7133GRT)
6 Mar 43	British steamer *Fort Paskoyac* (7134GRT) damaged

26 Aug 43	American steamer *John Bell* (7242GRT)
26 Aug 43	American steamer *Richard Henderson* (7194GRT)
26 Sep 43	Norwegian steamer *Christian Michelsen* (7176GRT)
1 Oct 43	British steamer *Fort Howe* (7133GRT)
1 Oct 43	British tanker *Empire Commerce* (3722GRT)
14 Feb 44	British steamer *Fort St Nicholas* (7154GRT)
18 Feb 44	British light cruiser HMS *Penelope* (5270t)

14 Type VII, pp. 84-90.

15 *Zaunkönig* – Wren. *Falke* – Falcon.

16 *Destroy*, p. 164.

17 *U371*.

18 Djidjelli is now generally rendered Jijel.

19 According to one source (U-boat Net), this was the first example of a new tactic, new at least to the Mediterranean, codenamed 'Swamp'. The idea was literally to cover the area where the U-boat could be lurking with surface escorts and air patrols until it was forced to the surface or destroyed at depth. In fact, this idea wasn't new. If it differed at all from the hunter-killer group tactics used so successfully by the US Navy in the Central Atlantic and the Royal Navy in the North Atlantic, it was in the lavishness of the investment of assets.

Interlude: U534

1 The records on U534 are extremely sketchy. This author has been able to find no direct evidence of how the boat was employed between its commissioning and its one operational patrol and again between its leaving Kristiansand for Flensburg on 25 October 1944 and its sinking en route from Germany to Norway on 5 May 1945. To make matters worse, what sparse evidence does exist is contradictory. For this reason, the author has made some reasonable

assumptions that would account for the boat's employment during those long gaps in the record. Anyone with more complete evidence of this boat's employment during this periods is invited to contact the author.

2 Brinkmann.

3 Brinkmann. The story of this incident is told on p. 61 of *Type VII*.

4 The absence of U534 from the official record of BdU between 25 August 1944 and the end of the war fuelled the speculation that it was involved in secret missions.

5 *Ten Years*, Chapter 22.

6 This author was unable to determine whether U534 was able to dive or not on this last voyage. An inability to dive would explain the boat being caught on the surface as it was.

7 Various sources give different numbers for the crew and for the dead. This number is from *Destroy*, pp. 258–9.

8 Brinkmann. Willi Brinkmann, a former officer on U534, spoke with the commander and various crew-members two weeks after the sinking and none of them mentioned anything unusual about the cargo or crew.

Chapter 13: U977

1 MoD, §487.

2 *U977* and Schäffer. Schäffer's book is short and rather sloppy with facts, but it provides a good insight into his thoughts. U977 is also a short account, but gives a clear, high-level account of the boat's activities.

3 *Success*, p. 195.

4 *U977*. This statement was written, in English, by Schäffer. He was fluent in English, having visited the United States and even attended part of a year of high school in Cleveland, Ohio.

5 Ibid. The crew stated emphatically that the corpsman was the only petty officer who was missed during the long voyage.

Bibliography

DIRECTLY REFERENCED SOURCES
Primary Sources

UB68   Dönitz, Karl, *The Sinking of U.B.68*, 1918. This account was written by Dönitz while in captivity at Malta immediately after the sinking of his boat. It was transcribed and made part of the official German records of the First World War in 1938, was captured by the Americans after the war and is now part of the 1914–18 records stored in the US National Archives and Records Service storage facility at Suitland, Md.

Wong   *Extract from Narration of Cruiser Wonganella from Malta to Gibraltar, 5–13 March 1917*. This document is part of the material in the log of UC74 in RG45 at the US National Archives and Records Service storage facility at Suitland, Md.

Invest   *Investigation of Movements and Activities of Enemy Submarines in the Mediterranean, #84: Oct. 1918*, French Ministry of Marine, 1918. A translated copy of these informal notes is in RG45 at the US National Archives and Records Service storage facility at Suitland, Md.

UB81   *'U.B. 81' Interrogation of Survivors*, O.X.O., C.B. 01400, Copy 315, December 1917. This copy was logged into the files of the office of Admiral Simms, the Commander of US Naval Forces, London, on 3 January 1918. It subsequently made its way into the CNO records at the US National Archives and Records Service storage facility at Suitland, Md.

UB72   *'U.B. 72' Interrogation of Survivors*, O.X.O., C.B. 01448, Copy 25, June 1918. This copy was logged into the files of the office of Admiral Simms, the Commander of US Naval Forces, London, on 1 July 1918. It also made its way into the US National Archives and Records Service storage facility at Suitland, Md.

U66   *Report on the Interrogation of Survivors from U-66 Sunk 6 May 1944*, US Navy Dept., Office of the Chief of Naval Operations, Washington, DC, 5 August 1944. This is part of the CNO records stored at the US National Archives and Record Service, Washington, DC.

U185 A variety of notes concerning U185, including raw interrogation notes, rough drafts of several chapters of a narrative based on these interrogations and later drafts of some of these chapters are collected in the records of the G-2 (Intelligence) Division (MIS-Y) stored in RG165 at the US National Archives and Record Service, Washington, DC. None of these were official documents. Even the later drafts are heavily marked up in pencil and crayon. Together, these notes constitute a remarkably complete account of the life and death of U185.

U371 *Report on the Interrogation of Survivors from U-371 Sunk 4 May 1944*, US Navy Dept., Office of the Chief of Naval Operations, Washington, DC, 21 August 1944. This is part of the CNO records stored at the US National Archives and Record Service, Washington, DC. This report also includes some chapters on the history of U410.

U604 An account of U604's sinking, because its survivors were picked up by U185, is included as a separate draft document in U185's records.

U977 *Report on the Interrogation of Survivors from U-977 Surrendered at Mar del Plata 17 August 1945*, US Navy Dept., Office of the Chief of Naval Operations, Washington, DC, 21 August 1944. This is part of the CNO records stored at the US National Archives and Record Service, Washington, DC. The only version of this report in these records is a hand-written draft.

U1059 Like the case with U185, the file on U1059 in the records of the G-2 (Intelligence) Division (MIS-Y) stored in RG165 at the US National Archives and Record Service, Washington, DC contains not only the final version of the sinking report, but early drafts and raw interrogation notes, often half in German.

KTB For various boats, use was made of translations of the boat's KTB (*Kriegstagebuch* – daily war log). These have been microfilmed and are stored as RG 242 at the main branch of the US National Archives and Record Service, Washington, DC. When referenced in this book, log references are of the form: 'KTB, <boat name>, <date>'. E.g. 'KTB, U47, 13 Oct 39'.

BdU The KTB of the *Befehlshaber der Uboote*, Karl Dönitz. Listings are by date. E.g. 'BdU, 24–30 May 41'. These records are now available in microfilm form at the US National Archives and Record Service, Washington, DC.

Wahoo *U.S.S. WAHOO – Third War Patrol, report of*, 7 February 1943, US Naval Historical Center, Washington, DC. These records are now available in microfilm form at the US National Archives and Record Service, Washington, DC.

Some of the material in this book came from conversations between the author and individual U-boat survivors. Most of these took place as a result of introductions made by Ken MacPherson in Toronto in 1978.

Schmidt   Ernst Schmidt, IWO, U821.
Brinkmann   Willi Brinkmann, IWO, U534.

SECONDARY SOURCES

The following list contains bibliographic notations for all the books used as references during the writing of this book. Each listing is preceded by a short tag-name used in the footnotes to identify sources.

Bagnasco   Bagnasco, Erminio, *Submarines of World War Two*, Arms & Armour Press, Ltd., London, England, 1977.

TL   Botting, Douglas, *The Seafarers: The U-Boats*, Time-Life Books, Alexandria, Va, 1979.

Boot   Buchheim, Loathar-Günther, *The Boat*, Alfred A. Knopf, New York, NY, 1975. Originally published in German as *Das Boot*, by R. Piper & Co. Verlag, Munich, 1973. This is a work of fiction, but is based on two patrols made by the author in U96.

Ten Years Dönitz, Karl, *Memoirs: Ten Years and Twenty Days*, Greenhill Books, London, England, 1990.

Wolf   Edwards, Bernard, *Dönitz and the Wolf Packs*, Arms & Armour Press, London, England, 1996.

Killing   Gray, Edwin A., *The Killing Time: The German U-Boats 1914–1918*, Charles Scribner's Sons, New York, NY, 1972.

Convoy   Kemp, Paul, *Convoy Protection: The Defence of Seaborne Trade*, Arms & Armour Press, London, England, 1993.

Destroy   Kemp, Paul, *U-Boats Destroyed: German Submarine Losses in the World Wars*, Arms & Armour Press, London, 1997.

Black   McKee, Alexander, *Black Saturday*, Holt, Rinehart & Winston, New York, NY, 1960.

MoD   Ministry of Defence, *The U-Boat War in the Atlantic 1939–1945*, HMSO, London, England, 1989. This is a facsimile edition (with new notes) of a study commissioned by the Admiralty after the war. In this source, each chapter is page-numbered starting at zero, but the sections are numbered continuously across chapters, so references for this source are by section number, e.g.

'MoD, §234'. The author was Günther Hessler, formerly CO of U107 and staff officer to his father-in-law, Karl Dönitz.

Success   Rohwer, Jürgen, *Axis Submarine Successes 1939–1945*, Naval Institute Press, Annapolis, Md, 1983. This is an updated translation of the original German edition, *Die U-Boote-Erfolge der Achsenmachte 1939–1945*, published by J. F. Lehmanns Verlag, Munich, Germany, 1968.

Rössler   Rössler, Eberhard, *The U-boat: The evolution and technical history of German submarines*, Naval Institute Press, Annapolis, Md, 1989. The original English edition with the same title was published by Arms & Armour Press, Ltd, London, England, 1981. Originally published as *Geschichte des deutschen Ubootbaus* by J. F. Lehmanns Verlag, Munich, Germany, 1975.

Schäeffer   Schäffer, Heinz, *U-Boat 977*, Ballantine Books, Inc., New York, NY, 1957.

Type VII   Stern, Robert C., *Type VII U-Boats*, Arms & Armour Press, London, England, 1991.

Tarrant   Tarrant, V. E., *The U-Boat Offensive 1914–1945*, Arms & Armour Press, London, England, 1989.

Pict   Von der Porten, Edward P., *Pictorial History of the German Navy in World War II*, Thomas Y. Crowell Co., New York, 1976.

Conway   *Conway's All the World's Fighting Ships 1922–1946*, Conway Maritime Press Ltd, London, England, 1980.

GENERAL SOURCES

The following sources were not referenced directly in the text, but provided invaluable background information.

U-Boats and T-Boats 1914–1918: Guides to the Microfilmed Records of the German Navy 1850–1945, No. 1, US National Archive and Records Service, Washington, DC, 1984.

Records Relating to U-Boat Warfare, 1939–1945: Guides to the Microfilmed Records of the German Navy 1850–1945, No. 2, US National Archive and Records Service, Washington, DC, 1985.

uboat.net: The U-boat War 1939–1945. This is a WWW site *(http://uboat.net)* developed by Gudmundur Helgason. I recommend it highly to anyone interested in U-boats who has Internet access. I used it frequently to check out its extensive glossaries of U-boat terminology and its excellent thumbnails of boats and men.

Picture Sources

The following sources supplied the photographs used in this book. When no source is given for a photograph, it is because the source was never known or that information was lost over the years, something which has happened far too frequently. My apologies to any individual or organisation whose photograph I am using without proper acknowledgement.

Ahme	Jochen Ahme.
Albrecht	Johan Albrecht.
BAK	Bundesarchive Koblenz.
ECPA	*Établissement Cinématographique et Photographique des Armées.*
Hirschfeld	Werner Hirschfeld.
NARS	US National Archives & Records Service.
NHC	US Naval Historical Center.
NPC	US Naval Photographic Center.
Schmidt	Ernst Schmidt.

Index

217

INDEX